The Spaces of Neoliberalism

The Spaces of Neoliberalism
Land, Place and Family in
Latin America

Edited by

Jacquelyn Chase

Kumarian
Press, Inc.

The Spaces of Neoliberalism: Land, Place and Family in Latin America
Published 2002 in the United States of America by Kumarian Press, Inc.,
1294 Blue Hills Avenue, Bloomfield, Connecticut 06002 USA

Production, design, indexing, and proofreading by
City Desktop Productions, LLC.

The text of this book is set in New Caledonia 11/13.
Printed in Canada on acid-free paper by Transcontinental Printing and Graphics,
Inc.

Text printed with vegetable oil-based ink.

∞ The paper used in this publication meets the minimum requirements of the
American National Standard for Information Sciences—Permanence of Paper for
Printed Library Materials, ANSI Z39.48-1984.

Library of Congress Cataloging-in-Publication Data

The spaces of neoliberalism : land, place and family in Latin America / edited by
Jacquelyn Chase.
    p. cm.
    Includes index.
    ISBN 1–56549–144–0 (pbk. : alk. paper)—ISBN 1–56549–145–9 (cloth : alk.
    paper)
    1. Latin America—Economic policy. 2. Land reform—Latin America. 3.
Privatization—Latin America. 4. Latin America—Economic conditions—1982–
I. Chase, Jacquelyn, 1956–

  HC125 .S688 2002

338.98—dc21

2001050824

11 10 09 08 07 06 05 04 03 02   10 9 8 7 6 5 4 3 2 1

First Printing 2002

Contents

Foreword

On September 11, 2001 the terrorist attack on the World Trade Center and the Pentagon prefigured as a *historical possibility* the end of capitalist modernity under Western hegemony in its latest incarnation of neoliberal globalization. To be sure, thinking about this possibility in no way condones the hideous acts of September 11. But societies have to re-examine at times their most cherished constructs. For more than two hundred years, Europe and the United States have enjoyed the socio-economic, cultural, and ecological privilege of building societies and life styles that asserted their primacy and rights in their own lands and the world over. Capitalist modernity has reigned with confidence, even when challenged. It is precisely the cultural values of individualism and rationality and their assumed superiority that are now being taken to new levels with neoliberal globalization.

There is a connection between our affluence and poverty elsewhere, between our high levels of consumption and the rate of depletion of natural resources in other places and between our cultural preeminence and the cultural crisis of other societies. This frequently means that "things fall apart" at their end, to recall the title of Chinua Achebe's famous work. This is why, in contrast to the external debt owed by poor countries to the international lending institutions and private banks, some raise a notion of the ecological debt owed by high-consumption regions to resource-rich and low-consumption ones. To this I would add a cultural debt owed by dominant cultures over Third World cultures. The former have enjoyed tremendous material and ecological privileges as a result of how cultures have been defined and arranged worldwide.

To suggest the target of the attack on September 11 was this system of civilizational privilege is not a farfetched historical proposition. It does not of course explain everything, but it accounts for a lot of the opposition and malaise felt worldwide about the accumulated effects of capitalist modernity and the recent neoliberal project. This is why it is so important to learn a different and enduring lesson from these events. Heeding this lesson means examining seriously the neoliberal model and, in general, what goes on under the rubric of globalization.

This book is part of this rethinking of neoliberalism and globalization. It is a special volume in a number of ways. First, it brings together three disciplines that have been at the forefront of thinking about globalization: geography, anthropology, and political economy. Geography is concerned with the transformation of the spatial orders that has accompanied the globalization of capital. This angle has been underplayed in all other disciplines, perhaps with the exception of the interdisciplinary field of city and regional planning (one thinks here of the work of Manuel Castells). Anthropology, for its part, seeks to examine the new modes of cultural production and production of difference that characterize the global order in ascension. Anthropologists emphasize the fact that globalization is by no means only an economic phenomenon, and that perhaps first and foremost it entails a deep cultural transformation. Finally, political economy analyzes the social and economic changes brought about by capital. It continues to do so today, in part reinvigorated by new tools of analysis, for instance, in the case of the feminist political economy represented in this book. The volume's value lies in its ability to bring into dialogue for the first time these three perspectives to arrive at a more complex understanding of neoliberalism and globalization: one that does not shun culture by emphasizing the economic, one that does not overlook the material by focusing on the cultural, or one that looks at space without regard for culture and locality.

As Jacquelyn Chase says in her introduction, this multifaceted approach can be made possible by understanding the geographies of neoliberalism as a complex process of spatial, cultural, and economic processes. This complexity and integration is largely made possible by the relatively new concept of place. Developed initially in geography, in part as a corrective to the abstractions of space and capital, the concept of place has found an auspicious home in anthropology and begins to make inroads into feminist political economy (e.g., the work of J.K. Gibson-Graham). "Place" enabled analysts to improve their understanding of the local imprint of neoliberal globalization. As Doreen Massey put it some years ago, "a global sense of place" is not an oxymoron nor does a defense of place need to be reactionary. On the contrary, this concept illustrates the many forms in which local groups both engage with and resist globalization. The idea of a global sense of place shows how local groups are transformed by globalization as these groups also change its local modes of operation. Globalization, rather than being a single process of worldwide homogenization, is characterized by unity and fragmentation; by cultural dominance and by heterogeneity; by the transformation of space by capital and the defense of place by social movements. In sum, neoliberalism does not do away with difference. One of the important lessons of these chapters is that place-based cultural, ecological, and economic differences continue to be created. These differences are never static. On the contrary, they are dynamically produced today and it is within these differences that we might look for clues about how to transform the world alongside people who have ordinarily been powerless to act. The second important aspect of the book is thus the reconstructive outlook enabled by the focus on geographies of neoliberalism as complex cultural, economic, and spatial configurations.

The third important aspect of the book is, of course, its focus on Latin American cases. This gives the book a solid grounding and specificity. How has neoliberal globalization affected land tenure systems, state action, sexual divisions of labor, indigenous peoples, and ethnic minorities? In what ways is the increasingly tight connection to world markets transforming long-standing models of the peasant economy, labor markets, or gender relations? Does the insistence of indigenous peoples, and ethnic minorities on collective territories, as opposed to a private land holding system, constitute an important resistance to neoliberal cultural and economic reconversion? What has been the cost of "success stories" of neoliberal integration in cultural and ecological terms? In what concrete ways have the intersections of space, place, and culture been redrawn today by global integration? How have various social actors produced mutations of this process? Are Latin Americans becoming the ideal "market citizens" of neoliberal dogmas, or are they being able to re-create a semblance of collective existence as they rework creatively neoliberal constructs?

In avoiding the extremes of gloom and romanticism that characterize a good deal of writing in this area, the case studies in this volume paint a realistic picture of neoliberal globalization in Latin America. The volume, however, is not a detached statement from the neutral perspective of the social sciences. To the contrary, its spirit is very much in keeping with the inspiring concept of the first Global Social Forum held in Porto Alegre, Brazil, in January 2000: Another World Is Possible. By turning this dictum into a question ("is another world possible?"), this volume contributes clues towards the long journey of redefining and reconstructing local and regional worlds that is envisaged by many social movements of today. Let us hope that, in the spirit of Porto Alegre and learning from volumes such as this one, we can bring this lesson home to the United States, so that we can also dream of the goal of living in a shared globe with all other human and non-human beings, in a pluriverse and finite planet.

Arturo Escobar
*Kenan Distinguished Teaching
Professor of Anthropology,
University of North Carolina, Chapel Hill*

Preface

The inspiration and most of the material for this volume came from a conference at the University of Massachusetts, Amherst, in the fall of 1998 entitled Space, Place, and Nation: Reconstructing Neoliberalism in the Americas. The participants were enthusiastic and politically engaged, and I thank them all for their commitment to making the conference a success and for their support of the book. The conference provided a forum for interdisciplinary reflection on how people's lives in Latin America and the Caribbean had been affected by neoliberalism. Participants discussed alternative visions, practices, and claims that have emerged from within the lived spaces of neoliberalism. The focus in this book on land, family and place reflects the interest displayed at the conference in shifting the critique of neoliberalism away from its typical emphasis on state-sponsored reforms to the ecologically and culturally diverse nature of neoliberal reforms and of people's complex reactions to them.

There are several people I wish to acknowledge for their assistance and encouragement during the elaboration of this volume. My former graduate assistants at the University of Massachusetts, Ugo D'Ambrosio, Karen Graubart, Ernesto Pavel, Lori Tanner, and Joanna Wheeler, helped me tremendously. Without them, neither the conference nor the book would have been possible. Gloria Bernabe-Ramos and Anne Tessier of the Center for Latin American, Caribbean, and Latino Studies at the University of Massachusetts gave unrelenting logistical support for the conference that led up to this book. Arturo Escobar, Jeffrey Rubin, Julie Graham, and Gilbert Joseph participated enthusiastically in organizing the conference and have made helpful suggestions along the way as well. The Geosciences Department at the University of Massachusetts kindly provided me with a home and with technical support to work on the manuscript. The students in my Latin American Studies graduate seminar in spring of 2000 were especially thoughtful critics of an early manuscript. Susan Place also read and commented on parts of the manuscript. I am extremely grateful to The William and Flora Hewlett Foundation, which generously supported the conference as well as research for and production of this book. Finally, a special thanks goes to Linda Beyus of Kumarian Press for her patience and support.

1

Introduction:
The Spaces of Neoliberalism
in Latin America

Jacquelyn Chase

Neoliberalism and globalization have become the common frames for understanding and critiquing development in Latin America for the last twenty
years. The state-led, inward-oriented development programs and philoso-
phies put in place after 1930 and extending to the early 1980s have been
replaced by market-friendly approaches to development and by an explicit
approximation and subservience to world markets and financial institutions
(Mohan, Brown, Milward, and Zack-Williams 2000). The idea of market efficiency and the election of numerous neoliberal presidents throughout the
last twenty years point to a broad disillusionment with state-led development
programs. The disintegration of communism in Eastern Europe and the
Soviet Union supported arguments against central planning, and has served
to strengthen the belief that the market is best suited to resolve problems
of inequality and poverty (Gore 2000). Specifically in Latin America the
source of neoliberal policies can be traced to the international economy, and
especially to the piling up of foreign debt by Latin American countries in
the early 1970s. Governments were faced with rising interest payments and
an increasingly stingy and organized international banking system throughout the 1980s that used anti-state rhetoric to justify reduced public spending.

Often at the behest of this banking system through institutions such as
the International Monetary Fund and the World Bank, Latin American governments have reversed land reforms, interrupted social programs, shut
down regional development schemes, and privatized national industries.
The globalization of commerce created renewed interest in resource extraction in some regions and induced the conversion of millions of acres to
nontraditional exports such as flowers and soybeans, while bankrupting small

farmers who have been unable to compete in the export sector. Neoliberalism also supports an increasingly narrow view of society and exhibits impatience with diversity. The doctrine of competitive efficiency has no room for subsistence peasants, Indians with historical claims to communal land, or unionized workers (Bebbington 2000). As an example of this attitude, the Latin American director of the United Nations World Food Program recently denied the urgency of assisting rural Hondurans in face of a devastating drought, stating that "These people are subsistence farmers in a world that is not a subsistence world . . . They live an outdated routine" (Gonzalez 2001).

Neoliberal reforms have redefined how people relate to each other, to vital resources, and to the state. An invigorated free market celebrates competitive individualism (Polanyi 1957; Leiva 1998, 36; Gore 2000; Sen 1999; Ong 1999). It favors a view of self-reliant urban individuals who would perform their "market citizenship" through practicing labor flexibility and mobility, and by loosening their dependency on the state and on labor unions (Schild 1998). Employment is increasingly precarious and flexible, pitting workers against each other and against the institutions that once gave them a measure of social and economic security (Leiva 1998; Soto 2001). Private property rights have replaced communal landholding in peasant and indigenous communities in Mexico, in parts of the Andes, and in Central America. Successful rural people also are expected to come together primarily as landowners and commercial farmers rather than as members of cultural or ethnic associations with deep roots in specific regions and localities (Bebbington 2000; McDonald 1999). According to Gwynne and Kay (1999, 13), Latin American governments in charge of neoliberal restructuring have been ". . . repressive . . . to the demands of the social losers of the new economic model. . . . On the whole, less protection has been given to certain sectors (such as the industrial working class and peasantry) than to others such as the entrepreneurial middle class and the new financial groups that have emerged)."

At the same time, the governments that are responsible for implementing neoliberalism and promoting globalization often display remarkable disinterest in the geographic diversity that is the stage upon which these changes are carried out. Despite its promise to reduce state interference in the market, neoliberalism in Latin America is mostly top-down in both an administrative and a geographical sense. In Mexico, one of the region's earliest and most devoted converts to neoliberalism, the agencies for designing and implementing policies, are mostly in Mexico City, and state- and local-level control over the process is fraught with corruption and lack of resources (McDonald 1999). According to McDonald, at least until the Zapatista uprising federal bureaucrats had been largely unaware of, or insensitive to, regional differences that might influence how these policies were carried out on the ground. Otero (1996, 3) maps these regional differences in his study of neoliberalism in the same country, stating that

> . . . capitalism has developed most intensely and economic integration with North America is most advanced in the western and northern regions, along with the metropolitan area of Mexico City. In contrast, the south and southeast, the most densely populated regions and with the largest proportions of indigenous peoples, still suffer from archaic social and power structures; poverty is pervasive. The fact that this neoliberal reform has exacerbated social polarization is in part the result of its sweeping application with little regard for regional diversity.

But as several chapters in this volume will show, within the vortex of neoliberal reform and structural adjustment policies, many Latin American people have begun participating in social movements that claim ecological, political, and economic citizenship, and the right to retain key aspects of their cultures. The claim to cultural difference, especially in the case of indigenous people, usually involves a demand for territorial integrity of the places that have historically provided them with a livelihood and with their identity as a group. The last two decades, while coincident with the hegemonic push to absorb all people and territories into the global market, have also been a time of remarkable activism by groups that have used a global stage to organize their demands for autonomous control over territory. Thus, as the chapters by Hvalkof and by Deere and León show, the pan-indigenous movement begun in Ecuador has been successful in pushing Andean countries to recognize the claims of Indians to communal land, even when other countries such as Chile, Nicaragua, and Mexico were rapidly reversing land reform and dismantling communal access to land. Other examples of local demands for control over resources are not the result of organized movements but are still suggestive of a kind of resistance to the logic of neoliberal market reforms. For example, some of the Guatemalans that Gudeman and Rivera-Gutiérrez discuss in their chapter draw on their community economies to negotiate access to municipal lands in a way that privileges sustainability over market competition, even though most of the people they encounter also participate in the market economy.

Neoliberalism as Narrative

Despite some of these countercurrents, even some of the most critical thinkers on neoliberalism and globalization today see these two processes as cohesive, powerful, unavoidable, and tending towards integration and uniformity. The objects and outcomes of neoliberalism and of the supportive institutions of globalization are often implicitly spatial, however, and produce new forms of spatial difference. Recently, critical geographers have looked at the twin processes of neoliberalism and globalization as powerful narratives, utopias, or metaphors that produce uncomplicated views of the geographies in which these policies are carried out in Europe, the United States and most of the Third World (Gibson-Graham 1996; Harvey 2000; Coronil 2001; Santos 2000). Neoliberalism is an extreme version of the "utopia" of the free capitalist market (Blaikie 2000) and it presupposes that geographical difference will melt away through market diffusion. Coronil (2001, 63) shows that ". . . these discourses set in motion the belief that the separate histories, geographies, and cultures that have divided humanity are now being brought together by the warm embrace of globalization, understood as a progressive process of planetary integration."

But, as David Harvey (2000, 178) states ". . . the purity of any utopianism of process inevitably gets upset by its manner of spatialization." He goes on to show that the market encounters new spatial discontinuities and makes new ones as it changes social relations and ecologies in places:

> As free market capital accumulation plays across a variegated geographical terrain of resource endowments, cultural histories, communications possibilities, labor quantities, and qualities . . . so it produces an intensification of uneven geographical development in standards of living and life prospects. Rich regions grew richer leaving poor regions poorer . . . Circular and cumulative causation embedded within utopianism of the market process produces increasing geographical differentiations in wealth and power, rather than gradual progress toward homogeneity and equality (2000, 178).

J.K. Gibson-Graham (1996, 120–21) argues that the narrative of globalization is based on an image of fatalistic convergence and penetration of markets into all geographic and social frontiers of capitalism:

> What I mean by "globalization" is that set of processes by which the world is rapidly being integrated into one economic space via increased international trade, the internationalization of production and financial markets, the internationalization of a commodity culture promoted by an increasingly networked global telecommunications system . . . The dynamic image of penetration and domination is linked to a vision of the world as already or about to be wholly capitalist—that is, a world "rightfully owned" by capitalism.

Piers Blaikie (2000, 1043) describes the hegemony of the neoliberal narrative in a similar way:

> The neoliberal paradigm . . . is highly totalizing and universalizing. Its view on the role of local people in applying their knowledge and skills in action is therefore myopic. Local knowledge is sidelined and reduced both theoretically and practically to market information on the technical choices available, and the local appropriateness of these choices to their environment and individual or household endowments. The paradigm is indifferent to the "localness" of appropriate institutions which should be induced to meet market demand.

What kinds of impact do all these critiques of a globalist narrative have on people who must figure out how to survive when their environments, economies, and social lives are shifting ground so rapidly and so profoundly? It is important to recognize that the narratives of globalization and neoliberalism have consequences for how people imagine alternatives to global capitalism. But a focus on these narratives is insufficient without probing how geographic difference underscores the many negotiated responses, institution-building, and forms of active or passive resistance to market reforms taking place in Latin America. Fortunately, anthropologists, geographers, political economists, and others are offering a more textured account of neoliberalism and globalization in regional and local case studies (Loker 1999; McDonald 1999). This book contributes to the effort of understanding how markets and market ideology come into people's lives through their communities, their culture, their resource base, their local labor markets, and their households. It examines how some people's attachment to places is redefined but not erased by the introduction of liberalized labor and land markets. After two decades of neoliberal reforms, the regions and localities of Latin America remain incredibly distinctive, yet share similar pressures to conform to global cultures and market opportunities. The case studies will show that these distinctive geographies help us understand the ways in which people engage with the market. None of the authors embrace the view that ordinary people consciously and overtly reject neoliberalism. None of the people studied in these chapters consciously seek full autonomy from markets. Actors sometimes coalesce around values that are absent in, indeed vilified by, market competition, but other times they do not. Consumption, market participation, migration, and changing gender relations are faces of these contradictions, many of which are laid out in the chapters that follow. Nonetheless, the industrial workers, artisans, farmers, housewives, households, Indians, and others who participated in these studies are not, indeed cannot be, the "market citizens" that neoliberalism implies they should be. People's market participation is only partial and is entangled with family life and gender relations, with local and other institutions, and with different kinds of communities. This creative mixture of resources and actions is a more realistic picture of people's encounter with neoliberalism than a story of compliance or resistance to this model (Bebbington 2000). However, people's actions are circumscribed by new forms of geographic difference in Latin America that are taking shape in the shadow of intensified global trade and neoliberal policies within their national borders, a subject I will turn to next.

The Geographies of Neoliberalism in Latin America

Neoliberalism and globalization have drastically changed rural landscapes, produced new regional discrepancies, and reinforced old and new patterns of urbanization. These changes are tied to the social, spatial, and ecological conditions that existed long before neoliberalism became hegemonic. Colonialism and its aftermath in Latin America were responsible for an incredibly skewed land distribution that persists today. In many highland regions, indigenous people still are a majority of the population, and Indians in most lowland areas have been all but decimated. All countries, large or small, are noted for extreme internal regional differences that have led to high levels of mobility and urbanization. Rural poverty and ecological degradation have sent millions of peasants to cities and to the United States over the past century. Descendants of African slaves have been segregated into impoverished coastal communities or into areas once occupied by marooned slaves. The presence of modern authoritarian states encouraged other geographical dualities. Urban-industrial regions captured most growth in manufacturing, even though by the 1960s and 1970s many governments tried ambitious policies to reverse this spatial concentration with little success. Zones of capitalist agriculture tended to spring up around urban markets, while indigenous and peasant regions went largely ignored by rural development policies.

The geographies of neoliberalism are in some ways extensions of these older inequalities, but they offer new patterns and trends that emerge from what some authors see as the increasing integration of localities with global markets and investments (Gwynne and Kay 1999). Old patterns of "core and periphery" that once marked Latin American space have been replaced by new spatial inequalities and relations, but also by new ways of seeing and describing spatial difference. For example the city and countryside are no longer the mutually distinctive categories they once were—or were thought to be—by policymakers and scholars. The rural is no longer essentially agricultural in many Latin American regions, and the urban comports strong daily ties to agricultural production (da Silva 2001). Regional differences are no longer best described by dualistic polarizations of backwards and developed regions, or of cores and peripheries. Instead, new dynamic regions have come about that possess many internal inequalities but appear otherwise to converge with the logic of globalization by specializing in exports and tourism. Communities are no longer the impermeable containers of culture and socialization they once were thought to be in anthropology. The case studies in this book portray a complex relationship between the places that are geographic referents to people's lives, and the many networks that intersect them and connect them with other places. It is possible to see oneself today as both a global and local actor, to take advantage of opportunities at both scales and to use global relations, networks and markets to defend the survival and well-being of local communities.

Much of rural Latin America is being subjected to a reinvigorated market economy. Central America, Brazil, Chile, Ecuador, and Mexico all rushed to develop their nontraditional exports sector as they switched from a more inward-oriented industrialization to export-driven growth in the early 1980s. Although countries like Brazil, Chile, and Mexico have complex export portfolios that include much more than agricultural goods, they embarked, along with their less industrialized neighbors, on a plan to massively support new export crops such as soybeans and flowers. The overall proportion of primary exports across Latin America continues to decline, but the mix of exports and their value to policies of global competition has changed dramatically (Murray 1999). New export crops have redefined the distinction between underdeveloped and developed regions. Production complexes in export-oriented rural areas consist not only of the cultivated earth, but transportation infrastructure, processing plants, storage capacity, and social infrastructure and housing for workers. The potential for new forms of exclusion is also enormous in these productive regions. The mandate in these new activities is to pursue modernity in the name of international quality controls and global competitiveness, but many family farmers and peasant households cannot afford the credit, machinery, seeds, and other inputs to production to make them competitive (McDonald 1999). When these activities move into lands once settled by peasants, the result is usually the disappearance of families from the land and their transformation into wage laborers.

Governments also remake rural spaces by redefining and policing access to land. As studies in this volume show, countries with large indigenous and peasant sectors, such as Chile, Peru, Bolivia, and Mexico, have rewritten the rules of access to land. These changes have enabled the growth of a land market in new regions of Latin America, opening the door for further private investments and for the concentration of land and rural credit. Institutional and legal challenges to communal and reformed lands have been critical steps for rural enterprises seeking new investments in the Latin American countryside and for states eager to implant market rationality in the countryside. In some countries with large indigenous populations, neoliberal policies have endorsed the privatization of communal lands, envisioning a rural space that is undifferentiated by ethnicity, history or recent memory of land struggles. In Brazil, where community landholding was never widely diffused, the current government has violently opposed any redirection of land toward collective use. Since the early 1980s, the Landless Rural Workers Movement (MST) has been challenging the government with organized occupations of land that usually lead, when allowed to prevail, to some form of cooperative or collective production (see Kay, this volume; Deere 2001). Ironically, the ongoing threat to territory and resources has driven many indigenous and peasant groups to new levels of national and global activism, as Hvalkof's chapter shows.

Pressures to create land markets in Latin America do not only remove land from the repertoire of resources that poor people use for survival. They also remove access to other communal resources such as forms of reciprocity, common practices, wild and domesticated plants and animals, and ancestral knowledge that are part of the foundation of economic life in rural areas (Gudeman 1996). Because these features of communal economic life are often metaphorically bound together in stories, myths, and practices, removing the landed base of these combinations weakens the foundations of community itself (Gudeman 1996, 107; Gudeman and Rivera-Gutiérrez, this volume). In ecological and social terms, David Barkin (2001, 186) argues pointedly that neoliberalism reduces the natural resource base in rural areas and thus has direct implications and responsibility for the loss of sustainability of communities and for increased poverty and displacement: "Official development theory seeks the solutions to poverty in market-led structural changes. International development experts and environmentalists alike join in an effort to wrench these groups from their regions, blending the arguments of economic efficiency with those of natural destruction to justify their removal." The chapters here on rural people show a kind of middle ground between the stability of rural communities—which all of them seem to want to protect—and the outright exodus that Barkin predicts will happen as a result of market-driven policies, which they would like to avoid. Whether or not they will be successful at living in the new rural geographies of neoliberalism will depend on how they negotiate the terms of these two extremes (Bebbington 2000).

Neoliberal reforms have also reinforced urban primacy, and strengthened the role that some cities play in promoting the global economy. Loss of union-based jobs and the constant downsizing and flexible restructuring of formal employment have made informal occupations the only source of robust employment growth in cities, as Escobar Latapí and González de la Rocha show in their chapter. Still, some cities—especially most national capitals—are command centers for multinationals. On the whole, foreign investment and management continue to flow to core urban regions in Latin America (Gwynne and Kay 1999, 21). The spread of neoliberalism brought a staggering enrichment of the region's ruling class, and most of these elite choose to or must live near the command apparatus of the global economy. The result has been that some cities of Latin America now take on characteristics typical of "global cities." Cities such as São Paulo have undergone frenetic building during the last decade that created entirely new financial districts to accommodate the growing international sector.

Although all large Latin American cities house an enormous informal sector, some cities are even more specialized in and dependent on informal and underground economies than others. In this book, Escobar Latapí and González de la Rocha show that Guadalajara has seen its artisan, informal and drug economies explode, but with little complementary growth in formal global economic sectors. In contrast, northern border towns in Mexico have been magnets for off-shore industrial plants that are attracted to Mexico and to this region because of its cheap, non-union labor (Cravey 1998; Gwynne and Kay 1999). In some countries, off-shore production sites have reinforced the growth of an urban system outside the largest cities by drawing people from rural Central America, Mexico, and the Caribbean to subregional centers of industry. Helen Safa's study in this volume of one such town in the Dominican Republic shows how contradictory and incomplete this integration can be for households and individuals. As women become more critical to the functioning of off-shore production sites, men are increasingly marginalized as workers in the global economy.

The privatization of basic industries—another pillar of neoliberal restructuring in Latin America—has enduring spatial outcomes as well. These industries are often resource-dependent and thus very much tied to place. Vast production complexes with permanent populations of workers and their families grew up around these sites, such as in the petroleum-producing regions of eastern Mexico and in Brazil's iron ore regions. The former sites of national industries—such as Itabira in my case study in Brazil—will stagnate as governments sell off their industries and as unemployment soars. People in these places are given pep talks that they must compete in a world economy and families scramble to gain what they believe are marketable global skills. These include learning English and computer skills, but there are few local opportunities to put these skills to use.

The city and the countryside may have already become leaky containers for the study of geographical change in Latin America during neoliberalism (Krupa 2001; Carneiro 1998; de Paula 2001; da Silva 2001). Increasing numbers of people in the countryside across Latin America are engaged in non-agricultural pursuits as traditional peasant-based economies wither and urban consumption and demand for services begins to tap into rural labor supplies. Rural households combine incomes from diverse sources, as do individuals through seasonal or even daily "crossings" between sectors. These changes include not only labor mobility strategies, but capital mobility as well. International factories locate in peripheral regions in the Caribbean and in Central America to take explicit advantage of a population that is no longer tied firmly to the land. Other regions where people move between sectors are tourist destinations that retain some of the "natural" characteristics of the place (including, in some cases, the rural indigenous inhabitants) but with the convenience of urban infrastructure of leisure and consumption close at hand. In the Guatemalan highlands—described in this book in the chapter by Gudeman and Rivera-Gutiérrez—communities are simultaneously engaged in market-oriented industries, wage labor, and farming. This common feature of Latin American rural areas has led to many calls to abolish the duality between city and countryside that has marked so much development thinking and literature over the past 75 years (Carneiro 1998; da Silva 2001; Abramovoy 2000). The ambiguous divide between the city and the countryside is especially salient to neoliberalism because it has emerged in the context of an increasingly exclusionary export-oriented agriculture, the construction of global tourist destinations, and the search by overseas industries for cheap rural labor in Central America and the Caribbean.

Regional inequality has always been a hallmark of Latin America's geography, but new configurations of regional difference and symptoms of more extreme chasms between regions are emerging. Gwynne and Kay (1999) argue that the major form of spatiality in Latin America in recent times has been the integration of new places and regions into the global economy. But for every story of integration into the world economy, new contradictions appear within and between places. Literature on the European experience provides useful comparisons for Latin America. The presentation of Southeast England as a "neoliberal region" that fed off of the neglect by Margaret Thatcher of the country's industrial periphery is informative (Massey 1994; Allen et al. 1998). First, we are reminded that "neoliberal regions" are in large part an ideological construction. The title confers status and access to further investments and state programs. Not surprisingly, the claim by London's elite that the city and its surrounding region are the European center of the high tech and financial sector obscures internal and systemic contradictions. As Harvey (2000) also notes, state investment in poor regions or neighborhoods in this phase has been made through private corporations, and has aimed at clearing the poor from desirable places to produce attractive new sites for middle and upper class consumption.

The literature on globalization and neoliberalism in Latin America brings numerous references to regions that are emerging as global or neoliberal "success" stories in that they have been able to take advantage of market opportunities for a series of historical, ecological, cultural, and ecological reasons. Liliana Goldin (1999), for instance, has studied the western and central highlands of Guatemala since they have been targeted as areas of investment by export agriculture and export industries for firms such as Nike. Within that area, she has identified a township that has a disproportionate number of independent farmers, businessmen and traders, higher-than-average incomes, and a need for land and labor such that the township receives migrant workers on a regular basis and rents land outside its area to fulfill demand for export-oriented agricultural production. The rise of such regions throughout Latin America is often used to showcase the success of the global market at work, but Goldin's ethnography revealed that this story far from legitimized neoliberalism and globalization. Instead it drew attention to social and spatial differentiation that neoliberalism and globalization were inducing in Guatemala. As successful townships went through their supplies of land and labor very quickly, other neighboring regions and localities grew dependent on supplying farmers and entrepreneurs with cheap labor and land. In the process, land that once may have supplied subsistence economies to highland people was being earmarked for export crops, driving people further into the labor market. Bebbington (2000, 5) has used his Andean case studies to argue similarly that a unitary view of regions under neoliberalism—either as failures or successes—obscures ". . . new and changing cultural practices [that] have . . . been played out, creating landscapes that continue to be distinctive, and indeed alternative to modern, capitalist landscapes even as they incorporate many ideas, practices and technologies of modernity."

A key example from this book on rapidly changing neoliberal regions is the case of the Yucatán's tourist zones studied by Oriol Pi-Sunyer. There, locals are experiencing both the clash and mutual accommodation between ethnic subsistence and tourist economies. The past is important in understanding the current contradictory conditions in Quintana Roo. The federal government of Mexico had for generations painted this area of Quintana Roo—once inhabited exclusively by surviving fragments of Mayans—as a marginal region of Mexico. It now serves as a dubious example of regional development, but the people that were once the target of national derision in a "backwards region" discourse remain extremely poor and unable to gain full membership in the bustling tourist economy just outside their traditional lands. So by national standards, if Quintana Roo has emerged as an example of a "neoliberal region," by internal standards it has shut out the Maya from most jobs and from government-led development schemes.

Market Arrogance and the Place of Culture

Most criticisms of neoliberalism in Latin America have focused on the deprivation it has caused among the poor and middle classes. The poor have ended up with a smaller piece of national wealth in almost every Latin American country since the early 1980s, and the very wealthy have become indecently rich (Gwynne and Kay 1999; Veltmeyer and O'Malley 2001; Escobar Latapí and González de la Rocha, this volume). Some groups have been struck more than others with state cutbacks in services and have needed to work harder for less money and under worse conditions. Other people have lost access to key resources such as land, water, and forests (Barkin 2001). The focus on deprivation, however, does not challenge the market-based representation of social life that neoliberal philosophy itself promotes and feeds upon. A deprivation account of neoliberalism ignores the vast heterogeneity of economic restructuring in Latin America by focusing on average changes in the distribution of income or poverty and on categories of people such as women, peasants, workers, and Indians. These social categories are removed from the geographic context of their lives and serve to generalize rather than specify neoliberalism in Latin America. Reliance on these abstractions obscures the fact that people may be fashioning place-based responses to neoliberalism out of this geographic diversity in ways that indicate new directions in people's defense of their livelihoods, environments, and cultures (Friedmann and Rangan 1993).

Global spaces of capital are often contrasted to the embodied places that provide meaning, sustenance, and social connections for the majority of the world's people (Escobar 2001; Dirlik 2001; Coronil 2001; Yúdice 1998). Many authors have thus embraced the locality or "place" to counter the totalizing discourse of globalization and support a geographically grounded account of neoliberalism (Dirlik 2001; Bebbington 2001). There are dangers of romanticizing local authenticity (Harvey 2000; Cloke and Jones 2001), but most discussions about the political significance of place assume that global space and concrete places are mutually constitutive of each other. Massey (1994) argues for instance that place should not be subjected to a dichotomy that puts it at the traditional end of things, and space at the apex of modernity. Arturo Escobar (2001, 205) talks similarly of reconceptualizing place as a project, in which he imagines a kind of traffic between the global and the local. The idea of transnational locations of places may also help bridge the divide between the unique characteristics of place, and a convergent space of global markets that is at the heart of neoliberalism's utopia. The concept of transnational locations challenges the ways that anthropologists and geographers once created meaningful boundaries for their studies in Latin America and suggests that the traffic between the global and the local will increase. Thus, Goldin (1999, 107) points out that in Guatemala,

> Many of the communities that we see today are essentially transformed communities in that they are global and transnational in nature. The boundaries, real or imagined, that anthropologists described in the 1940s, 1950s and 1960s were boundaries that held the township and the nation-state as the organizing categories. The boundaries (meaningful contexts) that we find today extend to the fields, cities and refugee camps of Mexico and the United States and the factories of Korea and Japan.

Research in such places shows people engaging in a complicated mix of global and local practices. These practices combine defiance with accommodation, situated habits with momentous changes in culture and the economy, and attachment to place with increased mobility between places and within networks (Cloke and Jones 2001). Most of the chapters in this book show people living at various scales simultaneously, shaped by the cultures of the places they have lived in, but not bound to place or to an authentic culture associated with any single place.

As people increasingly inhabit transnational places and become to some extent transnational actors, we should expect to find conflicts over the meaning of place and the way this meaning informs politics (Alvarez, Dagnino, and Escobar 1998). As Hvalkof's and Pi-Sunyer's chapters show, the ways that development planners or governments assign people or groups to a given regional space affects people's livelihoods and informs their political relationships with other groups. Regional histories and past representations of places underscore how people enter, leave, and change labor and land markets during neoliberalism. Historical views by Latin American governments on different regions inform how people living in these regions today can respond to neoliberal reforms and how they come to represent themselves as a group. Hvalkof describes how the Peruvian state defined its regions in ways that once made it possible to ignore the presence of indigenous people such as the Ashéninka. Occupying the marginal interstices between the Andean highlands and the Amazonian resource frontier, they were neither absorbed into the labor market for resource extraction, shunted into reservations, nor completely killed off. Instead, the Ashéninka were exposed to varying waves of resource extraction and colonist settlement, and they eventually learned successfully to "traffic" between their local territorially-based communities and the world of global NGOs and Peruvian electoral politics.

Pi-Sunyer shows that the Mexican state has historically criminalized or neglected the Yucatán periphery, and assisted in building an image of the Mayan people as marginal or even antagonistic to the national project. The lack of government support for the Maya during the development of tourism on and near their lands can help explain their poverty today. This poverty now makes the descendants of the builders of pyramids and cities uninteresting or invisible to tourists who want to enjoy the natural beauty of beach and jungle, and are disappointed by the fact that the Mayans work for wages, wear western dress, speak Spanish, and drink Coca-Cola. In this case, the representation of place by the Mexican state in the past had a direct influence on Mayan identity and survival today.

The politics of identity can also shape how the state influences different people's access to territory, as Deere and León show. In their study of several Latin American countries, the authors discovered a strong negative correlation between the legal endorsement of indigenous rights to land and state support for women's land rights. This contradiction complicates the picture of community claims to land in rural areas of Latin America that are undergoing agrarian counter-reforms. Indigenous women sometimes claim their individual rights over communal rights to defend their own access to land, even though this may seem to undermine the culture and solidarity of indigenous life.

The ongoing negotiation over control and maintenance of common property and communal relations in Latin America illustrates the tension between community and market-based definitions of resources that is simultaneously part of local people's matrix of decisions, and symptomatic of the division between the global and the local. Gudeman and Rivera-Gutiérrez propose in this volume that some rural communities in Latin America defend their common property and knowledge on the grounds that doing so will provide long-run security for themselves and their children. They do this while engaging selectively and cautiously in regional, national, and global market relations.

Organization of the Book

This book is divided into three parts. The first part focuses on the impact of neoliberalism on territorial rights in the agrarian and indigenous sectors. Cristóbal Kay leads off this section with an essay on the evolution of agrarian reforms and counter-reforms. The next two chapters address the privatization of land, and examine how Indians and peasants have responded to the emergence of land markets. While the chapter by Hvalkof emphasizes Peruvian Indians' relationships beyond their groups, with the state and with international organizations, Deer and León take on the ways that Indians have had to reshape internal relations, particularly those between indigenous men and women, in light of market reforms of land in several countries.

The second part of this book looks at how an examination of the private spaces of peoples' lives reveals a combination of market and non-market responses to neo-liberal policies. The chapters are committed to examining how neoliberal market reforms encounter historically constructed gender, community, and household relations. These authors are not interested in cataloguing the negative effects of neoliberalism on women, these having been well researched by others already. Instead, we bring information from case studies on how women use cultural and material resources to respond to the pressures of neoliberalism. In Safa's case, women do indeed work more, but in ways that, for some of them, are liberating. In my study, women draw on resources that can only peripherally be considered economic. Namely, by controlling their bodies' fertility they hope to maintain a standard of consumption that the privatization of the local company threatens to take from them.

The case studies of the first two parts of the book are situated in places where neoliberalism is strongly and unambiguously a factor in people's lives. In contrast, the third part examines how people in certain "marginal" or contradictory spaces (Coronil 2001, 83) of Latin America relate to the dominant paradigms of neoliberalism and globalization. These include the city of Guadalajara, highland areas of Guatemala, and the peripheral peasant communities just outside the tourist destinations of the Yucatán Peninsula.

Chapter Summaries

In the first part, Kay's chapter provides a comprehensive overview of agrarian politics and reform before and after neoliberalism in Latin America. His contribution shows the degree to which claims to rural land and territory have been central to market politics in the last twenty years. This chapter points out the diversity of responses by states and social movements around agrarian change, however, noting that there is no single predictable outcome of agrarian policies on people's poverty and social differentiation. A second important conclusion to Kay's chapter is the fact that territorial reforms in Latin America have provided examples of progressive redistribution of some categories of land (such as communal land) while opening the way for increasingly "globalized" social movements with the objective of establishing the right to territory.

Kay's chapter sets the foundation for the chapter by Deere and León on individual and collective land rights and gender. The authors demonstrate that institutional reforms in the agrarian sector have been quite heterogeneous. Women's and indigenous people's movements have contributed to this heterogeneity. The prominence of neoliberalism has coincided with the rise of women's and indigenous people's movements in Latin America, and with the globalization of both of these movements. This has led to a political situation of constant negotiation within the indigenous movement over the competing paradigms of universal and culturally situated human rights. In most critiques of neoliberalism, Indians and women share victimhood, and this treatment often leads to the incorrect conclusion that they are natural allies. Previous studies show that rural women were in fact excluded in most cases of agrarian reforms in Latin America and the authors show that it has been in the countries where communal lands have been most safeguarded that women's rights to land have seen the smallest gains. Deere and León push for a critical reconsideration of ethnic-oriented policies as these have had negative effects on women's rights in rural land reforms throughout Latin America.

Søren Hvalkof probes the meanings assigned to "land" and "territory" in the history of indigenous politics in Peru in the post-war period in order to assess indigenous movements' participation in civil society. Hvalkof is concerned with a broad notion of democracy that includes the right by indigenous peoples to "difference," and argues that indigenous territorial rights need separate treatment from agrarian property rights. In his case study of Peru, and more specifically of the Ashéninka, Hvalkof vividly illustrates the inappropriateness of assigning historical meanings of productive land in upland indigenous peasant communities to lowland groups. Thus, in his comparison of land and territory, and of upland and lowland agrarian politics, Hvalkof confirms the regionally specific path that neoliberalism and the struggle for place have taken in Latin America. He shows how the Ashéninka have been able, up to now, to find their own way through the Peruvian national state, global networks, and their regional and territorial past.

In the second part of the book, my chapter shows that private lives are as much a part of the economic dynamism of regions as are the industrial organizations that have been a focus of research on regional economic restructuring. This chapter is a study of a region in Brazil that has passed through a phase of sharp labor cutbacks after its main firm—a powerful state-owned mining industry—was privatized in 1997. I explore the responses of families and individuals to the threat of job loss as they reflect on a more secure and prosperous past and worry about an uncertain future. These responses are part of changing gender, family, and class identities in the region as people are moved out of the protective state sector and into the market. This study raises questions related to the way that household and community economies, gender, fertility, and migration are central to the outcome of neoliberalism in Latin American regions.

Helen Safa is concerned with policy controversies about female headship by Caribbean women living in an offshore production zone in the Dominican Republic. She places these debates within the context of global migration and economic globalization taking place in the islands. She begins her chapter with a summary of how female-headed households became a cultural feature of Caribbean women of color, and how race, colonialism, and family structure are still tightly intertwined. Safa relates economic pressures from neoliberal policies to the cultural features of family in the Caribbean, concluding that culture is not submissive to the economy. Gender, motherhood, marriage, and informal labor participation are flexible relationships that are both historically determined and responsive to social policy, economic conditions, and opportunities for migration. However, even as the economic basis of the male breadwinner model has corroded under the impact of free trade employment for women, patriarchy has reproduced itself at the level of labor institutions and the state. Men participate in creating a second myth about gender, associating women's economic responsibilities with sexual promiscuity and lack of commitment to family economies and values. Women respond to the economic and cultural pressures in the Dominican Republic by migrating in greater numbers than ever before to Europe, the United States, and Puerto Rico.

Opening the third part of this book, Gudeman and Rivera-Gutiérrez's chapter theorizes the relation between market and community economies, concluding that it is through this connection that we can better imagine the struggle for environmental sustainability in Latin America. The chapter is based on field research in Guatemala, where the authors have been studying the meaning and practices of community economies among peasant, indigenous, and urban groups. The chapter focuses on both cultural resiliency and flexibility, and how ethnographic research reveals a multitude of ways that communities relate to and define markets. The chapter addresses two issues that have particular resonance to geography. One of these is that beneath the apparently value-free surface of market exchange, market practices are rooted in specific places, community histories, values, and social learning. In other words, people participate in the market economy with the community economy in mind. The other is that many people connect their defense of and reliance on common property with a strong sense of place and time. People have an incentive to protect the *habitus* of community property and knowledge, so as to protect themselves and their descendants from uncertainty. The chapter is linked to the earlier section on agrarian and territorial politics because the people whose voices we hear are also confronting pressure to privatize their land and sell the land's resources. Gudeman and Rivera-Gutiérrez are able to show how resistance to this trend develops in particular places and contexts, but perhaps not in others. Far from asserting a fundamental conflict between traditional and modern cultures, Gudeman and Rivera-Gutiérrez show that in these struggles for common property people make, change, and reinforce communities.

De la Rocha and Escobar Latapí's paper connects urban restructuring and poverty in Mexico in the last 15 years to a new, more individualized, form of international migration. The authors argue that Guadalajara, despite its status as an important industrial city in Mexico, is a marginal space relative to the booming cities of the north and the continued concentration of global capital and political activity in the capital. The migration patterns stem from a notable decrease in opportunities for educated young people in Guadalajara, whose only option seems to be migration to the north or work in the informal sector. This selective and increasingly permanent migration and the economic crisis in Guadalajara hurt families that once benefited from migration. The breakdown in extended family culture has material and ideological reference points in the migration experience of communities. Materially, communities suffer two losses from selective migration of young unemployed adults: income from abroad, and the loss of grown children who in the past would usually return to Guadalajara to assist their parents in their old age. The meaning of family life and reciprocity between men and women, and between generations, has changed as a result of these new migration patterns. This chapter illustrates that beneath the surface of what appears to be a continuing pattern of northward migration from Mexico, certain cities, and certain families within those cities, are participants in what is a fundamentally different kind of migration in today's restructured global capitalism. Thus, the relationship between global and local works its way through many kinds of networks, the most basic one being the family, and the most extensive the international labor market.

In the closing chapter, Pi-Sunyer addresses the formation of a peripheral location within an international tourist region of Mexico. The chapter first deals with the representation of Yucatán as a periphery, both by Mexican national politics and by international travelers. Pi-Sunyer is interested in detailing how ordinary Mayan people understand these competing forces and gain new complex identities. He is not judgmental about Mayan farmers adopting and wishing for various features of modernity. Far from essentializing a Mayan tradition, Pi-Sunyer shows Mayan-ness to be present in many different forms of modernization. He does not limit his work to the impact of tourism on Mayan people, but explores the ongoing relationship by local people with the powerful forces of national memory and globalization. Pi-Sunyer's points are made in the context of renewed antagonisms by Mexican politicians against Mayan autonomy, and the increasing ability of Mayan activists to exercise global citizenship.

Together, by focusing on geographic differences, these chapters pull together new ways of observing, studying, and talking about neoliberalism in Latin America. They come from several disciplines that share a contemporary interest in alternative spaces of development and in the co-existence of these spaces. Most of the chapters build on field research and many of their authors engaged in ethnographic methods. People are therefore not reduced to silent victims of neoliberalism, nor are their actions recounted as straightforward acts of rebellion.

References

Abramovoy, Ricardo. 2000. *Funções e medidas da ruralidade no desenvolvimento contemporâneo.* Rio de Janeiro and Brazilia: Instituto de Pesquisas Econômicas Aplicadas (IPEA).

Allen, John, Doreen B. Massey, Allan Cochrane, and Julie Charlesworth. 1998. *Rethinking the Region.* London: Routledge.

Alvarez, Sonia, Evelina Dagnino, and Arturo Escobar, ed. 1998. Introduction: the cultural and the political in Latin American social movements. In *Cultures of Politics, Politics of Cultures: Re-visioning Latin American Social Movements.* 1–29. Boulder: Westview.

Barkin, David. 2001. Neoliberalism and sustainable popular development. In *Transcending Neoliberalis: Community-based Development in Latin America*, edited by Veltmeyer, Henry and Anthony O'Malley. 184–204. Hartford: Kumarian Press.

Bebbington, Anthony, 2000. *Reencountering Development: Livelihood Transitions and Place Transformations in the Andes.* Annals—Association of American Geographers, 2000, vol. 90, no. 3, 495–520.

Blaikie, Piers. 2000. Development, post-, anti-, and populist: a critical review. *Environment and Planning A.* 32:1033–1050

Carneiro, Maria José. 1998. Ruralidade: novas identidades em construção. *Estudos Sociedade e Agricultura.* 11:53–75.

Chant, Silvia. 1997. *Women-headed Households: Diversity and Dynamics in the Developing World.* New York: St. Martin's Press.

Cloke, Paul and Owen Jones. 2001. Dwelling, place, and landscape: an orchard in Somerset. *Environment and Planning A.* 33:649–66.

Coronil, Fernando. 2001. Toward a critique of globalcentrism: speculations on capitalism's nature. In *Millenial Capitalism and the Culture of Neoliberalism*, edited by Comaroff, Jean and John Comaroff. 63–87. Durham: Duke University Press.

Cravey, Altha. 1998. Cowboys and dinosaurs: Mexican labor unionism and the state. In *Organizing the Landscape: Geographical Perspectives on Labor Unionism*, edited by Herod, Andrew. 75–90. Minneapolis and London: The University of Minnesota Press.

Deere, Carmen Diana. 2001. *Gender, Land Rights, and Rural Social Movements: Regional Differences in the Brazilian Agrarian Reform.* Paper prepared for the meeting of the Latin American Studies Association. Washington D.C., September 6–8.

De Paula, Silvana Gonçalves. 2001. *Estilo de vida country no Brasil: o campo na cidade.* Paper prepared for the meeting of the Latin American Studies Association. Washington D.C., September 6–8.

Dirlik, Arif. 2001. Place-based imagination: globalism and the politics of place. In *Places and Politics in an Age of Globalization*, edited by Prazniak, Roxann and Arif Dirlik. 15–51. Lanham, Boulder, New York, and Oxford: Rowman and Littlefield Publishers.

Escobar, Arturo. 2001. Place, economy, and culture in a post-development era. In *Places and Politics in an Age of Globalization*, edited by Prazniak, Roxann and Arif Dirlik. 193–217. Lanham, Boulder, New York, and Oxford: Rowman and Littlefield Publishers.

Friedmann, John and Haripriya Rangan, ed. 1993. *In Defense of Livelihood: Comparative Studies on Environmental Action.* Hartford: Kumarian Press.

Gibson-Graham, J.K. 1996. *The End of Capitalism (As We Knew It).* Cambridge, Mass.: Blackwell Publishers.

Goldin, Liliana R. 1999. Rural Guatemala in economic and social transition. In *Globalization and the Rural Poor in Latin America*, edited by Loker, William M. 93–110. Boulder and London: Lynne Rienner Publishers.

Gonzalez, David. 2001. Drought creates food crisis in Central America. *New York Times*, August 28. Section A, Page 1, Column 4.

González de la Rocha, Mercedes. 1994. *The Resources of Poverty: Women and Survival in a Mexican City.* Oxford: Blackwell.

Gore, Charles. 2000. The rise and fall of the Washington Consensus as a paradigm for developing countries. *World Development.* 28: 789–804.

Gudeman, Stephen. 1996. Sketches, qualms, and other thoughts on intellectual property rights. In *Valuing Local Knowledge: Indigenous People and Intellectual Property Rights*, edited by Varese, Stefano and Doreen Stabinsky. 102–21. Washington D.C. and Covelo, California: Island Press.

Gwynne, Robert N. and Cristóbal Kay. 1999. Latin America transformed: changing paradigms, debates and alternatives. In *Latin America Transformed: Globalization and Modernity.* 2–30. London, Sydney and Auckland: Arnold.

Harvey, David. 2000. *Spaces of Hope.* Berkeley and Los Angeles: University of California Press.

———. 1996. *Justice, Nature, and the Geography of Difference.* London: Blackwell.

Krupa, Chris. 2001. *Producing Neoliberal Rural Spaces: Labor and Community in Ecuador's Cut-flower Sector.* Paper presented at the Latin American Studies Association Meeting, Washington, D.C., September 6–8.

Leiva, Fernando. 1998. *Neoliberal and Neostructural Theories of Competitiveness and Flexible Labor: The Case of Chile's Manufactured Exports, 1973–1996.* Ph.D. Diss., University of Massachusetts, Amherst.

Lima, Edilberto Carlos Pontes. 1997. Privatização e desempenho econômico: teoria e evidência empirica. Brasilia: IPEA (Instituto de Pesquisa Econômica Aplicada); discussion paper number 532.

Loker, William M., ed. 1999. *Globalization and the Rural Poor in Latin America*. Boulder and London: Lynne Rienner Publishers.

Massey, Doreen. 1994. *Space, Place, and Gender*. Minneapolis: The University of Minnesota.

McDonald, James H. 1999. The neoliberal project and governamentality in rural Mexico: emergent farmer organization in the Michoacán highlands. *Human Organization*. 58: 274–84.

Mohan, Giles, Ed Brown, Bob Milward, and Alfred B. Zack-Williams. 2000. *Structural Adjustment: Theory, Practice, and Impacts*. London and New York: Routledge.

Murray, Warwick E. 1999. Natural resources, the global economy, and sustainability. In *Latin America Transformed: Globalization and Modernity*, edited by Gwynne, Robert N. and Cristóbal Kay. 128–51. London, Sydney, and Auckland: Arnold.

Ong, Aihwa. 1999. *Flexible Citizenship: The Cultural Logics of Transnationality*. Durham and London: Duke.

Otero, Gerardo. 1996. Neoliberal reform and politics in Mexico: an overview. In *Neoliberalism Revisited: Economic Restructuring and Mexico's Political Future*. 1–23. Boulder: Westview Press.

Polanyi, Karl. 1957. *The Great Transformation*. Boston: Beacon Press.

Santos, Milton. 2000. *Por uma outra globalização: do pensamento único à consciência universal*. Rio de Janeiro and São Paulo: Record.

Schild, Verónica. 1998. New subjects of rights? Women's movements and the construction of citizenship in the "new democracies." In *Cultures of Politics, Politics of Cultures: Re-visioning Latin American Social Movements*, edited by Alvarez, Sonia, Evelina Dagnino, and Arturo Escobar. 93–117. Boulder: Westview Press.

Sen, Amartya. 1999. *Development as Freedom*. New York: Alfred A. Knopf.

Silva, José Graziano da. 2001. *Velhos e novos mitos do rural brasileiro*. Paper prepared for the meeting of the Latin American Studies Association. Washington D.C., September 6–8.

Soto, Eduardo Aquevedo. 2001. Poverty and local development in the Bio-Bio region of Chile. In *Transcending Neoliberalism: Community-based Development in Latin America*, edited by Veltmeyer, Henry and Anthony O'Malley. 95–124. Hartford: Kumarian Press.

Veltmeyer, Henry, James Petras, and Steve Vieux. 1997. *Neoliberalism and Class Conflict in Latin America: a Comparative Perspective on the Political Economy of Structural Adjustment*. Houndmills, Basingstoke, Hampshire, England: Palgrave.

Veltmeyer, Henry. 2001. The quest for another development. In *Transcending Neoliberalism: Community-based Development in Latin America*, edited by Veltmeyer, Henry and Anthony O'Malley. 1–34. Hartford: Kumarian Press.

Veltmeyer, Henry and Anthony O'Malley, ed. 2001. *Transcending Neoliberalism: Community Based Development in Latin America*. Bloomfield, CT: Kumarian Press.

Yúdice, George. 1998. The globalization of culture and the new civil society. In *Cultures of Politics, Politics of Culture: Revisioning Latin American Social Movements*, edited by Alvarez, Sonia, Evelina Dagnino, and Arturo Escobar. 353–379. Boulder: Westview.

I

Agrarian and Territorial Rights

2

Agrarian Reform and the Neoliberal Counter-Reform in Latin America

Cristóbal Kay

Introduction

This chapter provides an overview of the causes and consequences of the agrarian reforms that were implemented throughout most of Latin America from the 1950s to the 1980s. The era of agrarian reforms, which began with the Mexican revolution at the beginning of this century, appears to have ended with the spread of neoliberal policies across the region in the last decade (Herrera, Riddell, and Toselli 1997). It is thus an opportune time to reflect on the achievements and limitations of Latin America's agrarian reform as well as to explore the prospects of the neoliberal land policies. Part of this chapter analyzes the agrarian reforms in several countries in terms of their impact on agricultural production, income distribution, employment, poverty, and gender relations as well as from a social and political perspective. The other part reflects on the region's agrarian counter-reforms in the neoliberal period and the parallel social movements that are reinvigorating claims to land throughout Latin America today.

Governments have often underestimated the complexities of transforming the land tenure structure. They have also misjudged the intricate dynamic processes set in motion by the agrarian reform which frequently had unexpected and unintended consequences. The social and political struggles unleashed by agrarian reforms often provoked dramatic counter-reforms or neo-reforms. Their outcome has thus been varied and has given rise to a more complex and fluid agrarian system across Latin America. While initially some agrarian reforms were intended to benefit the peasantry, the predominant outcome has favored the development of capitalist farming (de Janvry and Sadoulet 1989). The recent shift to neoliberal economic policies has given an additional impetus to capitalist farming while further marginalizing peasant farming and sparking the emergence of new land claims based on ethnicity in many countries.

Although the era of agrarian reform appears to have come to a close, this does not necessarily mean that the land question has been resolved in Latin America. It only means that it no longer commands the political support of nation states it did during the 1960s and 1970s. Cold War concerns arising from the Cuban revolution and an emergent peasant movement at that time put agrarian reform firmly on the political agenda (de Janvry 1994). Neoliberal land policies have shifted priorities away from expropriation, which typified the populist agrarian reform period, towards privatization, decollectivization, land registration, titling, and land tax issues, as the following two case studies in this book will show.

The most significant symbol of the neoliberal winds sweeping through Latin America has been the change made in 1992 to Article 27 of Mexico's Constitution of 1917. This had opened the road to Latin America's first modern agrarian reform and enshrined the peasants' principal demand for "land and liberty." No government had dared to modify this key principle of Mexico's Constitution until the forces of globalization and neoliberalism proved too strong to resist (Barkin 1994; Randall 1996). The new agrarian law marks the end of Mexico's agrarian reform. It allows the sale of land belonging to the reform sector and the establishment of joint ventures with private capital including foreign capitalists. It also indicates Mexico's commitment to NAFTA—the free trade agreement with the United States and Canada—which Mexico joined in 1994.

The first part of this chapter analyzes the causes and objectives of agrarian reform. While governments often used agriculture's dismal growth record between 1945 and the 1960s to justify agrarian reform legislation, other internal and external pressures drove them to accept and promote agrarian reform.

The next section highlights the collectivist character of the more significant agrarian reforms in Latin America and examines their economic and social impact. This section helps contextualize the meaning of the neoliberal agrarian counter reforms in Latin America from the perspective of how they have potentially rearranged social life in the countryside. This section is followed by a discussion of the impacts of agrarian reform in Latin America. In this section I go beyond a strictly economic analysis of these reforms to highlight their social and political meanings.

Finally, the chapter explores the impact of neoliberal land policies in those countries where these have been followed for a significant period, such as in Chile and in Peru. This discussion includes a reflection on the implications for ecologically sustainable agriculture of these counter-reforms.

Experiences of Agrarian Reform: Causes and Objectives

Latin America's dismal agricultural economic performance from the end of World War II until the beginning of the agrarian reform period in the 1960s led to a lively debate between structuralists and neoclassical economists over the causes of this state of affairs (CEPAL 1963; ECLA 1968; Feder 1971; Lehmann 1978; Valdés and Siamwalla 1988). While structuralists stressed the unequal and bimodal land tenure system, neoclassical economists emphasized the ways they thought public policy discriminated against the emergence of a capitalist, productive agriculture.

Land tenure and labor structure in Latin American agriculture had already begun to change prior to the implementation of agrarian reforms. In the changing political climate of the 1950s and 1960s, landlords foresaw the prospect of agrarian reform legislation and took evasive action. In order to avoid expropriation, some landlords reduced the size of their estates by subdividing it among family members or by selling some land. In addition, they attempted to reduce the internal pressure for expropriation from rural labor by reducing the number of tenants and replacing permanent workers with seasonal wage laborers. Through these actions, landlords aimed to reduce the internal pressure for land from tenants who, as agricultural producers, were keen to expand their tenancy and reduce rent payments. Compared to permanent wage laborers, seasonal workers had fewer legal rights and could be more easily dismissed or laid off as the situation demanded. Mechanization allowed landlords to reshape the composition of their labor force and to reduce it substantially, thereby further weakening internal pressures for land redistribution and higher wages.

Thus the mere threat of an agrarian reform could precipitate the breakup and capitalization of the *hacienda*.[1] Agrarian reform legislation generally exempted farms below a certain size from expropriation and in some cases even farms that exceeded this limit so long as they were considered to be modern and efficient farms. Landlords attempted to evade expropriation by subdividing (often fictitiously) and/or modernizing their estates. Sometimes governments even encouraged landlords to undertake their own "private" land reform by giving them a time limit in which to dispose of their excess land by selling it to their tenants or other smallholders, as in El Salvador in the mid 1980s (Kowalchuk 1998), or even to other capitalists. The criteria of efficiency employed often referred to the existence of machinery and the use of wage labor rather than tenant labor. Tenancies were particularly frowned upon as they were considered to be part of a feudal and oppressive labor regime.

The most far-reaching agrarian reforms have tended to be the outcome of social revolutions. Such was the case in Mexico (1917), Bolivia (1952), Cuba (1959), and Nicaragua (1979). However, radical agrarian reforms were also undertaken by elected governments, as in Chile during the Frei (1964–79) and Allende (1970–73) administrations and even by military regimes as in Peru during the government of General Velasco Alvarado (1969–75). Civilian governments carried out less wide-ranging agrarian reforms in terms of the amount of land expropriated and the number of peasant beneficiaries in the remainder of Latin America. The major exception is Argentina, where to date no agrarian reform has taken place and agrarian reform has not formed part of the political agenda. The uniqueness of the Argentine case is explained in part by the relative importance of family farming and middle capitalist farms as well as by the relatively high degree of urbanization. Paraguay and Uruguay had colonization programs, but in neither country has a significant agrarian reform taken place.

Although often spurred on by deep social changes and pressures from below, agrarian reforms have generally been the outcome of political changes from above. In fact, few agrarian reforms in Latin America were the direct result of peasant uprisings. Urban social forces and even international forces, as in the case of the Alliance for Progress, played an important role in bringing about agrarian reform. While the peasantry was not an important social force behind agrarian reform legislation, it did significantly influence the process itself. Thus those areas where rural protest was strongest tended to receive the most attention from agrarian reform agencies.

Technocratic and reformist governments seeking to modernize agriculture and integrate the peasantry often initiated agrarian reforms. Not surprisingly they have confronted opposition from landlords who, in some instances, succeeded in blocking or reversing them. Agrarian reforms are social processes the unintended consequences of which may redirect the initial purpose of the agrarian reform along radical or conservative lines (but usually the latter) or in some instances derail it completely. In Guatemala President Arbenz's agrarian reform of 1952 was brought to an abrupt end in 1954 when he was overthrown by an armed invasion with support from the U.S. government. Arbenz's agrarian reform measures that had expropriated about one-fifth of the country's arable land and benefited close to one-quarter of the peasantry were quickly reversed (Brockett 1989, 100). In Chile Frei's moderate agrarian reform of 1964–1970 fuelled demands from the peasant movement for intensification of the reform process. The radicalization of the peasant movement was a factor helping Allende to win the presidency in 1970. Peasant radicalism in turn pushed Allende's democratic socialist program for expropriations beyond what was originally intended (Kay 1978). The subsequent military coup of 1973, which repressed and disarticulated the peasant movement, returned only a proportion of the expropriated land to former owners. Despite the political power of the military government, they did not undo the agrarian reform completely.

Governments pursued a variety of objectives with agrarian reform. A major objective, and the primary one of the more technocratic types of agrarian reform, was a higher rate of agricultural growth. Only inefficient estates were to be expropriated and the more entrepreneurial estates were encouraged to modernize further. It was expected that less land would be left idle and that land would be cultivated more intensely thereby increasing agricultural output. Another economic (and social) objective was equity. A fairer distribution of income was regarded as facilitating the import-substituting-industrialization process by widening the domestic market for industrial goods. A more dynamic agricultural sector would lower food prices, generate more foreign exchange, and create more demand for industrial commodities. Thus the underlying economic objective was to speed up the country's industrialization process.

Agrarian reforms also had social and political objectives. By distributing land to peasants, governments hoped to ease social conflicts in the countryside and to gain the peasantry's political support. By means of land redistribution and measures assisting the creation or strengthening of peasant organizations, governments aimed to incorporate the peasantry into the social and political system. Giving peasants a stake in society would strengthen civil society and the democratic system. More radical types of agrarian reforms were particularly keen to organize and mobilize the peasantry in order to weaken landlord opposition to expropriation.

Governments also aimed to increase their support among the industrial bourgeoisie whose economic interests could be furthered by agrarian reform. However, this was more problematic as industrialists often had close ties with the landed class and were fearful that social mobilization in the countryside could spill over into urban areas. Political links between landlords and the urban bourgeoisie were far closer than commonly thought and the bourgeoisie generally placed their political interests above temporary economic gains. They were well aware that agrarian reforms could gain a momentum of their own and spill over into urban unrest. This would intensify workers' demands for higher wages, better working conditions, and even lead to demands for the expropriation of urban enterprises. The Chilean agrarian reform experience is a good illustration of just such a situation. The increasing demands and mobilization of rural and urban workers strengthened the alliance between the rural and urban bourgeoisie, including some middle class sectors. In Peru the progressive military government of Velasco Alvarado undertook a sweeping agrarian reform in the expectation that this would help the country's industrialization process. However, it also failed to win the industrial bourgeoisie's support for such a development project and was unable to persuade expropriated landlords to invest their agrarian reform bonds, paid out as compensation for expropriated land, in industrial ventures. Such reluctance was not surprising given that the government was creating a social property sector in which the state controlled all major industrial and commercial firms and allowed a degree of worker participation.

Although agrarian reforms were largely instituted from above, once expropriation was underway conflicts in the countryside often escalated. Peasants demanded a widening and deepening of the agrarian reform process. Landlords opposed such demands and pressured the government, and in some instances the armed forces, to suppress the increasingly bold actions of the peasants. This was particularly the case in countries where political parties and NGOs used the reformist opening in the country's political system to strengthen peasant organizations and assist their social mobilization. Support, or lack of it, from urban-based political parties and urban social groups was often crucial in determining the outcome of the reform process.

Statist and Collectivist Character of the Reformed Sector

Collective and cooperative forms of organization within the reformed sector were far more common than the capitalist context of Latin America, with the exception of Cuba, would lead us to expect. In Mexico, the *ejido* dominated in the reformed sector particularly since the Cárdenas government of the 1930s. *Ejidos* are a communal type of organization, although farming is largely carried out on a household basis. Until recently it was illegal to sell *ejido* land. In Cuba state farms predominated since the early days of the revolution, and by the mid-1980s most individual peasant farmers had joined production cooperatives. Production cooperatives and state farms were the dominant farm organization in Chile's reformed sector from 1964 to 1973. This was also the case in Peru during Velasco Alvarado's agrarian reform of 1969 until their gradual dissolution in the 1980s, in Nicaragua during the Sandinista revolution of 1979 until 1990, and in El Salvador during the Christian Democrat regime of 1980–89. Only a small proportion of the expropriated land was distributed directly as private peasant family farms.

An important explanation for the statist and collectivist character of Latin America's most important agrarian reforms lies in the inherited agrarian structure. Prior to reform large-scale farming prevailed in the form of plantations, *haciendas, and estancias*. Governments feared that subdividing these large-landed estates into peasant family farms might erode economies of scale, reduce foreign exchange earnings as peasant farmers would switch from export-crop to food-crop production, impair technological improvements, limit the number of beneficiaries, and reproduce the problems of the *minifundia*.[2] Furthermore, a collective reformed sector reduced subdivision costs, allowed more direct government control over production and, in some instances, marketing, and could foster internal solidarity. In those countries pursuing a socialist path of development as in Cuba, Allende's Chile, and Nicaragua under the Sandinistas, a collectivist emphasis was also underpinned by political and ideological factors. In some cases collective forms of organization were regarded as transitory as in Chile and El Salvador. As beneficiaries gained entrepreneurial and technical experience a gradual process of decollectivization was envisaged.

Agrarian reform policymakers throughout Latin America greatly underestimated the relative importance of peasant farming, such as sharecropping and labor-service tenancies, within large landed estates. National census data generally failed to record, or to record accurately, the number of peasant tenant enterprises within the *hacienda* system (the "internal peasant economy"). This led them to underestimate the difficulties of organizing collective farming and the pressure that beneficiaries would exercise within the collective enterprise for the expansion of their own family enterprise. The new managers of the collective enterprises, generally appointed by the state, had far less authority over the beneficiaries than landlords had had over the peasantry and were unable to prevent the gradual erosion of the collective enterprise from within.

The enduring influence of large-landed enterprises on the post-reform situation is startling. In this sense the collectivist character of the reformed sector should not be overstated. This character was often more apparent than real. For example, in Peru about half the agricultural land of the reformed sector (collective and state farms) was cultivated on an individual basis. In Chile and El Salvador the figure was about a fifth and only in Cuba was it insignificant. These differences reflect the varying degrees of capitalist development and proletarianization of the agricultural labor force in each country before the agrarian reform.

The differences between types of estate, such as plantations and *haciendas*, were also reflected in the character of post-reform enterprises. Prior to expropriation, large coastal sugar plantations in Peru were capitalized and employed largely wage labor whereas the domestic-market oriented *haciendas* of the highlands relied more heavily on tenant labor. Evidently, it was far easier to set up centralized and collective management systems on the expropriated sugar plantations than on the highland *haciendas* and this had an important influence on the subsequent process of decollectivization.

One feature of Cuba's agrarian reforms (1959 and 1963), which is often overlooked, is the fact that the government greatly extended peasant proprietorship, giving ownership titles to an estimated 160,000 tenants, sharecroppers, and squatters. Before the revolution, peasant farmers had only numbered about 40,000 (Ghai, Kay, and Peek 1988, 10, 14). Cuba's agriculture was dominated by sugar plantations, and the agricultural labor force was largely proletarian. A large proportion of seasonal sugar cane cutters came from urban areas. The plantation sector was thus taken over by the state without much difficulty. Over time state farms were amalgamated into even larger units, becoming giant agro-industrial complexes under the direct control of either the Ministry of Agriculture or the Ministry of Sugar. Cuban policymakers were great believers in "large is beautiful." It was not until almost two decades after the revolution that the Cuban leadership launched a campaign for the cooperativization of peasant farmers. They were encouraged to form Agricultural and Livestock Production Cooperatives (*Cooperativas de Producción Agropecuaria* or CPA), having resisted joining state farms, and within a decade over two-thirds of all peasant farmers had done so. CPAs clearly outperformed state farms (Kay 1988b), eventually leading to the latter's transformation.

Impact of Agrarian Reforms

Like the neoliberal reforms of the 1980s, the agrarian reforms of previous decades can be assessed in narrow economic terms or in broader systemic and institutional terms. We can evaluate them in terms of their impact on growth, employment, income distribution, poverty, and socio-political participation, as well as in terms of a wider context of development. More recent evaluations have included the impact of agrarian reforms on gender divisions and on the environment, for example, as chapters by Deere and León and by Hvalkof in this volume also illustrate.

While agrarian reform may be a pre-condition for sustainable development, it is not a sufficient condition. Agrarian reform should not be regarded as a cure-all for all the ills afflicting Latin American rural economies and societies, despite the initial tendency for agrarian reform to be seen in this light. Agrarian reforms were perceived as a way of liberating the peasantry from landlordism with its associated feudal and exploitative conditions. They were seen as a way of achieving equitable rural development that would reduce rural poverty. They were also considered important for facilitating

Latin America's struggling industrialization process by expanding the domestic market and easing foreign exchange constraints.

Most agrarian reforms failed to fulfil expectations for a variety of reasons. In some instances, agrarian reform was implemented in a half-hearted fashion by governments paying lip service for domestic or foreign political purposes, be it to gain votes from the peasantry or aid from international agencies. In other instances fierce political opposition from landlords, sometimes with the support of sectors of the bourgeoisie, restricted reforms.

In this section I will consider four economic and social categories of potential impact of the agrarian reforms on the societies that implemented them. These are agricultural production, income distribution, gender relations (examined more closely in the following chapter by Deere and León), and political participation.

Agricultural Production

The impact of agrarian reform on agricultural production has been mixed. Most analysts agree that the results fell well below expectations. In Mexico agricultural production increased by 325 percent from 1934 to 1965, the highest rate in Latin America during this period. However, this was the result of the impetus given to agrarian reform by the Cárdenas government and the supportive measures for agricultural development. Thereafter, Mexican agricultural performance has been poor (Thiesenhusen 1995a, 41). Nevertheless, research has shown that the *ejido* reform sector, which is overwhelmingly farmed as individual family-plots, is as productive as farms of equivalent size in the private sector (Heath 1992). However, the most dynamic sector in Mexican agriculture is formed by private middle and large scale farmers. During the past few decades these have been the main beneficiaries of government policies favoring commercial agriculture. Major public investment in irrigation and provision of subsidized credits have principally favored large farmers and export agriculture while neglecting the *ejido* food producing sector.[3]

In Bolivia, marketed agricultural output in the years immediately after agrarian reform declined as reform beneficiaries increased their own food consumption. With respect to production, some argue that production levels were maintained; others say that it took almost a decade for production to reach its pre-revolutionary level (Thiesenhusen 1995a, 64). Subsequently much of agriculture's growth was achieved through the colonization of the eastern lowlands, a process encouraged by the state and designed to boost commercial farming and export agriculture.

In Chile, agrarian reform initially had a very favorable impact on agricultural production. This increased by an annual average rate of 4.6 percent between 1965 and 1968, three times faster than in the previous two decades (Kay 1978). However, growth slowed down in the last two years of the Frei (Sr.) administration. Under the Allende government production increased significantly in the first year, stagnated during the second year and declined sharply in 1973 as a result of socio-political upheavals and input shortages (Kay 1978). It is estimated that much of the initial increase in agricultural output came from the commercial farm sector. This is not surprising given that landlords often kept the best land and farm equipment. The reformed sector performed reasonably well at first, receiving much government support in the form of credits, technical assistance, marketing facilities, mechanization, and so on. This is no mean achievement given that landlords had decapitalized their estate before expropriation. However, as the expropriation process escalated and strained the administrative and economic resources of the state, the reformed sector faced increasing problems. Internal organizational problems began to arise as beneficiaries devoted more time to their individual plots than to the collective enterprise.

In Peru the agrarian reform did not lead to an increase of agricultural production. The growth rate of 1.8 percent from 1970 to 1976 was similar to the average pre-reform rate of the 1960s (Kay 1982, 161). From 1970 to 1980 the average annual growth rate of agriculture was even negative, Peru having been affected by drought in 1978 and by a severe economic recession in the late 1970s (ECLAC 1993, 76). During the 1980s agriculture recovered, growing by 2 percent yearly but this was still below population growth (IDB 1993, 261, 267). The reformed sector, plagued with internal conflicts between government-appointed managers and beneficiaries, was partly responsible for this poor performance. The state exacerbated matters by its failure to provide resources or adequate technical training to beneficiaries and by its continued adherence to a cheap food policy that reduced the reformed sector's profitability. Furthermore, reformed enterprises experienced land invasions by highland peasant communities and suffered from the violent activities of the Shining Path guerrilla movement in the 1980s.

In Nicaragua a series of factors conspired against the economic success of the 1979 agrarian reform. In the previous decade agriculture had been stagnant. After agrarian reform in the 1980s agricultural output declined on average by 0.9 percent yearly (IDB 1993, 267). Again, armed conflict between the *contras* and the government severely disrupted production. Other contributing factors were the insecurity of tenure which inhibited investment by private farmers, the mass slaughter of livestock by farmers facing expropriation, shortages of labor, disruption of the marketing system, and, last but not least, mismanagement of the reformed enterprises (Enríquez 1991).

In El Salvador the 1980 agrarian reform was implemented during a period of civil war that came to an end in 1992 (Seligson 1995; Paige 1996). Gross domestic product declined by 0.4 percent yearly while agriculture fell by 0.7 percent yearly in the 1980s (IDB 1993, 263, 267). The commonly-held view that individual farming is superior to collective farming is not born out in El Salvador. Yields achieved on the collective land of the producer cooperatives were often higher than those obtained on family plots either within or outside the reformed sector (Pelupessy 1995, 148).

Income Distribution, Employment, and Poverty

The gains in income distribution derived from agrarian reforms were also less than anticipated. Not surprisingly, the redistributive effects are greater where more land is expropriated and distributed to a larger proportion of the rural population, especially the rural poor. The less paid out in compensation to landlords and the less the beneficiaries have to pay for the land, the greater will be the redistributive impact. Similarly, an agrarian reform has a greater redistributive effect in countries with a relatively large rural economy and population. The redistributivist impact is also much influenced by social policy and by the performance of the economy as a whole. In Cuba, for example, the redistributivist impact of the agrarian reform was much higher than in Ecuador. This was not only because agrarian reform was far less significant in Ecuador but because health and educational policies in Cuba targeted the rural poor. In Peru, it is estimated that Velasco's agrarian reform redistributed only 1–2 percent of national income through land transfers to about a third of peasant families (Figueroa 1977, 160). Sugar workers on the coast, already the highest paid rural workers, benefited most while comuneros,[4] the largest and poorest group amongst the peasantry, benefited least (Kay 1983, 231–32).

The initial positive redistributivist impact of many agrarian reforms in Latin America was often subsequently cancelled out by the poor performance of the reformed sector (collective or private) and by macroeconomic factors such as unfavorable internal terms of trade and foreign exchange policy. If agriculture and the economy are stagnant, all that has been redistributed is poverty. In addition, by excluding the poorest segments of the rural population, such as members of peasant communities, minifundistas, and seasonal wage laborers from land redistribution, many agrarian reforms increased socio-economic differentiation among the peasantry. Tenant laborers and permanent wage workers, who generally became full members of the reformed sector, sometimes continued the landlord practice of employing outside seasonal labor for a low wage or renting out pastures or other resources of the reformed sector to *minifundistas* and *comuneros*. They could thus be perceived by non-members as the new landlords. This was particularly the case in Peru, El Salvador, and Nicaragua but also elsewhere in Latin America.

The income distribution effect of agrarian reform also depends on its influence on employment. In Peru it is estimated that the rate of male agricultural employment tripled in the decade following the Peruvian agrarian reform but this still only grew at a modest 0.9 percent per year (Kay 1982, 161). The net employment effects of the Chilean agrarian reform were also small as rural outmigration continued unabated. The *reservas*[5] used less labor per hectare than the former *haciendas*, owing to their higher degree of capitalization. However, a countervailing tendency existed in the reformed sector that employed more labor per hectare, particularly family labor, than the former estate. However, in some reform enterprises the amount of land cultivated declined due to capital and input shortages thereby reducing the employment effect.

Given the disappointing record of agrarian reforms with respect to agricultural production, income distribution, and employment, their impact on poverty alleviation is likely to be marginal. While standards of living generally improved for the direct beneficiaries of agrarian reform, these were not generally the poorest section of rural society. As mentioned earlier, the beneficiaries of agrarian reforms, with the exception of Cuba, did not include the *minifundistas*, seasonal wage laborers, and *comuneros* or members from the indigenous communities who account for the largest share of the rural poor and, particularly, of the rural destitute.

However, the Mexican and, to some extent, the Bolivian agrarian reforms did redistribute land to indigenous communities. As also discussed by Hvalkof in this volume, in Peru, following a decade of protests and land invasions of reformed farms by *comuneros*, some land was transferred to indigenous communities. Nonetheless any gains are easily eroded in periods of economic crisis, such as occurred during the so-called lost decade of the 1980s provoked by Latin America's debt crisis. Estimates of rural poverty vary because of the inadequacy of the data, and the different methodologies and definitions employed. At best rural poverty remained constant during the 1980s, arresting the improvements made in the previous decades (Feres and León 1990), while the incidence of destitution increased from 28 to 31 percent of rural households (Altimir 1994, 22–23). At worst rural poverty rose from 45 percent to over half of Latin America's rural population ("Mexico Survey: rural revolution" 1993, 43).

Gender Relations

With respect to gender inequalities the assessment is rather negative. As Deere and León show in their chapter, for the region's counter-reforms most land reform legislation ignored the position of women, failing to include them explicitly as beneficiaries, to grant them land titles, or to incorporate them into key administrative and decision-making processes in the cooperatives, state farms and other organizations emanating from the reform process. Even in Cuba, women made up only one-quarter of production cooperative members and even less on state farms (Deere 1987, 171). In Mexico women comprised 15 percent of *ejido* members, and in Nicaragua and Peru women were only 6 and 5 percent of cooperative members respectively (Deere 1987).

Women were excluded as beneficiaries due to legal, structural, and ideological factors. The stipulation that only one household member can become an official beneficiary tended to discriminate against women, given the assumption that men were head of the household (Deere 1985). The agrarian reform in Chile indeed reinforced the role of men as main breadwinners and provided few opportunities for women to participate in the running of the reformed sector, despite some legislation promoting this during the Allende government (Tinsman 1996).

Socio-Political Integration: Participation and Stability

The greatest contribution of agrarian reforms may lie in the stimulus given to institution-building in the countryside, a point that Hvalkof extends in his chapter on indigenous land titling in Peru. Governments facilitated the organization of the peasantry into trade unions and cooperatives of various kinds, such as producer, marketing, and credit associations. This brought about a considerable degree of integration of the peasantry into the national economy, society, and polity. Prior to reform, insurmountable obstacles lay in the way of peasants creating their own organizations. Political parties began to vie for the peasant vote and extended their networks to rural areas where, in the past, reformist and left wing political parties in particular had often been excluded by the landed oligarchy. With the agrarian reform, peasant participation in civil society was much enhanced. Many peasants, especially after being granted a land title, felt that only then had they become citizens. By weakening the power of landlords and other dominant groups in the countryside, agrarian reforms encouraged the emergence of a greater voice for the peasantry in local and national affairs. However, the peasantry's greater organizational and participatory presence did not embrace all categories of peasants and all regions of the country. There were also setbacks from which, in some instances, peasants have yet to recover.

Agrarian reform programs were usually accompanied by legislation or other measures to promote peasant organizations. Governments often sought to establish peasant organizations that would extend and consolidate their influence in the countryside. Although more successful in gaining the allegiance of peasants from the reformed sector who were the direct beneficiaries of government patronage, they were not always able to keep their allegiance. Some peasant organizations came to regard government patronage as a hindrance to the pursuance of their aims and sought a degree of autonomy from the government co-optation.

In Mexico, agrarian reform clearly contributed to the stability of the political system (although not necessarily to its democratic development). For many decades the PRI successfully co-opted the peasantry but in recent years their hegemony is being challenged by a variety of political forces and its grip over the peasantry has loosened, as evidenced by the Zapatista rebellion in Chiapas in southern Mexico and now of course by the recent national elections that ousted the PRI from its once trenchant position in the country. In Cuba the agrarian reform certainly strengthened the Castro regime as the reform was popular and benefited a large proportion of the rural labor force. In Bolivia the agrarian reform, by granting land to Amerindian peasants, reduced social conflicts in the countryside. The threat to political stability largely came from other social forces.

In the short term, however, agrarian reforms have tended to intensify social conflicts in the countryside and society at large. In Chile strikes and land seizures by farm workers escalated as peasants became organized, gained in self-confidence, and had less to fear from repression. Landlords could no longer so easily dismiss striking farm workers nor count on swift retribution from the state against a peasant movement which was demanding an acceleration and extension of the expropriation process. The intensification of conflicts in the countryside contributed to the military overthrow of the Allende government and brought an end to the democratic system that had distinguished Chile from most other Latin American countries.

The agrarian reform in Chile involved a major organizational effort. While in 1965 only 2,100 rural wage workers were affiliated to agricultural trade unions, this figure increased to 140,000 in 1970 and to 282,000 by the end of 1972 (Kay 1978, 125). This meant that about four-fifths of all rural wage workers were members of trade unions, an unusually high figure within the Latin American context. Pinochet's dictatorship greatly weakened peasant organizations to the extent that they have found it very difficult to rebuild their former strength with the democratic transition since 1990.

In Peru the military government of Velasco Alvarado set up the peasant organization Confederación Nacional Agraria (CNA) as a rival to the autonomous peasant organization Confederación Campesina del Perú (CCP) which was founded in 1947. However, CNA became increasingly independent of government tutelage, demanding a more radical expropriation process and a greater say in the running of the reformed enterprises that were largely managed by the state. As a result of CNA's growing independence and strength—at one point CNA had twice as many members as CCP—the government dissolved it in 1978. Conflicts between agrarian reform beneficiaries and peasant communities, whereby *comuneros* invaded the land of the reformed sector, subsided when the government transferred some land from the reformed sector to the peasant communities. Although the Shining Path guerrilla movement was partly spawned by the agrarian reform, it failed to root itself in the countryside and even less so in those regions with the greatest agrarian reform activity.

In Nicaragua the Sandinista agrarian reform also provoked a major organizational effort of the peasantry (Enríquez 1997). The government helped to set up the Unión Nacional de Agricultores y Ganaderos (UNAG) in 1981, and by 1987 one-fifth of all agricultural workers had joined (Blokland 1992, 154). UNAG also managed to wrench a greater degree of autonomy from the state over time and has remained the most important peasant and farmer organization in the countryside to this day.

In short, agrarian reforms were often restricted in scope and thwarted in their aims by opposition forces or by government mismanagement. However, in those countries where agrarian transformation went deeper and where poverty and social exclusion were significantly reduced, social stability and political integration are taking hold and facilitating economic development. Hence it is possible to argue that, from a longer term perspective, agrarian reforms have promoted albeit a precarious social stability and made a major contribution to the democratization of society. While agrarian reforms marked a watershed in the history of rural society in many Latin American countries, the root causes of social and political instability will remain as long as relatively high levels of rural poverty and peasant marginalization persist. It can be concluded from the above that agrarian reforms provide a framework for growth, equity, and sustainable development in rural society only when accompanied by complementary policies and appropriate macroeconomic measures. Whilst clearly facilitated by a favorable external environment, internal transformations remain critical for determining the outcome of the agrarian process. Rather than being seen as the answer to economic and political development, agrarian reform is best seen as an important instrument of transformation for attaining these objectives.

Counter-Reform and Land Titling in the Neoliberal Period

The neoliberal winds sweeping through Latin America (and indeed the world) since the 1980s have had major consequences for the rural sector. State enterprises that had provided a series of subsidized services to farmers and peasants, such as agro-industrial, marketing, technical assistance, and banking agencies, have been privatized. Reforms in the foreign trade regime and removal of price controls changed relative prices giving an incentive to agricultural exports. Commercial farmers were best able to adapt to these changing circumstances and to exploit some of the profitable export opportunities, particularly in non-traditional agro-exports. By contrast, peasant farmers were ill-equipped to meet the neoliberal challenge given their traditional disadvantage in the market. However, a minority of peasant groups with better resource endowment, entrepreneurial skills, locational advantages, or access to markets and support from NGOs, have adapted successfully.

In place of agrarian reform, neoliberalism favors a land policy that emphasizes free markets and security of property rights. An active and free land market in this view results in the reallocation of land to the most able producers. Furthermore, security of tenure would stimulate long term investment. International agencies such as the World Bank and NGOs financed programs of land registration and titling throughout Latin America to reduce the number of peasant farmers, especially in regions of colonization, with insecure or no titles. It was argued that secure and transparent property rights would facilitate land transactions and give producers access to credit as they could use their property as collateral.

Neoliberals strongly advocate individual property rights as these are seen to lead to greater efficiency and market transparency compared to collective or communal systems. They thus encouraged governments to introduce measures to privatize indigenous peasant communities' land as well as to break up the collectivist reformed sector (Bretón 1997; Zoomers 1997). In some cases these neoliberal measures formalized an ongoing unravelling of the reformed sector (and of communal arrangements within peasant communities). Beneficiaries had already begun to look for individual solutions to the collectives' or cooperatives' problems arising from mismanagement and inadequate state support. This generally meant expanding a peasant economy within the reformed sector. Collective agriculture encountered the familiar problems of inadequate individual work incentives and free-riders. Beneficiaries were generally paid the same wage regardless of work performance. Some members did not even bother to show up for work and many began to work for less than five hours per day. Management controls were often lax and collective resources and inputs were often misused or privately appropriated. Profits, if they did materialize, were often redistributed instead of being invested. At times management was too remote, failing to consult or involve members of the collective in the decision-making process. This pressure on collective agriculture was exacerbated by land seizures by those peasants living in indigenous peasant communities or in smallholder areas left out of the agrarian reform process.

Under neoliberal governments—be they democratic or military—cooperative, collective, and state farms have been dismantled. With the parcelling out of the reformed sector, land reform beneficiaries now became the owners of a plot of land, often known as the *parcela*. The growth of this new group, referred to here as *parceleros*, has greatly expanded the peasant farm sector in many Latin American countries. Chile was the first to initiate this process in late 1973. Peru has followed more gradually from 1980, Nicaragua since 1990, and Mexico and El Salvador since 1992. Some expropriated land has been returned to former owners (particularly in Chile) but most was distributed as individual family farms to members of the reformed sector. In some countries a significant proportion of reform sector members was unable to secure a parcel and thus joined the ranks of the rural proletariat. This parcelization doubled or even tripled the land area under the ownership of the peasant farm sector. To what extent this will lead to the development of a peasant road to agrarian capitalism remains to be seen. The prospects, however, are not favorable as a fair proportion of peasants who initially gained access to a piece of land have had to sell it as they were unable to keep up their repayments or finance their farm operations. The process of peasantization has turned sour for many who are facing "impoverishing peasantization" or complete proletarianization.

In Chile, under the counter-reform of Pinochet's military government, about 30 percent of expropriated land was returned to former owners, almost 20 percent was sold to private individuals or institutional investors, and about half remained in the reformed sector (Jarvis 1992, 192). The reformed sector itself was subdivided into *parcelas* or *unidades agrícolas familiares* (agricultural family units) through a process of parcelization. Under half of the original beneficiaries were unable to obtain a *parcela* because the size of the reformed sector was reduced by half through the counter-reform and because *parcelas* were relatively generous, averaging about nine basic irrigated hectares.[6] *Parceleros* had, on average, roughly nine times more land (expressed in basic irrigated hectares) than *minifundistas*. In the allocation of *parcelas* there was clear political discrimination against peasant activists who were expelled from the reformed sector. *Parceleros* had to pay for the land that was sold to them by the state for about half its market value.

Nevertheless, in subsequent years about half of the *parceleros* had to sell up being unable to repay their debts (incurred when purchasing the *parcela* and consequent losses), or because they lacked capital, management, and market experience.

A notable difference between the pre- and post-reform land tenure structure in Chile is that in the post-reform period the 5 to 20 basic irrigated hectares (b.i.h.) farm sector more than doubled, while the over 80 b.i.h. farm sector was reduced by more than half (Kay 1993, 21). This sizeable growth of the 5–20 b.i.h. farm sector, which presently comprises about a quarter of the country's agricultural land, is largely due to the parcelization process. It is composed of middle and rich peasants as well as by small capitalist farmers. The formation of *reservas* and the partial return of expropriated estates to former landlords have also led to a significant expansion of middle and medium-to-large capitalist farmers (i.e., those with 20–80 b.i.h. who now own almost a third of the country's land). Large farms of over 80 b.i.h. have little in common with the former *hacienda* and comprise about a quarter of the country's land. The average farm size in this sector is far smaller than the *hacienda* having been reduced from 235 to about 125 b.i.h. (Jarvis 1992, 201). More importantly, the social and technical relations of production have been completely transformed into thoroughly modern large capitalist farms. Many middle and large capitalist farms shifted their production pattern to non-traditional agricultural exports that have formed the backbone of Chile's agro-export boom during the previous two decades. Few parceleros, let alone *minifundistas*, can participate in agro-export production and reap the benefits of this boom (Murray 1997).

In Peru, agricultural production cooperatives on the coast, with the exception of the sugar cooperatives, were subdivided into *parcelas* and transferred to members of the cooperative. *Parcelas* were typically between 3 to 6 hectares in size and averaged 4.5 hectares. In the highlands, part of the cooperatives' land was transferred collectively to adjacent peasant communities (a process referred to as *redimensionamiento*) and part was distributed to individual members of the cooperative as *parcelas*. It has taken many years to legalize this land transfer and titling process. Indeed, both are still ongoing. The Peruvian parcelization process is the largest to date in Latin America. The under 10 hectares farm-size sector, of which a significant part is *parcelas*, currently controls about one-half of Peru's agricultural land and about two-thirds of the country's livestock (Eguren 1997, 132). However, lack of finance, among other factors, greatly hampers the development of the *parcelero* farm sector.

Cuba has not remained unaffected by the neoliberal turn. The demise of the Soviet Union and the transition of the former socialist countries from a planned to a market system mean that Cuba has also had to adjust its social-ist system. Greater opportunities and economic incentives have been provided for peasant farmers and producer cooperatives. In 1994 private agricultural markets were introduced in which prices are not controlled by the state and where producers can sell any surplus that remains after meet-ing their quota to the state market. Given the higher achievement of the cooperative sector since late 1993, the enormous state-farm sector is being decentralized into cooperative type management units through the creation of Basic Units of Cooperative Production (*Unidades Básicas de Producción Cooperativa* or UBPC). The UBPC members are given a certain amount of productive resources, negotiate their production plans with the state, and can distribute any profits among themselves. The cooperative-farm sector is now far more important than the state-farm sector which once owned four-fifths of Cuba's land. Indications are that UBPCs have significantly improved the performance of the former state farms (Deere 1995).

In short, agrarian reform and the subsequent unravelling of the reformed sector have given rise to a more complex agrarian structure. It reduced and transformed the *latifundia* system, and enlarged the peasant and the commercial middle- and middle-to-large-farm sectors. Privatization also increased heterogeneity among the peasantry as the leveling tendencies of collectivist agriculture have been removed. Following the introduction of neoliberal policies the commercial-farmer road to agrarian capitalism is gaining the upper hand. Capitalist farmers are the ones who stand to ben-efit from the liberalization of land, labor, and financial markets, the further opening of the economy to international competition, the new drive to exports, and the withdrawal of supportive measures for the peasant sector. Their greater land, capital, and technical resources, their superior links with national and especially international markets, and their greater influence on agricultural policy ensure that they are more able to exploit the new mar-ket opportunities than peasant farmers.

New Meanings of the Land Question: Ethnicity and Ecology

The neoliberal project has certainly not gone unchallenged by peasants and other rural groups. The 1994 peasant rebellion in Chiapas, the most south-ern and indigenous region of Mexico, was fuelled by the exclusionary impact of Mexico's agricultural modernization on the peasantry and by fears that Mexico's integration into NAFTA would marginalize them further (de Jan-vry, Gordillo, and Sadoulet 1997; Harvey 1998). Indeed the Chiapas rebel-lion has come to symbolize the new character of social movements in the countryside in Latin America. The peasantry is striking back and it would be a serious mistake to dismiss these new peasant and indigenous movements in Latin America as the last gasp of rebellion. Over the last decade the peasantry has reemerged as a significant force for social change not only in Mexico but also in Brazil, Ecuador, Bolivia, Paraguay, Colombia, and El Salvador, among other Latin American countries.

In Brazil the principal protagonist in the countryside has been the landless workers movement of the MST (*Movimento dos Trabalhadores Rurais Sem Terra*) that has spearheaded over 1,000 land invasions or take-overs of estates, demanding their expropriation. This comes as no surprise as land inequality is particularly acute in Brazil where only 4 percent of farm owners control 79 percent of the country's arable land (Veltmeyer, Petras, and Vieux 1997, 181). In these land occupations a variety of peasants were involved: rural semi-proletarians or proletarians, such as wage workers, squatters, sharecroppers, and tenants. By 1994, through direct action, which include blocking highways and occupying the local offices of the state's agrarian reform institute (INCRA), they had pressured the government into settling over 120,000 families on land since the beginning of their actions ten years earlier (Veltmeyer 1997, 192). In this struggle there have been many casualties as *fazendeiros* (landlords) and their hired guns (*pistoleiros*) have taken the law into their own hands. Many protestors have also died or been wounded in clashes between the militarized police and the landless peasants.

The Cardoso government promised in 1994 to grant land to 280,000 peasant households in four years under pressure from the MST with its campaign of selective invasion of fields belonging to large estates, occupation of town halls, and massive demonstrations. By the end of 1998—a year later than planned—the target had been achieved. However, far more needs to be done to satisfy the demand for land. According to the MST, 5 million families need land, while 340 million hectares are underused or lie idle. In reply Cardoso has pledged that a further 400,000 families, who have been occupying land abandoned by previous owners, will be granted formal title by the end of his second term of office in 2003 ("Land reform in Brazil" 1999, 60).

The land issue has been revived with the growing political prominence of environmental and ethnic movements. Furthermore, the environmental movements have evolved into struggles for social justice to prevent native groups from being displaced and their livelihoods threatened by the depredatory actions of commercial companies engaged in logging, mining, oil extraction, the building of dams for hydroelectric power stations, deforestation for pastureland and cattle raising, and so on. In Brazil the building of the Transamazon and other highways from the 1970s on led to large-scale deforestation and the expansion of pastureland, as big capital was lured to Amazônia by tax rebates, subsidies, and cheap credit. This led to a large scale migration of settlers, largely from the impoverished northeast to the tropical forest areas, contributing to environmental deterioration. This expansion of grazing and mining, or what Dore (1995, 262) has called the most extensive enclosure movement in history, encroached on the lands used by indigenous groups and rubber tappers. This sparked off the rubber tappers' movement as well as actions by native indigenous groups in defense of their livelihoods, bringing the Amazon environmental issue to world attention. The assassination in 1988 of Chico Mendes, the leader of the Amazon rubber tappers' movement, provoked an international outcry. His murder led to strong national and international pressure and prompted the government to accede to some of the rubber tappers' demands by establishing extractive reserves, the first of which was created in 1990, with many others following thereafter (Hall 1996).

During the past decade the resurgence of Indian ethnic identity in many Latin American countries has revitalized the social movement in the countryside and the struggle for land. (See Hvalkof's chapter for a detailed analysis of one of these struggles, and Deere and León's chapter for an overview of indigenous women's movements.) For example, in Ecuador, two major social mobilizations took place in 1990 and 1994 organized by the Confederation of Indigenous Nationalities of Ecuador (CONAIE). The action in 1990 led to a national Indian uprising, in which for an entire week tens of thousands of Indian peasants blocked highways, organized marches in various capitals, and occupied government offices (Zamosc 1994). Their protest was brought about by the economic recession resulting from the structural adjustment package. In the second mobilization of 1994 the protest was directed specifically against the introduction of neoliberal policies, and especially the new so-called "Agrarian Development Law." This law threatened the communal lands of indigenous groups, facilitating their privatization and ultimately favoring their transfer to capitalist farmers through the market mechanism. Thousands of indigenous communities, representing all of the country's ethnic nationalities, participated in this major 1994 mobilization. Peasants, small farmers, trade unions, and popular organizations also joined this protest and international environmental and human rights organizations offered their support (Pacari 1996). In Bolivia, a historic "march for territory and dignity" took place in 1990 where hundreds of people from lowland indigenous groups "trekked from the Amazon rainforest through the snow-capped Andes on route to the capital city to protest logging on indigenous lands and to demand legal rights to these lands" (Albó 1996, 15).

As Hvalkof shows us in this volume, ethnic groups have a higher profile in these new peasant movements than in the past, and in some ways have gone their separate ways from peasant-based movements. There is also a greater degree of ethnic consciousness and, in some cases, even demands for national autonomy, self-government, and territorial sovereignty. Indeed, indigenous territorial (as opposed to simply "land") politics offer a new vantage point unto a critique of neoliberalism, as Gudeman and Rivera-Gutiérrez also demonstrate in their chapter on Guatemala. While governments have not yielded to the claim for national autonomy, countries like Bolivia, Ecuador, Colombia, and Brazil have modified their constitutions to take the multi-ethnic character of the nation into account and to include provisions that recognize the linguistic, cultural, social, and territorial rights of the various indigenous groups. These processes are described in more detail in the following two chapters of this book.

This new character of the social movement in the countryside does not mean that traditional concerns have vanished. Demands for better wages and working conditions, land, improved prices for peasant products, greater and cheaper access to credit and technical assistance, among others, continue to be made, and in some instances with even greater urgency than in the past. However, new issues, such as the environment, are raised and some older issues have become less prominent or have acquired a different meaning. For example, the land question has acquired a new connotation with the conflicting territorial claims made by capitalists, small settlers, and indigenous groups as well as by the new ecological concerns. However, the increasing problem of landlessness in Brazil has given rise to a major class-based rural workers' movement under the leadership of the MST, and its demand for agrarian reform is reminiscent of past struggles for land. Furthermore, this social movement has been able to develop a national political agenda transcending narrow sectoral interests (Petras 1998).

Conclusions

The impact of agrarian reforms on the economy as well as on social and political participation is at best mixed. However, the institutional changes they entailed have undoubtedly contributed to capitalist development. Land and labor markets have become more flexible and investment opportunities in agriculture have improved, thereby enhancing agriculture's responsiveness to macroeconomic policy and global market forces. The main legacy of agrarian reform is its part in hastening the demise of the landed oligarchy and in clearing away the institutional debris that prevented the development of markets and the full commercialization of agriculture (albeit after the unravelling of the reformed sector). Thus the main winners have been the capitalist farmers. Although a minority of peasants gained some benefits, the promise of agrarian reform remains unfulfilled for the majority.

Poverty, exclusion, and landlessness are still far too common in Latin America. The land issue has not yet been resolved as the Chiapas uprising in Mexico (Burbach 1994; Barkin, Ortiz, and Rosen 1996) and the contemporary struggle for a piece of land by the mass of landless peasants in Brazil, spearheaded by the MST illustrate (Petras 1997). The era of radical type agrarian reforms, however, is over. Despite the continuing arguments by scholars and activists in favor of agrarian reform (Lipton 1993; Barraclough 1994; Thiesenhusen 1995b), as well as the recent upsurge in ethnic and peasant movements for land redistribution, there has been a shift from state-led and interventionist agrarian reform programs to market-oriented land policies. Paradoxically, such land policies have turned out to be much driven from above by the state and international agencies. Thus future state interventions in the land tenure system are likely to be confined to a land policy which focuses not on expropriation but on progressive land tax, land settlement, colonization, land transfer and financing mechanisms, land markets, registration, titling, and secure property rights. For example, in Brazil the government recently established a Land Bank with financial support from the World Bank with the aim of providing loans to around 200,000 families to buy land. However, a variety of studies indicate that such land policies are not the promised panacea. While the potential benefits of clearly defined property rights may be substantial given that about half of rural households lack land titles (Vogelgesang 1996), the economic and socio-political context under which small farmers are operating conspire against them. Evidence so far shows that all that has been achieved is "modernizing insecurity" (Jansen and Roquas 1998; Thorpe 1997). It has to be recognized that custom-based land titles as well as rental arrangements in rural communities often offer peasants greater security and flexibility than World Bank type land titling schemes. In the end peasants turn out to be the losers from these land titling projects due to their weak economic position in the market and their political inability to protect their land rights (Shearer, Lastarria-Cornhiel, and Mesbah 1990; Stanfield 1992; Carter and Mesbah 1993).

While the search for agrarian reform continues (Thiesenhusen 1989), issues like prices, markets, credit, technical assistance, wages, regionalization, and globalization currently exercise a major influence on agriculture's performance and peasant well-being. It is vital for peasants, rural workers, and indigenous communities to organize and strengthen their representative institutions so that they can shape and secure their future survival in a world increasingly driven by globalizing forces. While major agrarian reforms, especially of a collectivist kind, are unlikely to recur, it is certainly premature to argue that current land policies and neoliberal measures are heralding the demise of the agrarian problem in Latin America. Any resolution will still require changes in the unequal and exclusionary land tenure system. The new social movements in the countryside, such as the struggle of the Zapatistas in Chiapas, the MST landless movement in Brazil, and of the various indigenous groups throughout Latin America have again emphasized the centrality of the land question and the alternative meanings being given to it than that of the neoliberal interpretation in capitalism's current globalization phase.

Notes

1. *Hacienda* refers to large estates, many of which originated in the colonial period.
2. A very small agricultural landholding, usually owned by or under the control of petty commodity producers or subsistence peasants.
3. It was only in the early 1980s that the Mexican government attempted to reinvigorate peasant agriculture and the *ejidos* by pursuing a food self-sufficiency policy (Sistema Alimentario Mexicano or SAM) financed by the influx of petrodollars and the boom in Mexico's oil export earnings. However, the experience was short-lived.
4. *Comuneros* refers to those mostly indigenous peasants who live on communal lands.
5. *Reservas* are lands within the reformed sector.
6. A basic irrigated hectare (b.i.h.) is a unit of good quality land so *parcelas* with poor quality land were larger than 9 physical hectares and commonly varied between 11 and 15 hectares.

References

Albó, X. 1996. Bolivia: making the leap from local mobilization to national politics. *NACLA Report on the Americas*. 29:15–20.

Altimir, O. 1994. Income distribution and poverty through crisis and adjustment. *CEPAL Review*. 52:7–31.

Barkin, D. 1994. The spectre of rural development. *NACLA Report on the Americas*. 28:29–34.

Barkin, D., I. Ortiz, and F. Rosen. 1996. Globalization and resistance: the remaking of Mexico. *NACLA Report on the Americas*. 30:14–27.

Barraclough, S.L. 1994. The legacy of Latin American land reform. *NACLA Report on the Americas*. 28:16–21.

Blokland, K. 1992. *Participación campesina en el desarrollo económico: la Unión Nacional de Agricultores y Ganaderos de Nicaragua durante la Revolución Sandinista*. Doetinchem: Paulo Freire Stichting.

Bretón, V. 1997. *Capitalismo, reforma agraria y organización comunal en los Andes: una introducción al caso ecuatoriano*. Lleida: Universitat de Lleida.

Brockett, C.D. 1989. *Land, Power, and Poverty: Agrarian Transformations and Political Conflict in Rural Central America*. Boston: Unwin Hyman.

Burbach, R. 1994. Roots of the postmodern rebellion in Chiapas. *New Left Review*. 205:113–124.

Cardoso, E. and A. Helwege 1992. *Latin America's Economy: Diversity, Trends, and Conflicts*. Cambridge, Mass. The MIT Press.

Carter, M. and D. Mesbah. 1993. Can land market reform mitigate the exclusionary aspects of rapid agro-export growth? *World Development*. 21:1085–1100.

CEPAL (Economic Commission for Latin America). 1963. *Problemas y perspectivas de la agricultura latinoamericana*. Santiago: CEPAL. (División Agrícola Conjunta CEPAL/FAO).

CEPAL and FAO (Food and Agriculture Organization). 1986. *El crecimiento productivo y la heterogeneidad agraria*. Santiago: División Agrícola Conjunta CEPAL/FAO.

De Janvry, A. 1981. *The Agrarian Question and Reformism in Latin America*. Baltimore: The Johns Hopkins University Press.

———. 1994. Social and economic reforms: the challenge of equitable growth in Latin American agriculture. In *Apertura Económica, Modernización y Sostenibilidad de la Agricultura*, edited by E. Muchnik and A. Niño de Zepeda. 79–98. Santiago: Ministerio de Agricultura and ALACEA.

De Janvry, A. and E. Sadoulet. 1989. A study in resistance to institutional change: the lost game of Latin American land reform. *World Development*. 17:1397–1407.

De Janvry, A., G. Gordillo, and E. Sadoulet. 1997. *Mexico's Second Agrarian Reform: Household and Community Responses, 1990–1994*. San Diego: Center for U.S.-Mexican Studies, University of California, San Diego, La Jolla.

Deere, C.D. 1985. Rural women and state policy: the Latin American agrarian reform experience. *World Development*. 13:1037–53.

———. 1987. The Latin American agrarian reform experience. In *Rural Women and State Policy: Feminist Perspectives on Latin American Agricultural Development*, edited by C.D. Deere and M. León. 165–190. Boulder, Colo.: Westview Press.

———. 1995. The new agrarian reforms. NACLA *Report on the Americas*. 29:13–17.

——— Deere, C.D. and M. León 1998. Mujeres, derechos a la tierra y contrarreformas en América Latina, *Debate Agrario*. 27:129–153.

Dore, E. 1995. Latin America and the social ecology of capitalism. In *Capital, Power, and Inequality in Latin America*, edited by S. Halebsky and R. Harris. 253–278. Boulder, Colo. Westview Press.

Dorner, P. 1992. *Latin American Land Reforms in Theory and Practice: A Retrospective Analysis*. Madison, Wis.: University of Madison Press.

Duncan, K. and I. Rutledge, eds. 1977. *Land and Labour in Latin America: Essays on the Development of Agrarian Capitalism in the Nineteenth and Twentieth Centuries*. Cambridge, Mass.: Cambridge University Press.

ECLA (Economic Commission for Latin America). 1968. *Economic Survey of Latin America 1966*. New York: United Nations.

ECLAC (Economic Commission for Latin America). 1993. *Statistical Yearbook for Latin America and the Caribbean 1992*. Santiago: ECLAC, UN.

Eguren, F. 1997. Viabilidad de la pequeña agricultura serrana. In *Pequeña agricultura en el Perú: presente y futuro*, edited by J. Alfaro, A. Figueroa, and C. Monge. 129–138. Lima: Proyecto de Apoyo a ONGs—PACT, Peru.

Enríquez, L.J. 1991. *Harvesting Change: Labor and Agrarian Reform in Nicaragua, 1979–1990*. Chapel Hill: The University of North Carolina Press.

———. 1997. *Agrarian Reform and Class Consciousness in Nicaragua*. Gainesville Flor.: University Press of Florida.

Feder, E. 1971. *The Rape of the Peasantry: Latin America's Landholding System*. Garden City N.Y.: Doubleday.

———. 1974. Poverty and unemployment in Latin America: a challenge for socio-economic research. In *The Rural Society of Latin America Today*, edited by M. Mörner. 29–67. Stockholm: Almqvist and Wiksell.

Feres, J.C. and A. León. 1990. The magnitude of poverty in Latin America. *CEPAL Review*. 41:133–151.

Figueroa, A. 1977. Agrarian reforms in Latin America: a framework and an instrument of rural development. *World Development*. 5:155–168.

Ghai, D., C. Kay, and P. Peek. 1988. *Labour and Development in Rural Cuba*. Basingstoke and London: Macmillan.

Goodman, D. and M. Reclift. 1981. *From Peasant to Proletarian: Capitalist Development and Agrarian Transformations*. Oxford: Basil Blackwell.

Hall, A. 1996. Did Chico Mendes die in vain? Brazilian rubber tappers in the 1990s. In *Green Guerrillas: Environmental Conflicts and Initiatives in Latin America and the Caribbean*, edited by H. Collinson. 93–102. London: Latin American Bureau.

Harvey, N. 1998. *The Chiapas Rebellion: The Struggle for Land and Democracy*. Durham N.C.: Duke University Press.

Heath, J.R. 1992. Evaluating the impact of Mexico's land reform on agricultural productivity. *World Development*. 20:695–711.

Herrera, A., J. Riddell, and P. Toselli. 1997. Recent FAO experiences in land reform and land tenure. *Land Reform, Land Settlement and Cooperatives*. 1:52–64.

Huber, E. and F. Safford. 1995. *Agrarian Structure and Political Power: Landlord and Peasant in the Making of Latin America*. Pittsburgh Penn.: Pittsburgh University Press.

IDB. 1993. *Economic and Social Progress in Latin America: 1993 Report*. Baltimore: The Johns Hopkins University Press for the Inter-American Development Bank, Washington, D.C.

Jansen, K. and E. Roquas. 1998. Modernizing insecurity: the land titling project in Honduras. *Development and Change*. 29:81–106.

Jarvis, L.S. 1992. The unravelling of the agrarian reform. In *Development and Social Change in the Chilean Countryside: from the Pre-land Reform Period to the Democratic Transition*, edited by C. Kay and P. Silva. 189–213. Amsterdam: CEDLA.

Kay, C. 1977. Review of *Agrarian Reform and Agrarian Reformism*, edited by D. Lehmann. *The Journal of Peasant Studies*. 4:241–244.

———. 1978. Agrarian reform and the class struggle in Chile. *Latin American Perspectives*. 5:117–140.

———. 1980. Relaciones de dominación y dependencia entre terratenientes y campesinos en Chile. *Revista Mexicana de Sociología*. 42:751–797.

———. 1981. Political economy, class alliances, and agrarian change in Chile. *The Journal of Peasant Studies*. 8:485–513.

————. 1982. Achievements and contradictions of the Peruvian agrarian reform. *Journal of Development Studies*. 18:141–170.

————. 1983. The agrarian reform in Peru: an assessment. In *Agrarian Reform in Contemporary Developing Countries*, edited by A.K. Ghose. 185–239. London: Croom Helm and New York: St. Martin's Press.

————. 1988a. The landlord road and the subordinate peasant road to capitalism in Latin America. *Etudes Rurales*. 77:5–20.

————. 1988b. Cuban economic reforms and collectivisation. *Third World Quarterly*. 10:1239–1266.

————. 1993. The agrarian policy of the Aylwin government: continuity or change? In *Change in the Chilean Countryside: From Pinochet to Aylwin and Beyond*, edited by E. Hojman. 19–39. Basingstoke and London: Macmillan.

Kowalchuk, L. 1998. *Peasant Mobilization, Political Opportunities, and the Unfinished Agrarian Reform in El Salvador*. Paper presented at the XXI International Congress of the Latin American Studies Association (LASA), 24–26 September.

Land reform in Brazil. 1999. *The Economist*. 352:60.

Lehmann, D. 1978. The death of land reform: a polemic. *World Development*. 6:339–345.

Lipton, M. 1993. Land reform as commenced business: the evidence against stopping. *World Development*. 21:641–657.

Mexico Survey: rural revolution. 1993. *The Economist*. 13 February.

Murray, W.E. 1997. Competitive global fruit export markets: marketing intermediaries and impacts on small-scale growers in Chile. *Agrarian Change and the Democratic Transition in Chile*, Special issue of the *Bulletin of Latin American Research*. 16:43–55.

Pacari, N. 1996. Ecuador: taking on the neoliberal agenda. *NACLA Report on the Americas*. 29:23–32.

Paige, J.M. 1996. Land reform and agrarian revolution in El Salvador: comment on Seligson and Diskin. *Latin American Research Review*. 31:127–139.

Pelupessy, W. 1995. *Agrarian Transformation and Economic Adjustment in El Salvador, 1960–1990*. Ph.D. diss., Katholieke Universiteit Brabant, The Netherlands.

Petras, James. 1997. Latin America: the resurgence of the left. *New Left Review*. May-June, 17–47.

————. 1998. The political and social basis of regional variations in land occupations in Brazil. *The Journal of Peasant Studies*. 25:124–133.

Randall, L. 1996. *Reforming Mexico's Agrarian Reform*. Armonk N.Y.: M.E. Sharpe.

Seligson, M.A. 1995. Thirty years of transformation in the agrarian structure of El Salvador, 1961–1991. *Latin American Research Review*. 30:43–74.

Shearer, E.B., S. Lastarria-Cornhiel, and D. Mesbah. 1990. *The Reform of Rural Land Markets in Latin America and the Caribbean: Research, Theory, and Policy Implications*. LTC Paper No. 141, Madison: Land Tenure Center, University of Wisconsin.

Stanfield, D.J. 1992. Titulación de tierra: alternativa a la reforma agraria en un contexto de ajuste structural. In *Honduras: el ajuste estructural y la reforma agraria*, edited by H. Noé Pino and A. Thorpe. 181–206. Tegucigalpa: CEDOH-POSCAE.

Thiesenhusen, W.C., ed. 1989. *Searching for Agrarian Reform in Latin America*. Boston: Unwin Hyman.

————. 1995a. *Broken Promises: Agrarian Reform and the Latin American Campesino*. Boulder Colo.: Westview Press.

————. 1995b. Land reform lives! *The European Journal of Development Research*. 7:193–209.

Thorpe, A. 1997. Adjustment, agricultural modernization, and land markets: the case of Honduras. In *The "Market Panacea:" Agrarian Transformation in Developing Countries and Former Socialist Economies*, edited by M. Spoor. 29–42. London: Intermediate Technology Publications.

Tinsman, H.E. 1996. *Unequal Uplift: The Sexual Politics of Gender, Work, and Community in the Chilean Agrarian Reform, 1950–1973*. Ph.D. diss., Yale University.

Utting, P. 1992. The political economy of food pricing and marketing reforms in Nicaragua, 1984–87. *The European Journal of Development Research*. 4:107–131.

Valdés, A. and A. Siamwalla. 1988. Foreign trade regimes, exchange rate policy, and the structure of incentives. In *Agricultural Price Policy for Developing Countries*, edited by W. Mellor and R. Ahmed. 103–123. Baltimore N.J.: Johns Hopkins University Press.

Valdés, A., E. Muchnik, and H. Hurtado. 1990. Trade, exchange rate, and agricultural pricing policies in Chile. *The Political Economy of Agricultural Pricing Policy*. 2 vls., Washington D.C.: World Bank.

Veltmeyer, H. 1997. New social movements in Latin America: the dynamics of class and identity. *The Journal of Peasant Studies*. 25:139–169.

Veltmeyer, Henry, James Petras, and Steve Vieux. 1997. *Neoliberalism and Class Conflict in Latin America: A Comparative Perspective on the Political Economy of Structural Adjustment*. Houndmills, Basingstoke, Hampshire, England: Palgrave.

Vogelgesang, F. 1996. Property rights and the rural land market in Latin America. *Cepal Review*. 58:95–113.

Zamosc, L. 1994. Agrarian protest and the Indian movement in the Ecuadorean highlands. *Latin American Research Review*. 29:37–68.

Zoomers, A. 1997. *Titulando tierras en los Andes bolivianos: las implicancias de la Ley INRA en Chuiquisaca y Potosí*. Amsterdam: CEDLA.

3

Individual Versus Collective Land Rights: Tensions Between Women's and Indigenous Rights Under Neoliberalism

Carmen Diana Deere and Magdalena León

The rise to dominance of neoliberal governments in Latin America coincided with the growth and consolidation of two new social movements: the women's and the indigenous movements. Besides their timing, they share a number of other factors in common. Both movements challenged the traditional conception of Universal Human Rights, drawing attention to its exclusionary biases. Both movements grew simultaneously at the international, national, and local levels, with the growth at the latter levels supported by international conventions to end discrimination based on sex and ethnicity. And both movements, although in diverse ways, challenged neoliberal agrarian legislation that sought to end the agrarian reforms of previous decades.

The main demands of the indigenous movement in the debate over the future of land rights have been as follows: (1) recognition of their historic land claims, including the recognition of indigenous territories; (2) recognition and/or affirmation of collective property rights and of the inalienability of collective property; and (3) recognition of customary law; i.e., the right of peasant and indigenous communities to follow traditional customs and practices. The main demand of the women's movement has centered on establishing equality between men and women in the adjudication and titling of land redistributed or titled by the state, principally through the joint adjudication or titling of land to couples irrespective of their marital status, and/or the prioritizing of female household heads in such efforts.

What is noteworthy is that it has been in the countries with the largest indigenous populations—Mexico, Guatemala, Peru, Bolivia, and Ecuador—where there have been the slimmest gains with respect to women's land rights.[1] The 1996 Bolivian Ley INRA has a strong preamble favoring gender equity in land rights, but no specific provisions of the law guarantee women's access to land on the same terms as men. In the Peace Accords signed in the mid-1990s, Guatemala professed its intention to guarantee gender equity in future land distributions, but the only concrete measure specified was with respect to the refugee population returning to Guatemala; female heads of household were to be given priority in resettlement and land distribution efforts.[2] The 1995 Peruvian land law professes to be gender neutral in that land rights are to be vested in natural or juridic persons, but no specific provisions are made with respect to gender equity, such as for the joint titling of land. In Ecuador's 1994 land law there is also no mention of gender. And the 1992 Mexican agrarian code represents the main setback in the region with respect to women's access to land, since what was family patrimony within the *ejidos*[3] in the process of privatization, is becoming the individual private property of household heads, the great majority of whom are male.

The focus of this chapter is on the tension between the demand for recognition of collective land rights and the demand for gender equity. In principle, collective land rights should promote gender equity to the extent that such guarantees all members of a community access to land. We argue that in the Latin American case collective land rights do not necessarily guarantee all members of a community access to land. Rather, how collective land is distributed—the rules through which it is allocated to families and to the men and women within them—and who participates in determining these rules is governed by traditional customs and practices (*usos y costumbres*) which often discriminate against women.

The potential tension between the rights of women and the rights of indigenous communities to follow their own traditional customs and practices is at the center of the debate between the feminist and cultural relativist critiques of universal human rights, a debate which we review in the next section. We subsequently turn to how women's and indigenous land rights have been treated in the international arena. Then, we focus on the cases of Ecuador and Bolivia, for it is in these two countries where the indigenous movement has achieved the greatest gains in terms of the defense of collective property rights under neoliberalism. It is also in these two countries where the strength of the indigenous movement seemed to close the space for discussion of women's land rights. In the next section, we consider why this was the case. We then turn to Mexico and Peru as examples of what can happen when collective land rights are lost or weakened without provisions for gender equity with respect to individual land rights. Finally, in the conclusion, we discuss how indigenous women leaders are beginning to confront these tensions.

Feminist and Cultural Relativist Critiques of Universal Human Rights

According to Rhoda Howard (1993, 316), in international law Universal Human Rights are defined as "rights held equally by every individual by virtue of his or her humanity and for no other reason."[4] What the feminist and culturalist critique of human rights share is that they both challenge the universality of human rights as derived from liberal thought. They contend that liberal thought, which gave birth to the concept of the universality of human rights, is a historical and cultural product of Western philosophy and politics which was exclusionary of other cultures and groups, such as women and indigenous groups (Brems 1997, 142–147; Pollis 1996, 318). For human rights to indeed be universal they must be inclusive of other groups. However, whereas feminists use a gender lens, cultural relativists use a cultural perspective, each challenging on different terms how these human rights are to be defined, prioritized, and applied.

The main claim of cultural relativism is that there is no such thing as a universal morality, but rather, morality is conditioned by culture and historical variation. Following Jack Donnelly (1984, 400), it is useful to distinguish two versions of this thesis: the "strong" version, which posits that "culture is the sole source of validity of moral right or rule,"[5] and a "weak" version, where culture is an important source of moral validity. Regardless of the degree of determinism, the critique of the cultural relativists is that the doctrine of the universality of human rights is based on a western notion of rationality that has elevated the concept of individualism to a level of abstraction not compatible with other cultures. They argue that an alternative notion of morality may be found in other, non-Western cultures which privilege the collectivity over individuals. Within these non-Western cultures, collective rights and obligations place limits on individuals in favor of the collective (Brems 1997, 146).

The source of validity of moral right or rule for most Latin American indigenous cultures is ancestral authority and longevity. From the perspective of cultural relativists, the history of colonialism can be summarized as one of the displacement of ancestral or collective authority. At the same time, the introduction of the concept of individual rights was limited, for it was applied only to the conquerors—at the expense of indigenous peoples. The indigenous position in the current debate over land rights is that collective rights to land must be privileged over individual rights, for two reasons. First, given the history of colonialism, there is a moral argument to be made for restitution of land and territories to indigenous peoples and communities. Second, collective land rights are the basis of indigenous cultural identity and are necessary to the very survival of indigenous peoples.

The feminist critique of universal human rights, besides demanding inclusion in the system of production of human rights, stresses the need to break the dichotomy between the public and the private domains (Brems 1997; Garay 1996). It highlights how in the liberal tradition, human rights were designed to regulate the relations between men and the state in the public sphere, a sphere from which women have traditionally been excluded. In addition, since the subordination of women is in large measure situated in the context of the private sphere—that is, in the practice and traditions of daily life—human rights must be extended so that the "personal is political," following the feminist battle cry (Brems 1997, 139). The demand to bridge the private and public must be thus understood in a double vein: so that rights are extended to private relations, and so that women participate in rights in the public sphere.

By limiting the focus of human rights discourse to the public sphere, or the civic and political, not only has the condition of women been excluded, but more generally, social, economic, and cultural rights. Feminists have challenged the priority given to civil and political rights over socioeconomic rights since the latter are so necessary to women's advancement (Brems 1997 139–40).[6] In addition, feminists argue that in light of women's differences from men, "the catalog of human rights" has to be revised to include new rights, such as reproductive and sexual rights (Brems 1997, 139). The slogan, "women's rights are human rights" best sums up this effort, as recently recognized in the 1994 Geneva Declaration of Universal Human Rights.

Where the feminist and cultural relativist critique of universal human rights come into conflict is that in most societies women and culture are closely connected. As Amanda Garay (1996, 24) notes "women are most frequently the transmitters of culture to their children and are often responsible for maintaining cultural traditions in the home and maintaining links to the community . . . The close connection of women to culture makes it difficult to recognize that the human rights specific to women are part of the atomistic rights regime." That women have a greater burden than men in terms of the preservation of culture makes cultural relativists particularly beware of any attempts to expand the universality of human rights to include women's rights. Similarly, the close identification of women and culture has made feminists wary of ceding grounds to cultural relativists, particularly the strong strand of cultural relativism where culture is seen as the principal and sole source of validity of moral right or rule.

In the subsequent sections we explore this conflict between the feminist and cultural relativist critique of universal human rights in the case of indigenous struggles over individual and collective land rights. We emphasize the difficulty of accepting ancestral or collective authority when this authority is exclusionary and discriminatory of women. Further, we argue that collective property rights per se are not the problem, but rather, the problem rests with the traditional customs and practices through which collective land rights are allocated to families and the individuals within them.

Women's and Indigenous Land Rights in the International Arena

A central aim of the 1975 World Plan of Action approved at the First U.N. Conference on Women in Mexico City was to secure constitutional and legislative guarantees of non-discrimination and equal rights, including the provision of parity in the exercise of civil, social, and political rights pertaining to marriage and citizenship.[7] Specifically, it was recommended that legislative measures be undertaken to "ensure that women and men enjoy full legal capacity relating to their personal and property rights, including the right to acquire, administer, enjoy, dispose of, and inherit property."[8] No mention was made in the concluding report regarding women's access to land, although concern was expressed with the particular problems of rural women worldwide.

In contrast, by the time of the 1995 U.N. World Conference on Women in Beijing women's land rights formed an important component of the strategic objectives of the Platform for Action. Moreover, women's land rights had passed from being solely an element in efficiency arguments, focused on raising women's productivity, to being treated as an economic right, with clear recognition of the importance of land to rural women's empowerment and pursuit of economic autonomy.

The watershed in this evolution was the 1979 U.N. Convention on the Elimination of All Forms of Discrimination against Women. In Article 2 of the Convention, signatory states condemned all forms of discrimination against women and agreed to eliminate these through all appropriate measures, including constitutional and legislative changes. Moreover, governments agreed to modify or abolish all existing laws, regulations, and *customs and practices* which discriminated against women.[9]

Specific attention was given to the measures required to eliminate the discrimination against rural women and to assure that women participated and benefited from rural development on a par with men. Women's access to land, nonetheless, is considered in the context of programs of agrarian reform, rather than as a general right: "To have access to agricultural credit and loans, marketing facilities, appropriate technology, and equal treatment in land and agrarian reform as well as in land resettlement schemes."[10] The sections on property rights, however, make clear that efforts to end the discrimination against women must include recognition of women's rights to own, inherit, and administer property in their own names: "State parties shall accord to women, in civil matters, a legal capacity identical to that of men and the same opportunities to exercise that capacity. They shall in particular give women equal rights to conclude contracts and to administer property and treat them equally in all stages of procedure in courts and tribunals."[11] Moreover, within the family, men and women are to be accorded: "the same rights for both spouses in respect of the ownership, acquisition, management, administration, enjoyment and disposition of property, whether free of charge or for a valuable consideration."[12]

Subsequent U.N. Conferences on Women—at Copenhagen in 1980 and Nairobi in 1985—were to strengthen these provisions and to draw attention to the discriminatory role of not only national laws, but also traditional practices in limiting women's land rights. In the 1995 Beijing Conference Platform for Action, women's access to and inheritance of land was treated in the context of required strategic actions in four of the twelve critical areas of concern: Women and Poverty; Women and the Economy; Women and the Environment; and the Girl Child. Governments agreed to: "Undertake legislative and administrative reforms to give women full and equal access to economic resources, including the right to inheritance and to ownership of land and other property, credit, natural resources, and appropriate technologies" and to abolish and modify all existing laws, regulations, customs, and practices which discriminate against women.[13]

International Labor Organization Accord #107 of 1957 was the first international legal instrument specifically developed to safeguard the rights of indigenous and tribal peoples. Fourteen Latin American and Caribbean governments had ascribed to it before it was replaced by ILO Accord #169 of 1989 (OIT 1987). Accord #107 was based on an ethnocentric conceptualization in which indigenous populations were considered in need of integration to national societies (OIT, 1987, 4). That is, the overall objective was "to reduce them to civilization," since they were seen as inferior, temporary societies destined to disappear under the forces of modernization.[14] The role of the state was paternalistic, to protect these vulnerable groups in the transition. The dominant national ideologies in Latin America in this period were economic modernization and racial *mestizaje* (racial mixing), and the concepts of integration and assimilation fit well with advocates of indigenous rights from both the right and left: Indians were to be transformed into peasants and citizens (Dandler 1996; Black 1998; Hvalkof, this volume).

A major factor motivating the revision of ILO Accord #107 was that since the 1950s indigenous people worldwide began to form their own organizations to defend and protect their interests, an effort which attracted considerable support from international NGOs in the 1980s (Conferencia Internacional del Trabajo 1988, Ch. 2; Dandler 1996, 3). After three years of discussion, ILO Accord #169 on Indigenous and Tribal Peoples in Independent Countries was adopted in 1989 by the 76th International Labour Conference of the ILO in Geneva. It represents a fundamental change in approach to indigenous issues on a number of counts. Rather than considering indigenous populations as temporary societies, doomed to disappear, it assumes that indigenous populations are permanent societies. It also gives indigenous and tribal peoples equal status to other nationalities of a given country in terms of fundamental rights, which is why it is considered an instrument of inclusion rather than of integration.

Traditional rights are strongly affirmed and supported in the convention. It is recognized that to promote the full effectiveness of indigenous social, economic, and cultural rights requires respect for indigenous identities, traditional customs and practices, and institutions.[15] At the same time, it makes clear that for the above to be applicable, traditional customs and practices cannot be incompatible with fundamental rights as defined in the national juridical system, nor with recognized international human rights (Article 8.2). The accord also stipulates that the dispositions of the convention should be applied without discrimination to men and women (Article 3.1).

Part II of the Convention deals with indigenous land rights. The following points are worth highlighting:

- The special relation of indigenous people to the land and territory which they occupy or use is recognized, and in particular, "the collective aspects of this relation" (Article 13.1).

- The use of the term lands "shall include the concept of territories, which covers the total environment of the areas which the peoples occupy or otherwise use" (Article 13.2).

- The indigenous peoples' right of property and possession of the lands which they traditionally occupy is also recognized (Article 14).

- ◆ With respect to inheritance, following the norms already established with respect to traditions and customs, the Convention requires respect for the procedures for transmission of land rights established by these peoples (Article 17.1).

- ◆ In terms of agrarian reform programs, indigenous and tribal peoples are to be assigned additional lands on the same terms as other groups when those which they are possess are insufficient (Article 19).

A concern of feminists is whether countries who are signatories to Accord #169 will take their commitments seriously under other conventions to undertake the necessary measures to end the many forms of discrimination against indigenous women, particularly those forms embodied in traditional customs and practices. It is worth noting that in the Preamble to Accord #169, mention is made of a number of the international accords which prevent discrimination,[16] but no specific mention is made of the 1979 U.N. Convention to Eliminate All Forms of Discrimination against Women, a convention which has had the force of international law since 1981. Moreover, while the accord states that its dispositions are to be applied to men and women without discrimination, in the section on inheritance no explicit mention is made of women's lands rights, with inheritance left to be determined by the traditional customs and practices of the indigenous and tribal communities.

Specifically, Accord #169 seems to ignore Article 2f of the 1979 Women's Convention which obliges signatory states to modify or abolish all existing laws, regulations, and customs and practices which discriminate against women (UN 1980, 2–3), a commitment which was again reiterated in the 1995 Beijing Platform for Action (UN 1996, 93, 96).

It might be argued that Accord #169 is compatible with both the Women's Convention and the Beijing Platform of Action since the accord states that traditional customs and practices cannot be incompatible with fundamental rights as defined in the national juridical system nor with recognized international human rights. This position was apparently the majority position at the Beijing Conference, for the 1995 Platform of Action explicitly endorsed Accord #169, calling for governments to consider ratifying this international treaty.[17] Nonetheless, the lack of explicit guarantee of women's land rights remains a weakness in Accord #169, particularly since changing gender-discriminatory traditional practices and customs with respect to land rights is so difficult to carry out in practice. Indigenous rights expert Jorge Dandler concedes that "there is probably a gender bias [in Accord #169]. Gender issues could be made more explicit, particularly on the topic of land. The emphasis was on collective rights to land; it was based on an advanced conceptualization of peoples and their rights to territories."[18]

Ten out of nineteen Latin American countries have thus far ratified Accord #169. The main countries with large indigenous populations which have not are Brazil, Chile, El Salvador, Nicaragua, and Panama. All Latin American countries have signed the 1979 Women's Convention and endorsed the 1995 Beijing Platform for Action.

The Defense of Collective Land under Neoliberalism: Ecuador and Bolivia

The greatest gains with respect to indigenous land rights in Latin America in the 1990s have been made in Ecuador and Bolivia, countries where organized groups of indigenous Amazonian peoples built strong organizations during the 1980s, and where the Amazonian and highland peasant/indigenous organizations were able to form either one all-encompassing organization, or a strong alliance. In both countries the indigenous movement was able to defeat neoliberal attempts to weaken collective forms of property; moreover, in both collective rights were strengthened and extended in scope in the new agrarian legislation. Here we consider these two cases in more detail and then how gender rights were subsumed in the discussion of indigenous demands.

In 1986 the two main peasant and indigenous organizations in Ecuador, ECUARUNARI, formed in 1972 of peasant federations in the *sierra*,[19] and CONFENIAE (the Confederación de Nacionalidades Indígenas de la Amazonia Ecuatoriana), formed in 1980 of indigenous organizations in the Amazon region,[20] joined together to form CONAIE, Confederación de Nacionalidades Indígenas del Ecuador. During the late 1980s CONAIE grew in strength through the actions leading up to the 1992 Quincentennial under the banner of "500 Years of Indigenous Resistance." It consolidated its role as the legitimate voice of the indigenous population during the "Indigenous Uprising of 1990" (Levantamiento Indígena) which centered on conflicts over land and the demand for recognition of indigenous territories.[21]

This uprising began with the peaceful occupation of the Santo Domingo church in Quito in May of that year, followed by a national strike. Indigenous communities in the highlands and Amazonian region closed down markets and set up roadblocks until the government was forced to negotiate. One of the main issues in the negotiations was the legal recognition of indigenous territories in the Amazon.[22] According to Chad Black (1998, 2), CONAIE pushed a threefold agenda of land, culture, and national identity: "The centrality of cultural claims, mediated through an alternative conception of the nation, and the organizational process that gave birth to CONAIE and a unified national Indian movement represented a significant break from traditional leftist and popular social movements." Moving beyond land reform and traditional labor concerns, CONAIE pushed the concept of plurinationality center-stage, "going beyond recognition of the diversity of cultures and languages within Ecuador to a redefinition of the very nature of national-democratic participation" (Black 1998, 22).

Although the Indigenous Uprising had considerable support from a broad range of civil society, the Social Democrats who had negotiated with CONAIE lost the 1992 elections and the neoliberal government of Sixto Duran Ballen was ushered in. This government promptly promulgated a very neoliberal land law—one that envisaged the break-up of the indigenous communities—and this act provoked a second uprising of peasants and indigenous people in June of 1994. This uprising, called the "Mobilization for Life," included demonstrations in all the major cities of the highlands and the occupation of major oil wells in the Amazonian region. As explained by one of CONAIE's women leaders:

> The indigenous peoples could not accept a law that would promote the concentration of land in the hands of those who have always held it, and which would make it prohibitive for indigenous communities to get access to land. Without any means of expanding, we would die of hunger and misery in the large cities . . . Land can't be sold or negotiated. A people without a territory is a dead nation. That is why one of our fundamental objectives is the defense and recuperation of our territories.[23]

After ten days the government was again forced to negotiate, for the courts had declared the neoliberal law unconstitutional on procedural grounds. The main actors in the negotiations were CONAIE and the various regional chambers of agriculture. The main victory of CONAIE was in having the state recognize the right of indigenous, afroecuadorian, and montubian communities to their ancestral lands; moreover, these lands would be adjudicated to them free of charge. This is considered to be one of the most positive aspects of the Law of Agrarian Development and is innovative in the case of afroecuadorian and montubian communities, since up to this time, only indigenous communities had been adjudicated ancestral lands.

CONAIE had wanted the state to commit itself to recognize territories, defined "as a geographic area or natural space under the cultural influence and political control of a people" (de la Cruz 1995, 8). This implies the possibility of controlling the use of the subsoil, which the government was not about to give up, given that Ecuador is an oil-producing nation. Also, it may be one thing to recognize indigenous territory in the *selva* (particularly in non-oil-bearing regions), but quite another in the highlands. Recognition of a Quichua territory in the highlands would challenge the very legitimacy of private property rights and, probably, the very concept of the nation state as traditionally defined.

Among the various forms of organization of production recognized in the 1994 land law are communal forms, which CONAIE had also insisted upon. However, the law does allow communal lands to be parcelized and sold if two-thirds of the community members so wish; a similar vote is required to transform the community structure into another form of association. CONAIE claimed victory in that it forced the provision that any change in tenure or structure would require a two-thirds, rather than a simple majority, vote of community members. Also, at its insistence, the law provides that communal pastures at high elevations and forest land cannot be subdivided, and attempts to privatize water rights in the legislation were defeated (Ecuador 1994; Macas 1995).

No explicit mention is made of gender or of women's right to land in the Law of Agrarian Development. The law presumes to be gender neutral in that property owners, "be they natural or juridic persons" are guaranteed their right to work the land (Article 19). In the regulations supporting the 1994 law, the beneficiaries are defined as "peasants, indigenous people, montubios, afroecuadorians, agriculturalists in general and agricultural entrepreneurs . . ."(Article 1). The only explicit mention of women is in the section in the regulations on training where it states that "training should take into account women's participation in agriculture and should incorporate them actively in the respective programs" (Article 3).

That ethnicity and race were mentioned explicitly in the law and its regulations, but that gender did not merit parallel treatment when it came to land rights, reflects the fact that during the whole debate over the Agrarian Development Law gender was never an issue. The main demands of CONAIE centered on securing government recognition of indigenous territories and guaranteeing the right to collectively-held land; why CONAIE paid no attention to gender issues is explored in the next section.[24]

The omission of gender concerns from the Law of Agrarian Development was partly corrected in the 1998 Constitution where it states that "the State will guarantee the equality of rights and opportunities of women and men in access to resources for production and in economic decision making with respect to the administration of the conjugal society and the management of property" (Ecuador 1998).[25] These measures were largely the result of the efforts of DINAMO, the national women's office, which launched a vigorous lobbying effort to introduce gender concerns throughout the constitution. Moreover, CONAIE continued to lobby for the inalienability and indivisibility of collective property in the debates regarding Ecuador's constitutional reform and it was successful in securing these in the 1998 constitution (Article 84; Ecuador 1998), as well as securing Ecuador's ratification of ILO Accord #169. In addition, Ecuador was officially recognized in the constitution as a pluricultural and multi-ethnic state, although not one that was plurinational, as CONAIE had wanted.[26]

In Bolivia, as well, peasant and indigenous organizations played a key role in the effort to place the discussion of a new agrarian reform, one which would defend communal lands and recognize indigenous territories, on the national agenda. The CSUTCB (Confederación Sindical Unica de Trabajadores Campesinos de Bolivia), which led this effort, had been characterized up through the 1970s by its traditional, class-based demands, but by the 1980s was very marked by the influence of the Katarista indigenist movement, one which privileged ethnic identity. Also, during the early 1980s a number of regional organizations had been consolidated which also privileged ethnic identity: the Central Indígena del Oriente de Bolivia, la Central de Pueblos Indígenas del Beni, and the Asamblea del Pueblo Guarani. The main demand of all of these groups—particularly after they joined together to form CIDOB (Confederación Indígena del Oriente, Chaco y Amazonia) in 1982—was recognition of the territories which they had traditionally occupied. In contrast to Ecuador, however, at the moment of discussion of the new agrarian code, the highland and *selva* organizations had not structurally merged to form one, united indigenous organization.

With the return to democracy in 1982, the CSUTCB proposed a new agrarian reform law based on the principle of land for those who work it directly and the strengthening of communal property, while the other indigenous groups began pressing for recognition of their right to the territory which they have traditionally occupied. Throughout the next year there were large peasant mobilizations in support of a new agrarian reform, and a presidential commission was appointed to study CSUTCB's proposal (Urioste 1992, 137–141).

Then in 1985 Víctor Paz Estenssoro became president and in the context of structural adjustment, neoliberal ideas began to gain currency in government circles. There was discussion of the need for a new land law, but one quite different than that envisioned by the CSUTCB: one which would focus on making land a commodity—which could be bought and sold without impediment—and would tax all rural property. Both ideas met with tremendous peasant opposition. Peasant land has been exempt from taxes since the 1953 agrarian reform; in addition, the attempt to get rid of the inalienability and inembargability of communal land and peasant property met with much hostility.[27]

The land issue exploded during 1990 when the first indigenous march, the 40-day "Indigenous March for Territory and Dignity" from Trinidad to La Paz took place in the context of the hemispheric preparations in commemoration of the 500 Years of Resistance Campaign.[28] Up until then, the Bolivian state had not recognized the rights of indigenous peoples and communities to their original territory and this became the main demand of the increasingly vocal association of indigenous peoples, CIDOB. Their other demands were in terms of respect for their traditional uses and customs and for bilingual, inter-cultural education.

In response, the government of Paz Zamora was forced to issue four Supreme Decrees in September 1990 recognizing the major indigenous peoples of the Amazonian region and their right to their original lands. In 1991 the government also ratified ILO Accord #169. However, the government refused to recognize these lands as indigenous territories, calling them "original communal land" and reserving for itself the right to dispose of the subsoil. Moreover, several years went by without the government developing the necessary regulations to implement the decrees, such as surveying the land and relocating the lumber mills which were operating in these territories (Ruiz 1993, 20).

In 1992 there was another major march from the lowlands to La Paz and, in response, the government issued eight Supreme Decrees recognizing the ancestral lands of various other indigenous groups (Muñoz and Lavadenz 1997, 6). The 1994 constitutional reform also made explicit the right of all indigenous people to their original communal lands, the inalienable character of collective property (Article 171), and the recognition of Bolivia as a multi-ethnic and pluricultural state (Article 1).[29]

The new agrarian law was developed in the context of a contentious, national discussion involving peasants, indigenous peoples, medium and large growers, the political parties, and the different instances of civil society. While there was recognition of the need to find consensus, this was a difficult process. When the law was about to be discussed in the national congress, in August 1996, there was another massive march, the "March for Land and Territory," by peasants and indigenous people, marked by a high participation of rural women (Ybarnegaray 1997, 32). The main issue of indigenous groups from eastern Bolivia was the titling of territory, with full rights over the subsoil, and not just the titling of their original, communal land. Peasant groups (Aymara and Quechua) continued to be concerned that land be for those who work it directly.[30]

Strangely silent in this national debate over land, until the last minute, were gendered perspectives. None of the rural women's associations raised the issue of gender and land rights. This is somewhat surprising given the level of organization of rural women over the past decade, and the high visibility of rural women in the various peasant and indigenous marches to La Paz—it is said that at least half of the protesters have been women. But the central demand of these mobilizations has been access to and the titling of indigenous territory, or communal access to land. The traditional practices and customs by which the internal redistribution of land would be governed did not emerge as an issue. The main topics raised by women in these national mobilizations were access to health care and education.[31]

An NGO, TIERRA, was largely responsible for any recognition at all of gender issues in the proposed legislation. TIERRA and the Sub-Secretary for Gender Issues of the Ministry of Human Development held a workshop on the issue and, subsequently, a consultancy report was commissioned by TIERRA. This report (Camacho 1996) served as the basis for the discussions which were then held with congresswomen and others to garner consensus on how to introduce gender concerns into the law. The main recommendation of this report—which was incorporated into the law—was that mention be made of gender equity, independent of a woman's marital status, in the distribution, administration, tenancy, and use of land. According to Isabel Lavadenz, then Director of INRA, by the time of this consultancy report and the subsequent workshops, it was quite late in the process to introduce major modifications in the proposed law. There was consensus, nonetheless, that a paragraph on gender equity should be introduced into the law. The Parliament approved the paragraph on gender equity without much discussion or dissent.[32]

The main accomplishment of the INRA law was that it guaranteed indigenous peoples and communities the land to which they traditionally had access. Land titles were to be issued immediately to those indigenous peoples and communities recognized by previous Supreme Decrees.[33] These lands could not be sold, subdivided, used as collateral, or expropriated by the State. The indigenous groups of the Amazon basin lost out on their demand to be titled territories; the subsoil remains the patrimony of the State, as provided for in the Bolivian constitution. They also lost out with respect to the rights of third parties who can establish legitimate titles to land located within their regions. The compromise worked out was that indigenous communities who lost land in this fashion would be given comparable land in another, contiguous area. Another major accomplishment is that agrarian reform efforts in Bolivia are to continue; moreover, in the adjudication of public lands or those expropriated by the state, priority is to be given to the collective adjudication of land to indigenous or peasant communities without sufficient land.

To recapitulate, the main gains achieved by the indigenous movement in Bolivia and Ecuador have been with respect to the recognition of historic land claims in the Amazon region, although neither movement succeeded in having these recognized as indigenous territories. What is interesting is that although there was greater unity between highland and *selva* organizations in Ecuador than in Bolivia—a joint organization, CONAIE, having been formed as opposed to an alliance—the potential gains to the peasantry and indigenous movement from the new legislation are far greater in Bolivia. In Ecuador, CONAIE basically had to run a defensive campaign, to protect the dismemberment of Andean highland communities. While this was also an issue in Bolivia, in this country there was a stronger consensus behind the maintenance of collective property. In addition, whereas in Ecuador agrarian reform efforts for all practical purposes have concluded, in Bolivia, these are to continue. With respect to gender, the Bolivian land law is much more favorable than that of Ecuador, since it states that women have a right to land independent of their marital status, and that gender equity criteria are to be applied in the distribution of land. However, this provision, rather than being a demand of organized indigenous and peasant women, was a result of the pressure of the feminist and women's movement.

Organized Indigenous Women and the Defense of Collective Land Rights

As we have seen, in neither Ecuador nor Bolivia in the negotiations leading to the new agrarian codes were gender and land rights raised as an issue by the national peasant and indigenous organizations, nor by organized indigenous women leaders. A national female leader of CONAIE went so far as to say that the whole topic of gender and land rights was irrelevant, for " . . . the indigenous people have not taken up the individual demand [for land]; it has always been collective, from the perspective of the community" (Torres Galarza 1995, 79). The topic seems irrelevant, for the very preservation of indigenous communities—their identity as indigenous people—is seen to be based on communal access to land. To question how that communal land is then going to be distributed—through what rules will it be allocated to families and to the men and women within them, and who will participate in determining those rules—is seen to be divisive and a threat to indigenous unity.

It is argued that issues of class and ethnicity—issues which unite peasants and indigenous people—must come before all other issues, because it has been as peasants and indigenous people that men and women in Ecuador have been exploited over the centuries. Blanca Chancoso (n.d., 22), a former Secretary General ECUARUNARI in the 1980s, explains the position of organized indigenous women this way: ". . . indigenous women do not have their own revindications, as women, for we are not separate from the people. Our indigenous people are exploited and discriminated against, and together with the people, we suffer this same discrimination."

The primary demand of indigenous women must be for the defense of the community, which they see as being based on collective access to land, for it is this factor which gives cohesion and meaning to indigenous identity. Thus one of the principal demands in the 1994 Forum of Indigenous Women, which preceded the debate on Ecuador's Agrarian Law, was as follows:

> Ask the leaders of our *cabildos*, of the provinces, regions, and nationally, that communal lands not be divided nor sold. They are for the benefit of all and were acquired through great sacrifice. These should be maintained communally, for the family. Our *compañeros* have to assume responsibility for the care of land and women, for to divide the land is the same as dismembering a woman (CONAIE 1994, 41).

The defense of land (*la tierra madre*) is equated with the defense of women, for women are seen to be identified more closely with nature and culture. According to Ruth Moya (1987), "one of the characteristics of the organization of indigenous women is that it is based in the valorization of the indigenous movement regarding the important role of women in the reproduction of indigenous culture and as the main agent of socialization." The defense of culture is, in turn, based on an appeal to a mythical, ancestral culture where women were venerated as the source of life, together with land. This is quite evident in the following testimony:

> Land and the woman is one and the same mother, both produce, give life, they feed us and clothe us. We say that it is one and the same mother, because for us indigenous women, land is what gives us life . . . We women are similar to land for we give life, we are the reproducers. Since land is

our mother, it cannot be divided. It would be like dividing our own mother (CONAIE 1994, 38).

While CONAIE is made up of representatives of diverse indigenous cultures—ranging from the majority Quichua populations of the highlands and *ceja de selva* to heterogenous tribal groups in the Amazon basin—this theme of the relation between woman and land and of the centrality of both to the reproduction of indigenous culture is often generalized as the "essence" of indigenous culture.

In Andean indigenist discourse this mythical, ancestral culture was based on the complementarity of male and female roles.[34] The basis of complementarity was the alleged equality between men and women, linked to the essential role that each played in the process of production and reproduction. Each gender had authority derived from these complementary roles and each participated in decision making. In this analysis, it was colonialism and/or capitalism that was responsible for introducing gender inequality:

> . . . Before in our culture, when our society was free [Aymara] men and women had the same rights. Women had authority . . . The current system tries to impose that "men are superior to women." In the traditional system men and women both participated and made decisions. Since this traditional system has been under attack for over four centuries, our objective is to defend it and protect it (ISIS International 1987, 45).

Whether such a mythical, ancestral culture ever existed is beyond the scope of our inquiry. Our concern is with how, within this discourse, gender equality is to be attained. According to a Bolivian indigenist women leader,

> . . . Once we are able to break with colonial structures, we can live in complementarity . . . In the society in which we live, colonialist and patriarchal, it is impossible to ask a man to show solidarity to a woman, it is impossible to ask a woman with a machista, patriarchal and colonial mentality to show solidarity to another poorer, indigenous woman. We need to break with all this.[35]

In other words, since patriarchy is a European import, and men and women complement each other in the division of labor, there is no need for gender-specific demands in current struggles.[36] Class and ethnic solidarity must come foremost, for what is necessary in the present context is collective access to land and autonomy for indigenous communities so that they can eventually return to the ways of the past, a past in which complementarity in the gender division of labor was synonymous with gender equality, rather than today's inequality.

This is one of the reasons why the growth of the indigenous movement and the increasing participation of women within it has not led to an automatic questioning of women's role within indigenous society. Rather, the participation of women is a consequence of the need to strengthen the indigenous organizations, for they are key players (as reproducers of life and culture) in the resistance offered by indigenous peoples to assimilation into the dominant culture (Prieto 1998, 15–16).

In a detailed study undertaken in Ecuador of indigenous female leaders, it is suggested that one of the reasons that these leaders promote the discourse "that in complementarity there is equality," is that "the same process of re-valuation of one's culture, of the traditional, that is used to recuperate the values, knowledge, and identity of indigenous people, is being used to revalue the position of women" (Cervone 1998, 185). According to Emma Cervone (1998, 185–186), indigenous women leaders have to defend two spaces simultaneously: first, the ethnic space for the defense of difference and the equality of rights before white/*mestizo*[37] society; and second, their space as women leaders within the indigenous movement, a space where they must be validated by male indigenous leaders. She thus argues that the equality ideology, "highlighting the feminine in the symbolic order of the value system," be seen as a strategy by women leaders to defend their space as women.

Nonetheless, there are a number of contradictions in this position, as she recognizes, including the fact that the re-valuation of the position of women is taking place more at the symbolic than the political level. In addition, the gender equality discourse is often at odds with the lived experience of indigenous women at the base, particularly with respect to such issues as domestic violence, and could lead to a rupture between female leadership at the national level and at the local level over issues of inequality (Cervone 1998, 186–187).

There is recognition among organized indigenous women leaders that they suffer discrimination within the mixed indigenous organizations. They are underrepresented in numbers both within the membership and in leadership positions. One of the main demands of women within CONAIE, for example, is for equal participation by men and women in the organization: "We demand that we be taken into account so that participation in assemblies, congresses, etc. is egalitarian between men and women; i.e., if ten people are to participate, it should be five men and five women" (CONAIE 1994, 7).

There is also awareness among the female indigenous leadership of the difficulties of women participating on the same terms as men in local and regional mixed organizations. In both Bolivia and Ecuador, local-level organizations of women proliferated over the past two decades, but participation in women's-only groups has been slow to result in women's greater participation in male-dominated local institutions.

In Ecuador, the primary form of local-level organization in the highlands has been the *comunas*, associated with communal access to landholdings and local governance. By law membership in these is open to all men and women over 18 years of age; however, in practice, households are represented by the male household head.[38] The main form of local-level governance in the Bolivian highlands has been through the village peasant syndicate structure, where representation is based on one member per household, again usually the male household head (Sostres and Carafa 1992; Paulson 1996).[39] As in Ecuador, although indigenous women are increasingly participating in their own women-only groups, this has not automatically led to their growing representation in traditional structures of governance and power within their communities, although in recent years their participation in these has been growing.

It is primarily within women's own organizations at the local or regional level where women are beginning to address not only practical, but also strategic gender issues. In women's meetings concerns are raised about women's lack of access to land and of the problems this fosters. The NGO preparatory activities for the 1995 Beijing Conference in Bolivia included five regional meetings of indigenous and peasant women in different parts of the country and illustrate this point.[40] Women's land rights emerged as follows:

- The agrarian syndicates prefer men when it comes to distributing lands and property rights. We women don't have our own lands. Many times if the husband dies our lands are returned to the community. Parents give preference to male sons, discriminating against women (Salguero 1995, 23);

- Among our proposals to enhance our situation are the following: access to education for women at all levels; technical training and credit; the right to property of land . . . (Salguero 1995, 25);

- Women have a right to land and we want this to be legalized for we are the ones that work the land: land belongs to whomever works it (Salguero 1995, 28);

- Families own the land although we don't have formal titles. Nonetheless, we women suffer because we don't have the right to our own land, to plant our own crops, which is what we need for economic survival (Salguero 1995, 35).

The problems associated with women's lack of legal access to land become most apparent in the case of male migration, for often access to credit or technical assistance depends on their being landowners or having land in their own name. Moreover, when seasonal migration by the spouse turns into permanent migration, without secure land rights, women are placed in a situation of great insecurity in providing for their families, since sometimes, the family's usufruct plot reverts to the peasant syndicate or community. According to traditional customs and practices, there is no certainty that community authorities will cede land to women who are abandoned.

What is worth noting here is that when these concerns of indigenous women at the local and regional level were taken to the national meeting, what was privileged was the general demand for recognition of indigenous territories and defense of communal land. Of the various concerns regarding women's land rights which had been expressed earlier, only one—regarding inheritance—was preserved in the final recommendations: "When it comes to inheritance of these territories from parents and spouses, we want to have property rights over these" (Salguero 1995, 48). According to the coordinator of these meetings:[41]

> Many indigenous women highlighted the role of complementarity and in how in the complementarity of roles there is not discrimination . . . Nonetheless, no topic is clearer in terms of breaking the conception that in complementarity there is no discrimination than the topic of inheritance of land rights.

This suggests the following points: 1) that traditional patterns of inheritance based on customary law and practices often discriminate against women;[42] 2) that indigenous women are increasingly becoming aware of this discrimination; and 3) that there is often a great distance between the concerns of indigenous women at the base and what is expressed by their leaders in national-level meetings, particularly in meetings where the male leadership of the mixed associations is also present.

Within the majority of today's peasant and indigenous communities in the Andes, gender inequality is pervasive, as seen in inheritance patterns, land tenure, the structure of power and representation of communities, and in daily life. Thus the demand for respect of traditional customs and patterns is rarely, in practice, a call for gender equality based on complementarity, but rather, a call for the reproduction of practices which subordinate women to men. The only way to guarantee that men and women will have equal access to land within collective forms of landholding is if the rights of individuals to land are clearly specified and guaranteed within the collectivity.

Consequences of Ignoring Individual Land Rights: The Counter-Reforms in Mexico and Peru

Perhaps the best case that can be made in terms of why it is important to specify women's land rights explicitly within collective forms of property is by considering what is happening to women's access to land under the counter-reforms underway in Mexico and Peru. In both countries, neoliberal agrarian legislation now allows, upon majority vote,[43] for collective landholdings to be divided up and eventually sold. Before the counter-reform, women's rights to collective land were much more explicit in Mexico and Peru than in either Bolivia or Ecuador. In Mexico, which was the first country to establish legal equality between men and women in its agrarian legislation, since 1971, either men or women could become *ejiditarios* and enjoy equal rights within *ejido* decision-making structures. However, following traditional practice (and usually embodied in the regulations established by each *ejido*), each household was entitled to be represented by only one *ejidatorio*, who by custom was the male household head. Thus while the state had granted all adult women the legal right to participate in *ejido* decision making, the ability to practice this right was limited by local regulations based on traditional custom and practices, effectively limiting formal participation by women to female household heads.

Nevertheless, usufruct rights on the *ejido* were considered to be the family patrimony, entitling each member within the household access to land and other resources. Inheritance provisions on the *ejidos* protected this family patrimony by restricting the inheritance of *ejido* parcels, if a will had been made out, to the spouse or partner and/or the children, or if there were no will, giving first preference to the spouse/partner and then the children.

In the current counter-reform, all major decisions regarding the future of the *ejido* (such as whether to parcelize and/or dissolve the *ejido*) are to be made by recognized *ejido* members. This means that spouses of *ejido* members are excluded from decision making, and in effect excludes most women (since women represent less than one-fifth of total *ejido* membership) from participating directly in determining the future of their communities. Moreover, upon a vote of *ejido* members, individuals holding usufruct rights may acquire a title to the family parcel and dispose of it as they see fit, either renting it or selling it.[44] In addition, changes in inheritance provisions no longer assure that access to the parcel will remain within the family. Now the *ejidatario* may decide the preference ordering, which may include the spouse or partner, one or all of the children, or any other person. Only in the case in which the *ejidatario* dies intestate does the previous preference ordering rule, which granted first priority to the spouse/partner, or in her absence, one of the children.

What we want to highlight is that what was a family resource—the *patrimonio familiar*—has given way in the counter-reform to a process of individualization of land rights which has excluded women. It has excluded women because traditional norms and practices grant household representation to only one sex. Moreover, since married women have no rights of direct representation within the *ejido*, they have no voice and vote in the decisions determining the privatization of communal land. The family patrimony thus becomes the individual property of the male household head (Lara Flora 1994, 86; Esparza, et.al. 1996; Stephen 1996; Botey 1997).

Turning to Peru, since 1987 men and women in Peru have had equal rights to be members of the officially recognized peasant communities. However, the Law of Peasant Communities, which pledged the state to respect and protect "the customs, uses, and traditions of the Community," also distinguished between community membership and the category of *comunero calificado*, or qualified *comunero* (Perú 1987, Article 1). To be the latter required having civil capacity, to have lived in the community for at least five years, to be inscribed in the community registry, and to meet whatever other prerequisites might be established in the community statutes. While all *comuneros* have the right to use the goods and services of the community, one must be a qualified *comunero* to participate with voice and vote in the community assembly and to be elected to a position of leadership in the community.

While theoretically, the qualified *comunero* can be a man or woman, following customary practice, there is only *one* qualified comunero per family, and it is the man who, as head of household, represents the family before the community. Traditionally, the only women who participate in communal decisions are widows (del Castillo 1997). For example, in the highlands of the Department of Lima:

> Mayobamba men say that each family is represented by a single *comunero* and as long as there is a male to take on this role, it should be done by a man. In any given family, brothers become *comuneros* while sisters must gain access to representation and resources through their fathers and

husbands who are *comuneros*. Only when a woman has been widowed or when she is a long-term single mother and no longer attached to her father's family does she receive *comunera* status (Bourque and Warren 1981, 157).

In some cases, if widows remarry they lose their right to represent their family, and their direct access to land (Casafranca and Espinosa 1993, 19, 26). Other researchers have also concluded that the highland peasant communities are characterized by widespread "discrimination with respect to the usufruct of land by sex, age, and marital status (ie., women, younger sons, orphans, widows, and the elderly" (Bonilla 1997, 72).

While it is only since the 1995 Land Law in Peru that peasant communities in the highlands or native indigenous communities in the *selva* may freely choose their form of association and disposition of communal land, this decision is to be made by a two-thirds majority vote of the qualified *comuneros*. As in Mexico, married women will not be participating in this crucially important decision-making process regarding the future of their communities, and if the individualization of land rights takes place, may also see the family usufruct parcel transformed into male private property.

Relatively little attention has been given in Peru to the gender implications of the parcelization of communal land. A recent report by a Working Group on Communities and Titling was concerned, nonetheless, about what would happen to the land rights of widows in the peasant communities:

> Traditionally, the right of widows to maintain a land parcel to sustain herself and her children has generally been respected, however, cases are found where widows have more restricted rights, such as access to less land than is usual, or to the poorest land, or even where they are not given any land rights at all. The latter might turn out to be a significant problem in those zones of the *sierra* which have been affected by the social and political violence and where the number of widows is quite high . . . (Coordinadora Nacional de Comunidades Campesinas 1997, 3).

If this group of women within peasant communities does not have assured land rights as household heads, the probability is slim that the interests of wives and daughters will be duly considered or their voices heard in the parcelization process.

Among these four countries, it is in Mexico—where the process of privatization of communal land is most advanced—where indigenous women have been most vocal in demanding land rights explicitly for women. As expressed at the 1994 NGO Preparatory Meeting for Beijing, the changes to Article 27 of the Mexican constitution which opened the way for privatization of the *ejido*:

> . . . affects us indigenous women because we cannot decide on the fate of our lands; it allows that land be sold, when previously it was inalienable, imprescriptible, inembargable. Now they can take away our lands. Besides, this article does not take us into account . . . we do not count . . . Parallel to the struggle for land must be the struggle for women's rights . . .[45]

In meetings in Chiapas, indigenous women have voiced concrete demands for land rights: "women have the right to property of land and to inherit it;" "that in granting land titles, women should be co-owners;" and that "if a man abandons his family, the parcel should automatically pass to the woman" (Rojas 1995, 203, 209). And of all indigenous movements, the EZLN (Zapatista National Liberation Army) has been the first to recognize in position papers that "land should be redistributed in an egalitarian form to men and women" and that "women must be included in tenancy and inheritance of land" (Rojas 1995, 251).

Conclusion

This chapter has illustrated the importance of the defense of community for indigenous people, and the centrality of the demand for collective rights over land and territory for indigenous identity and survival. At the same time, we have argued that it is one thing to support the demand for collective property rights, and quite another to defend traditional customs and practices in terms of how that land is allocated to families and the individuals within them. Our central concern is when respect for customary law or traditional customs and practices violates the individual rights of indigenous women.

In our view, accepting the strong cultural relativist position—that culture is the sole and principal source of validity of moral right and rule—requires accepting the subordination of women and negates women's individual human rights. While we are respectful of indigenous cosmovisions based on the link between women and land as the source of life, and the appeal that the complementarity thesis carries of a past where men and women might have been equal, we worry about where it leads: to the argument for the preservation of all aspects of a culture, no matter how discriminatory.

Besides idealizing the past and requiring the acceptance of a closed cultural system, the strong cultural relativist position ignores internal inequities and relations of power (Howard 1993, 329). By not recognizing the relations of power in which authority derived from tradition is based, this vision claims that the subordination of women is a product of external forces, such as colonialism and machista acculturation, and deflects attention from current inequities and injustices. This strong cultural relativist position is beginning to be challenged by indigenous women intellectuals. In the opinion of Amanda Pop, Kichie Mayan woman and scholar in Guatemala,[46]

> It is important to know the history of the atrocities to which our people have been subjected, but if I am consistently going to interpret the present according to some mystical past, which is not even a real history, then, where is this going to lead? I have to analyze what is currently most important and the present is the most important task. If I do not question whether there is discrimination, then other people are deciding the question for us, and those are our men. We can't waste time, for it really is not important how it [discrimination against women] came about, more important, is that it exists.

When women such as Pop express these ideas, demanding recognition of the rights of women, they have been denounced by male Mayan intellectuals as engaging in ethnocide (Alvarez 1996, 26).

Besides fear of confronting internal relations of power, one of the main reasons indigenous organizations have refused to consider the specific situation of women is that it is seen to be divisive for indigenous unity (Hernández and Murguialday 1993, 132). But increasingly in national and regional meetings, indigenous women are beginning to question relations of power when they demand equal participation in the mixed indigenous organizations. These demands were made very timidly at the 1989 Meeting of Latin American Peasant and Indigenous Organizations, organized in the context of the planning for the anti-1992 Quincentennial Events. The few women who were in attendance at this meeting first had to explain to the men that they were not against them before they spoke out about concerns regarding their participation (Comisión Mujer 1989, 29). Sometimes indigenous women in these meetings make very pointed criticisms but in order for these criticisms to be heard, they frame these in the language of the "external influences" of *machismo* and colonialism to make their main point: that *machismo* makes their participation in indigenous organizations difficult, in addition to supposedly being against their own indigenous cultural values (FENSUAGRO, ANUC, AND ANIC 1988, 82–83).

According to Hernández and Murguialday (1993, 157), it was at the Second Continental Meeting of the 500 Years Campaign, held in Guatemala in 1991, that indigenous groups first recognized the triple oppression of indigenous women. One of the resolutions of this meeting acknowledged that: "The struggle for women's emancipation must take place in an integral framework that takes into account the struggle against class inequality, ethnic inequality, and gender inequality" (Hernández and Murguialday 1993). By 1995, in the context of the preparatory activities for the Beijing U.N. Conference on Women, indigenous women in the various regional meetings were increasingly vocal regarding the mechanisms which reproduce gender inequality. For example, the following was concluded in the diagnostic elaborated at the 1995 Seminar of Indigenous Women of South America held in Bogotá:

> We women have begun to criticize the [indigenous] organizational structures for being exclusionary, for not being autonomous models, for not being internally democratic, and more than anything else, for ignoring and belittling our contribution. We have been very clear in expressing our wish to work together with the men within our organizations, even if we continue to face obstacles which lead us to be discriminated against within them. It hurts us that in many occasions we have to put up with excuses to maintain us in inferior positions, where we can't exert leadership, that our contributions are not taken seriously, and that our work with indigenous women is the first to be interrupted if there are financial problems . . . Indigenous women have been present in the organizations which fight for the rights of the originary peoples of the Americas. The invisibility of women does not mean that we have been absent. This is why it has become increasingly clear that we must struggle for the space in which to participate at all the different levels of power, where the vital decisions are made that affect the life and future of women and of the people . . . (ONIC 1996, 35–36).

In the process of demanding the right to full participation within the mixed indigenous organizations, there is growing recognition of the complexity of factors that reproduce women's subordination to men, down to the community level:

> In terms of politics, indigenous women recognize that in their communities many aspects of the dominant ideology are reproduced which emphasize that women should be maintained in a subordinate position in all spheres. This generates relations of power and inequality between men and women that go against the idea that women should be incorporated into the structures of decision making. The main obstacles with respect to the participation of women in the discussions and decisions of the community is the social structure of our country and of the indigenous

communities which consider that women are not capable of leadership (ONIC 1996, 86).

It is thus apparent that indigenous women leaders are beginning to struggle not only for broadening the scope for participation of women within the mixed indigenous organizations, but also in terms of the structure of decision making within indigenous communities. That is, they are beginning to demand a voice in determining how "customary" rules are determined and defined.

At the same time, the level of discourse in terms of women's land rights remains rather muted in most of these regional meetings, perhaps because these must be considered, in the first instance, part and parcel of the broader struggle for indigenous land and territories. Nonetheless, at the Second Meeting of the Continental Campaign 500 Years, the Commission on Women and Life demanded that the campaign support its struggle to attain: "the same rights as men to the property of land and housing, access to credit, the creation of jobs for women, and equal remuneration for equal work" (Hernández and Murguialday 1993, 158). Among the demands of the Forum on Indigenous Women and Political Participation at the NGO preparatory meeting at Mar del Plata in 1994 was the following: "To demand the right of indigenous and peasant women to land" (CEIMME 1995, 136). And at the 1995 Seminar of Indigenous Women of South America, the following point was agreed to: "That indigenous women, whether widowed or not, be given access to land and credit" (ONIC 1996, 56).

Thus while the topic of women and land rights has not always emerged as a primary demand, as organized indigenous women have begun to question in public forums the structure of gender inequality within their mixed organizations and communities, the relationship between material factors and relations of power are beginning to be uncovered, examined and struggled against.

Notes

The field research upon which this chapter is based was funded by a grant from The Ford Foundation's regional offices for Mexico and Central America, the Andes, and Brazil. The authors are very grateful for their support as well as that of the many feminist researchers and activists, too many to mention here, who facilitated our research. This chapter draws on Deere and León (2001).

1. The gains with respect to women's land rights in eight Latin American countries are reviewed in Deere and León (1998a and 1998b), and in twelve countries in Deere and León (2001).

2. Guatemala's 1999 legislation creating a new land bank program made joint adjudication and titling to couples mandatory. Female-headed households are to continue to receive priority (Guatemala 1999).
3. The *ejidos* were communal lands granted to peasants after the Mexican Revolution.
4. The Universal Declaration of Human Rights was adopted by the U.N. General Assembly in 1948. It was designed to reaffirm and reinforce the provisions of the U.N. Charter which affirmed explicitly in its preamble the equal rights of men and women and prohibited discrimination based on sex, race, language, and religion. Nonetheless, the writing of the Universal Declaration of Human Rights in relatively gender neutral terms was a major struggle. Early versions of the Declaration had begun with "All men are brothers." After considerable lobbying, the U.N. Commission on the Status of Women managed to introduce language focusing on "all human beings," the language which was eventually adopted (Tomasevski 1993, 98–100).
5. The strong version of this thesis is also referred to as cultural absolutism (Howard 1993).
6. Among the rights that feminists want to include as priorities, which have also been stressed by socialists, are the rights to food, clothing, shelter, work, heath, education, etc., as well as the general right to development (Brems 1997, 140).
7. World Plan of Action, pars.37, and 46–48, in Fraser (1987, 38–39).
8. World Plan of Action, pars. 120–130, in Fraser (1987, 45).
9. Our italics. UN (1980, 2–3), Article 2, pars. a and f.
10. UN (1980, 7), Article 14, par. 2 (g).
11. UN (1980, 7), Article 15, par. 2.
12. UN (1980, 8), Article 16, par. 2 (h).
13. UN (1996, 21–22, 93, 96), pars. 61b, 230g, and 232d.
14. Interview with Jorge Dandler, Senior Specialist in Rural Employment and Indigenous Peoples, ILO, February 21, 1999, San José.
15. Article 2.2b, "C169 Indigenous and Tribal Peoples Convention, 1989," International Labour Office, mimeo, 4/14/99. The Spanish version of the document may be found in Sánchez (1996, Appendix).
16. The predecessors which are mentioned in the Preamble include the Universal Declaration of Human Rights, the International Covenant on Economic, Social, and Cultural Rights, and the International Covenant on Political and Civil Rights, "and the many international instruments on the prevention of discrimination."
17. The 1995 Beijing Platform of Action is considered a victory for feminists over cultural relativists with respect to women's human rights for i) the Beijing Platform for Action explicitly adopted the key principles on women's human rights of the 1994 Vienna Declaration and Programme of Action; and ii) debates regarding whether the goal was equality between men and women versus equity were resolved in favor of equality (Brems 1997,150–152).
18. Interview, February 21, 1999, San José.
19. On the development of ECUARUNARI and its transformation from a peasant-oriented organization to a self-identified indigenous organization see Zamosc (1994) and Black (1998).
20. On the development of CONFENIAE from nine, ethnic-based organizations in the Amazon, and the evolution of their demands see Black (1998).

21. Prior to the uprising, some 600,000 hectares in the provinces of Napo and Pastaza had been titled to the Huaorani people. Now the OPIP (Organization of the Indigenous People of Pastaza) demanded that the bulk of the province of Pastaza be titled as the territory of the indigenous people who inhabited it. After a twelve day march from Pastaza to Quito in April 1992, which included representatives of all of the indigenous organizations, the government finally conceded and deeded 1.1 million hectares to the Quichua, Shuar, Achuar, and Zaparo peoples (Navarro, Vallejo, and Villaverde 1996, 28–30).

22. Other important issues included the settlement of some 72 specific land conflicts pending before IERAC, the agrarian reform institute; the creation of a land fund to subsidize land purchases; and that large landholdings be expropriated in areas of high population pressure (i.e., the continuation of the agrarian reform).

23. Carmelina Porate of CONAIE at the NGO Preparatory Meeting for Beijing in Mar del Plata, Argentina, 1994, in CEIMME (1995, 68–69).

24. Another reason that the issue of gender did not figure at all in the discussions surrounding the 1994 law was that land rights were not a primary concern of DINAMO, the national women's office, whose priority at that time centered on passage of a law against domestic violence. In addition, in that year, as part of President Sixto Duran's effort to trim the size of the state, the Department of Peasant Women in the Ministry of Agriculture had been eliminated, thus there was no strong lobby coming from the Ministry either. Interviews with Rocío Rosero, researcher at DINAMO, July 25, 1997, Quito, and with Dolores Casco, Director of the Office of Peasant Development of Ministry of Agriculture and Livestock, July 23, 1997, Quito.

25. Subsequently, a change was made in the administrative regulations of the land titling agency to allow the joint titling of land to married couples; couples in consensual unions are made co-property owners.

26. See Andolina (1998) on the process leading to the constitutional assembly of 1998 and on CONAIE's role in strengthening indigenous rights in the new constitution.

27. Interview with Miguel Urioste, Director of TIERRA, July 10, 1997, La Paz.

28. Interview with Paulino Guarachi, Sub-Secretariat of Rural Development, July 15, 1997, La Paz. Guarachi was a former Secretary General of the CSUTCB.

29. During this period there were major charges of corruption in the two institutions charged with agrarian reform and colonization, the CNRA, the Consejo Nacional de Reforma Agraria and the INC, the Instituto Nacional de Colonización. In the face of all of these problems and contending positions, the government of Jaime Paz Zamora intervened in these two institutions in late 1992. The National Intervention, as it was known, was charged with coming up with a new law to govern land rights and land redistribution, settling the morass of overlapping claims, and reorganizing the Servicio Nacional de Reforma Agraria. Meanwhile, a moratorium was placed on the titling or adjudication of any new land.

30. Interview with Julia Ramos Sánchez, Executive Secretary, and Emiliana Sarcido, General Secretary, Federación Nacional de Mujeres Campesinas de Bolivia "Bartolina Sisa," July 15, 1997, La Paz.

31. Discussion generated at the Seminar on Rural Women and Land Tenure, organized for the authors by CEDLA, CIDEM and Consultores rym "ac," July 11, 1997, La Paz.

32. The Director of INRA at the time considered that several of the other recommendations of the consultant's report, such as gender-neutral language, could be

dealt with in the subsequent regulations to accompany the law. Interview of July 14, 1997, La Paz. However, in the subsequent regulations, no additional gender-specific content was added (INRA 1997).

33. Some eight or nine had already been recognized; sixteen applications were pending at the time the law was passed and these were to be titled land within ten months of the signing of the law, a process which was underway during our research trip to Bolivia in July 1997. Interview with Luz María Calvo and Doris Vidal, Subsecretariat of Ethnic Affairs, July 10, 1997, La Paz.

34. Billie Jean Isbell (1978, 11) defines the notion of complementarity in terms of one entity's relation to another entity: "sexual complementarity is perhaps the most pervasive concept used to classify cosmological and natural phenomena. It also symbolizes the process of regeneration. Phenomena are conceptualized as male and female and interact with one another in a dialectic fashion to form new syntheses, such as new cycles of time and new generations of people, plants, and animals." She has called this dialectic the concept of "the essential other half."

35. Interview with Clara Flóres, Congressional Deputy and indigenous leader, July 12, 1997, La Paz.

36. Interview with researcher Gloria Ardaya, July 13, 1997, La Paz.

37. *Mestizo* refers to a racially mixed person of Indian and European descent.

38. It was estimated that in the mid-1980s less than 10 percent of the members were women, the vast majority of whom were widows or abandoned women (FIDA 1989,166). The leadership of the *comunas* has traditionally been all male, and while in recent years there appears to be an increase in the number of women in leadership positions, it is estimated that women comprise less than one percent of the elected leadership in mixed base-level organizations. Interviews with Dolores Casco, Director, and Julia Almeida of the Direction of Peasant Organizations, Ministry of Agriculture and Livestock, July 23, 1997, Quito.

39. In the four Mizque communities studied by Paulson (1996, 38), women represented 17 percent of the households. Most of these were widows or separated women, but some women who represented households did so because they were the owners or administrators of the household's land.

40. The pre-Beijing Conference process included the participation of peasant and indigenous women throughout the region for the first time, and in many cases, promoted the organization of national-level peasant and indigenous women's organizations and networks. In Bolivia, after Beijing discussions have continued on whether a National Confederation of Peasant Women should be created which would be totally independent of the mixed-membership associations (Salguero 1996).

41. Mercedes Urriolagoitia, NGO National Coordinator for Beijing, intervention at the Seminar on Rural Women and Land Tenure organized for the authors by CEDLA (Centro de Estudios de Desarrollo Laboral y Agrario), CIDEM (Centro de Información y Desarrollo de la Mujer), and the consultancy group "rym.a.c." in La Paz, Bolivia, July 1997.

42. This proposition is examined in detail in Deere and León (2001, Ch. 8).

43. In Peru, the decision to parcelize the peasant communities requires a 50 percent majority vote in the coast, and—as in Ecuador—a 2/3 vote in the highlands. In Mexico this decision only requires a simple majority vote. See Deere and León (2001, Ch. 3).

44. Women and children have the *derecho de tanto*, or right of first buyer, but they have only thirty days to make arrangements to purchase the land.

45. Sofía Robles, Grupo Iniciativa Indígena por la Paz, Chiapas, in CEIMME (1995, 52–3).
46. Interview by the authors, January 7, 1998, Guatemala City.

References

Alvarez, Francisca.1996. Las mujeres mayas etnocida. *El Periódico Domingo*. November 24, p. 26.

Andolina, Robert. 1998. *CONAIE (and Others) in the Ambiguous Spaces of Democracy: Positioning for the 1997–8 Asamblea Nacional Constituyente in Ecuador*. Paper prepared for the 1998 Congress of the Latin American Studies Association, September 24–26, Chicago, Ill.

Black, Chad T. 1998. *The 1990 Indian Uprising in Ecuador: Culture, Ethnicity and Post-Marxist Social Praxis*. Paper prepared for 1998 Congress of the Latin American Studies Association, September 24–26, Chicago, Ill.

Bourque, Susan and Kay Warren. 1981. *Women of the Andes: Patriarchy and Social Change in Two Peruvian Towns*. Ann Arbor: University of Michigan Press.

Bonilla, Jenifer. 1997. Tercer intento modernizador? In *II Encuentro Regional por la Agricultura: Contexto Económico y Pequeña Producción Rural Andina*, edited by Colectivo de Autores. 67–74. Cuzco: COINCIDE.

Botey, Carlota. 1997. Mujer rural: reforma agraria y contrareforma. In *Tiempo de crisis, tiempos de mujer*, edited by Josefina Aranda, Carlota Botey, and Rosario Robles. Mexico, D.F.: Centro de Estudios Históricos de la Cuestión Agraria Mexicana and Ford Foundation.

Brems, Eva. 1997. Enemies or allies? Feminism and cultural relativism as dissident voices in human rights discourse. *Human Rights Quarterly*. 19:136–164.

Camacho, Aida. 1996. *Incorporación del componente género en el proyecto de ley de modificación del servicio nacional de reforma agraria*. Consultancy report to TIERRA, April, La Paz.

Casafranca, Jazmine and Cristina Espinoza. 1993. *Análisis de la política del sector agropecuario frente a la mujer productora de alimentos en la región andina: Peru*. Documento síntesis, preliminary report, IICA/BID Rural Women Project, Lima, Peru, December.

CEIMME (Centro de Estudios e Investigación Sobre el Maltrato a la Mujer Ecuatoriana). 1995. *Encuentro Latinoamericano, Mujer Indígena y Participación Política, Memoria, Foro Alternativo de ONGs, Mar del Plata, Argentina, septiembre de 1994*. Quito: CEIMME.

Cervone, Emma.1998. Prof. Abelina Morocho Pinguil: entre cantares y cargos. In *Mujeres Contracorriente: voces de líderes indígenas*, edited by CEPLAES. 163–207. Quito: CEPLAES.

Chancoso, Blanca. n.d. Las indígenas no sabían de esta reunión. In *Mujeres Fempress: Especial la Mujer Indígena*.

Comisión Mujer y Autodescubrimiento. 1990. Conclusiones y resoluciones. In *Memorias encuentro Latinoamericano de organizaciones campesinas e indígenas, 500 años de resistencia indígena y popular. Bogotá 7 al 12 de octubre de 1989*, edited by ONIC, Organización Indígena de Colombia, ANUC, Asociación Nacional de

Usuarios Campesinos, and FENSUAGRO-CUT, Federación Nacional Sindical Unitaria Agropecuaria. 18–31. Bogotá.

CONAIE. 1994. *Memorias de las jornadas del Foro de la Mujer Indígena del Ecuador.* Quito: CONAIE-UNFPA.

CONAIE and CONAMIE/CONAIE. 1995. *Memorias: encuentro de mujeres indígenas de las primeras naciones del continente, 31 de julio al 4 de agosto de 1995, Quito, Ecuador.* Quito: CONAIE.

Conferencia Internacional del Trabajo. 1988. *Revisión parcial del convenio sobre poblaciones indígenas y tribales, 1957 (num. 107).* Geneva: International Labour Office, Report VI.

Coordinadora Nacional de Comunidades Campesinas, Grupo de Trabajo sobre Comunidades y Titulación. 1997. *Derechos individuales al interior de la comunidad.* Paper presented to the Primer Taller sobre comunidades Campesinas y Titulación, June, Lima.

Dandler, Jorge. 1996. *Indigenous People and the Rule of Law in Latin America: Do They Have a Chance?* Paper prepared for the Workshop on the Rule of Law and the Underprivileged in Latin America, November 19–16. Kellogg Institute for International Studies, University of Notre Dame.

Deere, Carmen Diana and Magdalena León. (1998). Mujeres, derechos a la tierra y contrareformas en América Latina. *Debate Agrario: Análisis y Alternativas.* 27:129–154.

———. 1998b. Gender, land, and water: from reform to counter-reform in Latin America. *Agriculture and Human Values.* 15:375–386.

———. 2001. *Empowering Women: Land, and Property Rights in Latin America.* Pittsburgh: University of Pittsburgh Press.

de la Cruz, Rodrigo. 1995. Los derechos de los Indígenas: un tema milenario cobra nueva fuerza. In *Derechos de los Pueblos Indígenas: Situación Jurídica y Políticas de Estado*, edited by Ramón Torres Galarza. 7–16.Quito: CONAIE-CEPLAES-ABYA-Yala.

del Castillo, Laureano. 1997. *Derechos de la mujer en el ámbito agrario.* Paper prepared for the Seminario/Taller Ley de Tierras y Titulación en Cajamarca, Cajamarca, Red de la Mujer Rural Flora Tristán and REPRODEMUC.

Donnelly, Jack. 1984. Cultural relativism and universal human rights. *Human Rights Quarterly.* 6:400–419.

Ecuador, República de. 1994. *Ley de desarrollo agrario y reglamento.* Quito: Congreso Nacional.

———. 1998. *Constitución política de la República de Ecuador.* Quito: Corp. de Estudios y Publicaciones.

Esparza Salinas, Rocío, Blanca Suarez, and Paloma Bonfil. 1996. *Las mujeres campesinas ante la reforma al Artículo 27 de la Constitución.* Mexico, D.F.: GIM-TRAP.

FENSUAGRO, ANUC, and ONIC. 1988. *Primer encuentro de mujeres campesinas e indígenas de América Latina y del Caribe, noviembre 28 a diciembre 2 de 1988, Bogotá, Colombia.* Bogotá: FENSUAGRO, ANUC, and ONIC.

FIDA, Fondo Internacional de Desarrollo Agricola. 1987. *Report of the Special Programming Mission to Ecuador.* Rome: FIDA.

Flores, Andrea, Felipa Gutierrez, and Arminda Velazco. n.d. Nosotras las mujeres Aymaras in *Mujer Fempress, Especial la Mujer Indigena*. N.p.

Fraser, Arvonne S. 1987. *The U.N. Decade for Women: Documents and Dialogue*. Boulder: Westview Press.

Garay, Amanda. 1996. Women, cultural relativsm, and international human rights: a question of mutual exclusivity or balance? *International Insights*. Spring: 19–33.

Guatemala. Congreso de la República. 1999. *Ley del fondo de tierras*. Guatemala City: Congreso de la República.

Hernández, Teresita and Clara Murguialday. 1993. *Mujeres indígenas ayer y hoy*. Managua: Punto de Encuentros.

Howard, Rhoda E. 1993. Cultural absolutism and the nostalgia for community. *Human Rights Quarterly*. 15:315–338.

INRA, Instituto Nacional de Reforma Agraria. 1997. *INRA: Una herramienta para la tierra*. La Paz.

Isbell, Billie Jean. 1978. *To Defend Ourselves: Ecology and Ritual in an Andean Village*. Austin: University of Texas Press.

ISIS Internacional. 1987. Las mujeres Aymaras se organizan. *ISIS Internacional, Edición de las Mujeres*. 6:45–48.

Lara Flores, Sara María. 1994. Las mujeres: nuevos actores sociales en el campo? *Revista Mexicana de Sociología*. 2:77–88.

Macas, Luis. 1995. La ley agraria y el proceso de movilizacion por la vida. In *Derechos de los pueblos indígenas: situación jurídica y políticas de estado*, edited by Ramon Torres Galarza. 29–43. Quito: CONAIE-CEPLAES-Abya-Yala..

Moya, Ruth. 1987. *Educación y mujer indígena en el Ecuador*. Paper prepared for the Regional Office of UNESCO, Quito.

Muñoz, Jorge A. and Isabel Lavadenz. 1997. *Reforming the Agrarian Reform in Bolivia*. Development Discussion Paper No. 589, HIID. Cambridge, Mass.: Harvard University.

Navarro, Wilson, Alonso Vallejo, and Xabier Villaverde. 1996. *Tierra para la vida: acceso de los campesinos ecuatorianos a la tierra: opción y experiencias del FEPP*. Quito: FEPP.

OIT, Organización Internacional del Trabajo. 1987. *Informe VI (1) Revisión Parcial del Convenio sobre Poblaciones Indígenas y Tribales, 1957 (Num. 107)*. Geneva: OIT.

ONIC, Organización Nacional Indígena de Colombia. 1996. *Mujer, tierra y cultura: ayer, hoy y mañana, taller suramericano de mujeres indígenas, memorias, Santandercito, Cundinamarca, Colombia, 10 al 14 de julio de 1995*. Bogotá: ONIC and Dirección Nacional para la Equidad de La Mujer, Presidencia de la República.

Paulson, Susan. 1996. Familias que no "conyugan" e identidades que no conjugan: la vida en Mizqe desafía nuestras categories. In *Ser mujer indígena, chola o birlocha en la Bolivia postcolonial de los años 90*, edited by Silvia Rivera Cusicanqui. 85–162. La Paz: Subsecretaria de Asuntos de Género, Ministerio de Desarrollo Humano.

Perú, República de. 1987. Ley general de comunidades campesinas, Ley No. 24656 de 13/4/87, *Diario "El Peruano."* Lima: Edited by "M.A.S."

Pollis, Adamantia. 1996. Cultural relativism revisited: through a state prism. *Human Rights Quarterly*. 18:316–344.

Prieto, Mercedes. 1998. El liderazgo en las mujeres indígenas: tendiendo puentes entre género y etnia. In *Mujeres contracorriente: voces de líderes indígenas,* edited by CEPLAES. 15–37. Quito: CEPLAES.

Rojas, Rosa, ed. 1995. *Chiapas, y las mujeres que?* Mexico, D.F.: Ed. del Taller Editorial La Correa Femenista.

Ruiz, Marta. 1993. Algunas consideraciones sobre tierra y territorio. In *Memoria: encuentro de mujeres de pueblos originarios,* 17–24. Santa Cruz: Fundación San Gabriel, MOSOC-CEPAS, UNICEF.

Salguero, Elizabeth, ed. 1995. *Memoria: primer encuentro de mujeres indígenas, campesinas y originarias, Cochabamba del 24 al 26 de julio de 1995.* La Paz: Federación Nacional de Mujeres Campesinas de Bolivia "Bartolina Sisa," Coordinación Nacional del Foro de ONGs de Bolivia para IV Conferencia Mundial sobre la Mujer, and Educación en Poblacion-UNFPA, 1995.

———. 1996. *Informe, reunión nacional de mujeres rurales.* I Encuentro Latinoamericano y del Caribe de Mujeres Rurales. La Paz, 21 y 22 de noviembre. mimeo.

Sánchez, Enrique, ed. 1996. *Derechos de los pueblos indígenas en las constituciones de América Latina.* Memorias del Seminario Internacional de Expertos sobre Régimen Constitucional y Pueblos Indígenas en Paises de Latinoamerica, Villa de Leyva, Colombia julio 17–22. Bogotá: COAMA and Disloque Editores.

Sostres, María Fernanda and Yara Carafa.1992. Propuestas de políticas agropecuarias para la mujer en la estrategia de desarrollo. In *Propuestas de Políticas Sectoriales para la Participación de la Mujer en la Estrategia de Desarrollo,* edited by Coordinadora de la Mujer. 49–87. La Paz.

Stephen, Lynn. 1996. Too little, too late? The impact of Article 27 on women in Oaxaca. In *Reforming Mexico's Agrarian Reform,* edited by L. Randall. 289–303. New York: M.E. Sharpe.

Tomasevski, Katarina.1993. *Women and Human Rights.* London: Zed Books.

Torres Galarza, Ramón Torres, ed. 1995. *Derechos de los pueblos indígenas: situación jurídica y políticas de estado.* Quito: CONAIE, CEPLAE, and ABYA-YALA.

United Nations. 1980. *Convention on the Elimination of All Forms of Discrimination Against Women.* New York: United Nations (reprinted by the Human Rights Program, Department of Secretary of State, Minister of Supply and Services, Ottawa, Canada, 1982).

———. 1996. *Report of the Fourth World Conference on Women, Beijing, 4–15 September 1995.* New York: United Nations, A/Conf.177/20/Rev.1.

Urioste, Miguel. 1992. *Fortalecer las comunidades: una utopía subversiva, democrática . . .y posible.* La Paz: AIPE, PROCOM, TIERRA.

Ybarnegaray, Roxana. 1997. Tenencia y uso de la tierra en Bolivia. In *Agricultura, hoy y mañana,* edited by Academia de Ciencias. La Paz: Academia de Ciencias.

Zamosc, León. 1994. Agrarian protest and the Indian movement in the Ecuadorian highlands. *Latin American Research Review.* 29:37–69.

4

Beyond Indigenous Land Titling: Democratizing Civil Society in the Peruvian Amazon

Søren Hvalkof

Introduction

Land and Territory in Latin America and Peru

The question of access and rights to land in Latin America is as old as the European colonization of the continent. Control of land means social control through the control of production and the economy, the control of labor, and political control. Land and land rights have been at the center of innumerable social and political conflicts in the modern Latin American states. These rights have been mostly articulated within the framework of class and class struggle, as Deere and León pointed out in the previous chapter. Land rights understood as individual or collective rights to the basic means of production and sustenance have been the prime mover of peasant movements in Latin America (and elsewhere in the world). Land rights have also had a high priority on the agendas of revolutionary movements in the continent. Although these struggles have been socially motivated by poverty, economic misery and social injustice, the claims for land have most often been contextualized within a general discourse of modernization, economic progress, and developmentalism with a rather conventional economic focus.

This discourse has left little room for divergence and there has been no conceptual or political means by which indigenous land claims might be distinguished from other types of land claims. Although indigenous groups in Latin America in the past occasionally have insisted on the special historical right to land, they have not had much resonance in national societies before the mid-1970s. Following the growing doubts and critique of the worn-down modernist paradigm and the failure of developmentalist strategies to deliver the expected social improvements (Escobar 1995), an "empty" or "vacant" political space was created in which indigenous peoples could find room to consolidate as a new social movement with qualitative characteristics different from those of former political campaigns. Indigenous people created a new political platform based on cultural characteristics and ethnic identities, challenging both Marxist and liberal political strategies. Ethnic struggles extended the meaning of the nation state itself. In the course of the 1980s a political reality of multiple meanings and truths was unfolding in many Latin American countries with an expanding indigenous movement as one of its major driving forces. As pointed out by Sonia Alvarez and Arturo Escobar (1992, 328), "Indigenous peoples present perhaps the most striking challenge to the dominant cultural and socioeconomic models of Latin American societies" . . . and further, "[Such] . . . movements can have a significant symbolic impact even when they involve a relatively small number of participants. The symbolic reach of movements . . . often exceeds their social reach or measurable policy impact." (Avarez and Escobar 1992; Van Cott 1995). Land and land titling was thus to attain a completely new meaning and significance in this period.

Before we enter into the intricacies of the Peruvian case, a summary of state strategies toward indigenous populations and their rights to land in South America and Peru is warranted. Although policies vary widely from country to country according to differences in social and demographic structures and diverse national histories, state policies toward indigenous groups have tended to follow the same historical sequence. Apart from more extreme strategies of outright extermination of native populations as obstacles to progress and development, or whose mere existence within the modern nation state was seen by the bourgeoisie as an insult to national "civilization," three main state policies have developed since the turn of the century (Davis and Wali 1994).

The first policy deployed early in this century was inspired by the Indian reservation policy of the United States, and could be named the protectionist strategy. It is based on the rationale that indigenous groups are closed tribal units representing earlier human stages of evolution and as such should be protected by the state as an interesting anachronistic phenomenon and object of scientific inquiry. It presupposes that such tribal groups are unable to take care of themselves in the modern state and that they are potentially dangerous to national society and have to be enclosed and isolated within bounded reserves or reservations. The strategy is based on a static and primitivist view of indigenous culture and represents an extreme paternalistic and objectifying position. Within this policy of "human zoos" all control over the allotted reservations is out of the hands of the contained native groups. Social and territorial control reside with the state and are administered from outside of the reserved area and out of reach of the indigenous group. In this scenario indigenous groups have no political relevance per se and may have neither political representation nor citizenship. Indigenous (land) rights are nonexistent in this context. This policy of establishment of state patronized reservations was mostly carried out in countries where the indigenous groups were relatively small, had an apparent minority status, and meant little in terms of labor.

In the Andean countries such as Peru, where large populations were identified as "Indian" and where their production and labor were important for the national economy, such a policy was not relevant. Although the highlands represented the majority of indigenous people in Peru, in the Amazon the bulk of production was also carried out by indigenous labor. When Indians became an obstacle to economic expansion, the extermination strategy rather than the reservation one, was applied. In the case of Peru, no protectionist reservations were ever established. Still, the paternalist notions on which the protectionist strategy was based prevailed all over Latin America until well after World War II. But as civil society developed and new notions of the state, development, and democracy were widely accepted, a new strategy of integration and assimilation followed.

A second policy emerged in this context that we could refer to as integrationist. From the end of the 1950s the large indigenous population (of the Andes in particular) was converted from Indians to peasants in national conceptualization and idiom. This followed a growing social unrest in the rural areas of the Peruvian Andes that had resulted in that region's agrarian reforms. The indigenous peasant population was to be integrated into the national life of the modern state as labor and productive potential for the liberalists, and as rural proletarians and revolutionary potential for the Marxist left. In this respect there was (and is) a right/left consensus about the appropriateness of modernization and a common allegiance to developmentalism. This consensus includes an agreement on the irrelevance, backwardness, and counterproductivity of indigenous cultures, values, and knowledge. The common agenda shared by the left and the right was the integration and assimilation of indigenous people into mainstream national society. One of the progressive means to this end was cooperativism—the "silver bullet" that would reorganize the entire rural economy. As discussed by Kay and by Deere and León in this book, several agrarian reforms tried this magic remedy, which indeed did transform the rural economy from a feudal structure to a state-controlled hybrid. The results were however usually disastrous because control still resided with the state and now also with the wider national market.

Although these highland populations had never been regarded as tribal, and only had little resemblance in their social organization or economy with the indigenous groups of the Amazon and tropical lowlands, the assimilation strategy of transforming Indians into peasants in cooperatives was also being transferred to the indigenous populations of the Amazon basin. The transfer was largely unsuccessful, but in several countries the model was later adapted to the Amazon and lowland reality in such a way that communal land rights could be granted. Although communal rights were not based on an explicit recognition of indigenous rights, they were a precursor of such rights. In Peru the corresponding legislation distinguished (and still does) between native communities of the tropical lowlands (Amazon) that are identified as "Indian" and indigenous, and the agrarian communities of the Andes, that are identified as "peasant." The qualitative differences between these two identifications are conspicuous. Thus, in Peru indigenous communities do not exist in the Andean highlands or on the coast as legally recognized social entities, but in the Amazon they do.

It is not possible legally and administratively to distinguish between indigenous and non-indigenous peasants in the Peruvian Andes, despite the fact that the area is inhabited by large indigenous Quechua speaking populations. Land rights are granted as communal rights as a means of production, not as territory. The legal unit is the *Comunidad Campesina*. The political ideology on which this model is based is the populist/corporate notion that "we are all Peruvians." This is a nationalist and populist idea that is constantly propagated as "democracy," indicating that no special rights should be granted to any particular social or ethnic group or class-based association. However, some people are 'more Peruvian' than others. Contrary to the unifying nationalist ideology is the recognition of *Comunidades Nativas* in the tropical forest lowlands (Amazon) of Peru. Their aboriginal rights to land as a community's collective right is guaranteed in the Peruvian constitution, and is the closest that one gets to a recognition of indigenous rights in Peruvian legislation. Although it presupposes the existence of identifiable communities that can be titled as delineated social units, which is seldom the case in the Amazon, the law still leaves room for interpretation, and this has permitted the local indigenous groups and their organizations to develop functioning territorial strategies. (We will discuss the concept of "community" in Peru later in this chapter.)

A third state strategy of control over indigenous lands and peoples in Peru, which emerged a decade after the previous one, is related to nature conservation. Protection of nature became a growing concern in the late 1960s and 1970s and soon captured a prominent place on the international agenda as conservation of endangered species and biodiversity became a public concern in Western industrialized countries. Without casting doubt on the urgency of dealing with the global ecological crisis, it will suffice here to note that nature conservation also became a new way of defining and controlling indigenous groups, especially in the tropical lowlands. Although the conservationist endeavor could be seen as the inversion of the developmentalist idea of economic growth and national integration, it still operated within a modernist Nature/Culture dichotomy, objectifying indigenous peoples as Nature and as rare species suited for "protection." Indigenous "culture" was really "nature" (understood as a simple collection of static "cultural" traits) and indigenous groups had to conform to Western essentialist expectations about their performance and behavior as primitive *naturvölker*. In many ways this is quite similar to the early protectionist strategy. The difference from the earlier version is that although control still is external, it is now increasingly in the hands of international agencies and supra-national anonymous bureaucracies. In Peru several such protected areas have been established where indigenous inhabitants are judged in terms of primitiveness and subsistence technology. If they do not comply with the responsible authority's stereotypes of primitiveness, they are not allowed to remain inside the reserves and must relocate. Indians must behave as "nature."

The conservationist strategy (and legislation) is obviously at odds with the legally recognized land rights of indigenous communities in the Peruvian Amazon. In other Latin American countries strategic alliances between environmental interest organizations and the indigenous movement have proved effective in several cases, resulting in co-management of protected areas, but the viability of such alliances is questionable (Conklin and Graham 1995; Little 1998).

National legislation in Latin American countries is commonly contradictory on aspects of land tenure and land rights, giving leeway for diverse interpretations and manipulations. The outline sketched here does not cover all the different nuances in various national strategies over time nor does it allow for a number of actual exceptions, but it gives an overview of the main tendencies that, although listed as sequential, may indeed exist simultaneously even today. These different schemes can altogether be seen as aspects of the same modernist episteme, and are now being challenged by the autonomous indigenous movements in Latin America.

From Land to Territory

A substantial change in these schemes came with the rise of the indigenous movement and the creation of a political space for a qualitatively different indigenous strategy. Given the earlier co-optation of the indigenous peasantry in the Andes by developmentalist oriented political organizations and systems, whether represented by the Marxist left or its liberalist adversaries, it is no coincidence that the alternative to these conventional political strategies grew out of the indigenous populations of the Amazon. Contrary to the indigenous populations of the Andes, the Amazonian peoples have never been regarded as political targets or objects for development (though often victimized by it), very much because of the dominant society's essentialist notions and stereotypes of Amazonians as savages.

Thus categorized as almost subhuman, the indigenous Amazonians have mostly been targeted as labor in the extractivist industries following a typical pattern of boom-and-bust cycles, the rubber boom (1885–1915) being one of the most infamous of such periods. Local patrons have seized indigenous labor through debt bondage or outright slavery, a practice used to this day. This commodification of the indigenous population has been followed by a notion in the non-indigenous national society of the native Amazonians as "Nature" and thus an extractivist resource like rubber, timber, or pelts.[1] But beings who belong to the natural realm are not seen as rational in any human way and hence do not act politically. The native Amazonians were not seen as having any political potential, and political co-optation was not an issue. However, from an indigenous position there were obvious reasons and a great social motivation for counteracting the exploitation of their labor and the general abuses that arose from the extractive sector. With increasing global integration and emerging human rights platforms after World War II, and with a vacant "undiscovered" political space at hand, the stage was set for unexpected achievements during the neoliberal turn of the 1980s in Latin America.

The first autochthonous indigenous organization in the Amazon based on a culturally oriented political platform was the Shuar Federation[2] in the Ecuadorian Oriente, created in 1964 (Salazar 1977). It grew out of a land conflict between settlers encroaching on Shuar territory and was created to counteract this encroachment and to obtain title and control of the land. At the same time, documentation of abuses of indigenous groups in the Amazon and elsewhere began to appear with increasing frequency. Parts of the international academic and intellectual community reacted, and after 1968 several indigenous support organizations were established in Europe and the United States with networks in many Third World countries (Hvalkof 1998c). The combination of support from these circles and growing political awareness and organizational effort among the indigenous groups of the Amazon themselves allowed an indigenous movement to take form. During the next two decades practically all indigenous groups in the

Amazon basin established their own local organizations mostly defined by ethnic affiliation and locality. Subsequently they joined in regional federations and national umbrella organizations. A similar process developed simultaneously in the Andes and Central America, but as the majority of indigenous populations in these regions are peasants, the political platform was generally less clearly based on cultural parameters and did not gain the same momentum as in the Amazon. Conventional Marxist oriented peasant unionism and organizational structures impeded a stronger and more united indigenous movement. Still, indigenous organizations kept growing.

This extraordinary pan-indigenous phenomenon emerged at a moment in modern history characterized by the collapse of fixed categories in the modernist episteme and a corresponding political frustration in the industrialized world with the gospel of development. In a 1998 article, Hanne Veber addressed the unexpected political success of the indigenous peoples under the eloquent headline "The progress of the victims" and quoted social movement theorist Alan Touraine to emphasize that "An analysis based on the idea of social movement can . . . help rediscover that these alienated and excluded categories are nevertheless actors and are more often able than the 'silent majority' to analyze their situation, define projects, and organize conflicts which can transform themselves into an active social movement" (Touraine 1985, 782; Veber 1998, 383–87). This definitely seems to be the case in Latin America.

The indigenous movement became further consolidated up through the 1970s and 1980s. Following the increasing internationalization of policymaking in these years, the need for a pan-American indigenous body to coordinate supra-national policymaking and international legislation became evident. Several attempts were made with varying success. The most politically dynamic of these has been the COICA (Coordinadora Indígena de la Cuenca Amazonica) which forcefully lobbied the international development establishment to acknowledge special indigenous rights. They lobbied to oppose conventional development programs threatening their existence and territorial integrity, and to support indigenous efforts to have their territories demarcated and titled. These lobbying activities motivated many international development institutions to elaborate special policies on indigenous peoples.[3]

In this process of political and organizational consolidation, a significant shift in the idiom of land claims took place: the change from "land" to "territory." The COICA focused on claiming "indigenous territory" as part of their strategy for indigenous self-determination, thus marking a conceptual shift from the liberal conception of land as a means of production, to territory as a spatial concept with much wider cultural and political connotations.

The significance of the term and notion of "territory" may be summarized as follows:

• "Territory" is related to the notion of nation and nationhood. "Territory" is a valid notion in international law connoting spatial integrity and collective rights for its inhabitants whereas "land" only refers to a means of production or a spatial unit for the individual dwellers. Speaking of "indigenous territories" and "indigenous nations" goes hand in hand, implying special rights including the right to self-determination and self-government. It also opened the possibility to use the only specific international legislation at hand at that time, the famous ILO convention 107 from 1957 that talks about direct aboriginal rights to territories within the nation state. (The ILO Convention 107 was substituted in 1994 by the Convention 169 which has been updated in accordance with the global steps toward recognition of indigenous rights, including territory).

• Control over territory signifies social control. This includes control of resources and control of development that ultimately may lead to self-government and self-determination in some form.

• "Territory" has new meaning, which includes the symbolic configuration of space inferring cultural identity, social organization, economy, health, and education. Territory means a supra-individual system defining collective rights as opposed to individual and individualized rights.

• "Territory" is part of collective responsibilities: constitution of groups, nations, and organizations and the accountability to the social collective. This also includes rights to political tools for access to national and international decision making.

The shift in discourse was evident, and it is beyond a doubt that the international acceptance of the notion of "territory" has been crucial for the consolidation of the indigenous movement. However, the most profound changes are not to be found in the discursive level but in the process itself of constructing and obtaining legal recognition of indigenous territories. The local struggle for territorial rights and the social enactment of the indigenous territory may be one of the most powerful instruments for social and political change in Latin America today. As we will see in our case from Peru, the process per se of obtaining legal title is at least as important as the title itself. To paraphrase Gregory Bateson in his discussion of logical types (1972), "the map is not the territory." A map is an abstraction, a symbolic representation most often depicted on a piece of paper. A territory is a living social entity, which only exists as part of the social enactment by its inhabitants. They exist on quite different levels of abstraction. Our case from Peru will demonstrate this point.

The Development Scenario

The Setting and the Indigenous Population

The tropical forest of central Peru, the Selva Central, is situated where the foothills of the Andes stretch out into the Amazon. The area is often referred to as the Montaña region (Steward 1963).[4] The area is characterized by a very rugged topography, heavy precipitation, dense montane tropical forest, and fast-running, only partially navigable, whitewater rivers. These physical features always cause infrastructure difficulties for colonization schemes in this region.

The indigenous populations inhabiting this zone are all of the Arawakan linguistic family. They are divided into six or seven main ethno-linguistic groups, numbering some 65,000–80,000, divided in several regional subgroups.[5] The largest of these groups are the culturally and linguistically closely related Asháninka and Ashéninka, formerly referred to generically as *Campa* in the ethnographic and historical literature.[6] Their territories cover most of the central part of eastern Peru extending from the foothills of the Andes to the lowlands of the Upper Amazon, and scattered groups are found as far east as Acre in Brazil.

As an intermediate area between the high mountains of the Andean sierra and the lower Amazon basin, the Montaña has always been a zone of cultural and economic brokerage between the highlands and the Amazon lowlands. After the European conquest this meant colonization pressure from the expanding agricultural frontier encroaching from the Andes and repeated pressure from the boom and bust cycles of ever-changing extractivist economies of the Amazon. Since the first Spanish and Franciscan attempts in the early 17th century to colonize the central Peruvian rain forest and evangelize the indigenous inhabitants, the Asháninka have periodically reacted violently against such impositions. This has created a cyclic historical pattern of colonization, resistance, and aborted conquest. The most forceful of these uprisings was the general indigenous rebellion 1742–1756, led by the charismatic mestizo figure of Juan Santos (with the opulent byname Atahualpa Apu Inka). The rebellious Asháninka and neighboring indigenous groups completely cleared the central Peruvian Amazon of Franciscan missions and Spanish colonies, and maintained a standing Asháninka militia for more than fifteen years with far-reaching effects on the development of the region that remained largely uncolonized until the late 19th century (Lehnertz 1972; Metraux 1942, Santos 1987; 1992; Varese 1973).

State and Modernization

After the war of independence and the initial turmoil in the mid 19th century during the establishment of the new Peruvian state, more long-lasting efforts to colonize the Peruvian Amazon took place. New plans for colonist settlements, agriculture, cattle raising, and infrastructure were made, all of them based on the erroneous idea that the zone held tremendous productive potentials and that the indigenous population would provide the necessary labor for the colonist endeavor in the phase of establishment. The idea was that the Amazon region was "empty" and that the few indigenous inhabitants eventually would be "civilized" and assimilated into mainstream national life. This is a fantasy that is reproduced up to this day in the nationalist rhetoric, despite the fact that the productivity of most of the Amazonian soils is low, logistic problems are enormous, and the indigenous population occupies considerable areas.

In the lower part of the Peruvian Amazon a logistic revolution occurred with the introduction of the steamship in the mid-1850s, boosting the extractivist economy. Within a few decades the extractivist industry grew to dominate all corners of the region and drastically changed its social and demographic structures. In 1891, as part of a deal for settling a major national debt with British creditors after a Peruvian state bankruptcy, the Peruvian government handed over a concession area of some two million hectares to the British-owned Peruvian Corporation in the higher central Peruvian rain forest. The area was targeted for agriculture, extraction, and other economic developments with all the native inhabitants as free labor in addition to the imported workers and contracted European colonists. Although the corporation actually succeeded in using "only" some 500,000 hectares, it established large plantations with coffee and other export crops, and was notorious for its inhumane labor conditions in closed colonies resembling concentration camps. It operated in the area until 1975, when the Peruvian government nationalized and eventually closed it down (Barclay 1989).

Historically the extractivist economy of the Amazon has been characterized by recurring boom and bust cycles related to specific products. It reached its climax with the rubber boom during the first decades of this century, making way for permanent settlements around trading posts. The social relations of the extractivist production in Peru have always been characterized by exploitation of indigenous knowledge and labor, procured by local patrons through debt bondage and indentured labor. The debts were and still are established through advance payments in kind to the indigenous worker. This method is known in Spanish as *enganche*, meaning to "hook up" or "hitch a horse to a carriage." The system is well known from the *haciendas*[7] in the Andean highland and from the agricultural corporations in the *montaña*. In the Upper Amazon it developed into a particular system of accumulation known as the system of *habilitación*, which has been the driving force of the extractive economy. The *habilitación* system functions as a hierarchy of interconnected debt relations in a chain of exploitation. At the top of the system, the exporter or commercial house prepays a contractor to deliver the product by a specified time. He in turn prepays several subcontractors, who "habilitate" local patrons. At the bottom of the chain we reach the actual producers, most often an Indian and his family.

A related system of chattel slavery developed, overlapping with the debt bondage system. Since debt was passed on from a father to his children, debts were accumulated through generations. Indebted indigenous families became real capital or property owned by the patrons and were a commodity that could be traded on the market. This commodification of the indigenous population rapidly evolved into real slave trade run by the contractors involved in extractive enterprises. With further colonization and with changes in production and labor requirements, the traffic in slaves became rampant in the Upper Amazon and developed into an independent "extractive" industry of its own. Armed slave raiding, so-called *correrías*, became widespread, and markets for Indian slaves developed in the few commercial centers of the Upper Amazon.

During the short peak period of the rubber bonanza between 1890 and 1915, hundreds of thousands of Indians were enslaved as tappers in rubber extraction. The atrocities committed by the rubber barons were numerous. Some cases are well documented, like the notorious Putumayo scandal where the London-based Peruvian Amazon Company Inc. was made responsible for the deaths of some 30,000 Indians in the extraction of four thousand tons of raw rubber. The scope of this violence is put into perspective when we recall that the Putumayo was just one rubber concession in one river area (Hardenburg 1913; US Department of State 1913; Valcárcel 1915; Taussig 1984; 1985; Gray 1990; Hvalkof 1998b). Slavery and trade in Indian individuals and entire families persisted in the Atalaya province of the Upper Ucayali until as recently as 1988 (Hvalkof 1994b; Gray 1997; Renard-Casevitz 1980).

Up through this century the pressure to colonize the Peruvian Amazon intensified. Many ambitious economic initiatives were initiated: large scale plantation and colonization schemes were set up, roads constructed and large amounts of foreign capital invested in cattle ranching, the rubber tapping industry, coffee and fruit plantations, the lumber industry, and saw mills. In addition, the MIR guerrilla movement swept through Ashéninka territory in the mid 1960s, only to be suppressed by counterinsurgency troops led by U.S. specialists (Brown and Fernandez 1991).[8] In effect, the Asháninka and Ashéninka populations have been exposed to every aspect of "development" through the past two centuries. They gradually developed pragmatic strategies to deal with this, ranging from going along with the colonist or extractivist strategies to get the resources they wanted, to the outright opposition to these ventures.[9]

The Latest Development Boom

In the late 1970s a new wave of development initiatives revived the old illusion that unlimited economic potential of the Amazon region would save the economy of the deeply indebted Peruvian state. Grand "integrated development" schemes were set up, sponsored by the international development establishment represented by the World Bank, the Inter-American Development Bank, USAID, and some European agencies. In the Asháninka territory of the *montaña* these so-called Special Projects mostly amounted to road construction and extension of credit for small-scale cattle ranching, which caused thousands of landless *mestizo* settlers from the Andes to flood into the area. This led to massive clearing of the forest and caused an ecological and economic disaster. Conflicts with the native population escalated and violence increased, as did illegal coca production for the Colombian drug mob. From the mid-1980s Peru was propelled into a deep economic, social, and political crisis that lasted a decade. The Shining Path and MRTA guerrillas were fishing in the muddy waters of this flood of progress. Fueled by the growing social unrest as a result of the massive influx of settlers, by the expanding cocaine economy in the Amazon, as well as by increasing military repression in the Andes, the two competing guerrilla groups established themselves in the Central Forest. Here they initiated forced recruitment campaigns among settlers and native communities. They soon found themselves at odds with the indigenous population and their organizations that turned out not to be natural allies of the guerrillas but instead had their own indigenous political agenda. A violent conflict with catastrophic results was unfolding (Benavides 1993; Hvalkof 1994b; 1997). The integrated development programs that triggered the tragedy were a complete economic and social fiasco. They were terminated after some years, and the international institutions backed out of Peru, leaving behind an even greater foreign debt than before.

Land Titling and the Reconstruction of Territory

Oppression and the Indigenous Response

The last three decades of cyclic boom-and-bust development of the Amazon have had a profound impact on the indigenous societies of the Central Montaña. The Ashéninka found themselves squeezed between the colonization frontier expanding from the Andes, and the lumber extraction frontier expanding from the lower Amazon, which now was increasingly followed by cattle ranching and new colonists moving in where logging had cleared the way. Especially in the zones of the Gran Pajonal and Atalaya in the upper Ucayali River this development boosted extreme forms of exploitation of the indigenous population, ranging from indentured labor to outright slavery violently enforced by local patrons and civil authorities (Hvalkof 1986a; 1986b; 1987; 1994a; 1997; 1998c; Gray 1997; Schäfer 1988).

However, in the inter-fluvial plateau of Gran Pajonal, the Ashéninka started to organize. Inspired by the emerging indigenous organizations in other parts of Peru they demanded titles to their territory. By pragmatically activating all human resource potentials within their reach (from protestant missionaries to anthropologists on fieldwork), they succeeded in gaining the attention of the World Bank (the major sponsor of the integrated development and colonization projects). The World Bank was (indirectly) held responsible for the social and ecological disaster that was developing (Hvalkof 1986a). To prevent a major social tragedy with violent clashes between settlers and native inhabitants, the latter requested immediate intervention in and demarcation of their community lands. The World Bank responded positively, confirming the allegations, and obliged their Peruvian counterpart in Lima to carry through a land titling process for all the indigenous communities in the Gran Pajonal.

From this process emerged a strong indigenous organization, the Organización Ashéninka de Gran Pajonal (OAGP). It duly established itself with its new leadership posts, statutes, a general assembly and corresponding rubber stamps for the newly elected representatives. Despite fierce resistance from the settler population, a series of complicated intrigues, and manipulation from the colonist establishment and their allies in the regional administration, the Ashéninka succeeded in getting the demarcation process started. From 1984 to 1988, 26 new Ashéninka communities were demarcated and titled in the area, forming an almost continuous indigenous territory, surrounding the settler zone.[10] These previously marginalized Indians had succeeded in organizing and regaining territorial control, hence curbing further colonist expansion and destructive cattle ventures.

The land titling took the heat off the explosive situation for a while, as the immediate conflicts with the local settlers decreased considerably (Hvalkof

1997; 1998c; Veber 1998). At the same time a similar conflict was developing in the bordering zone of Atalaya in the upper Ucayali River, but here the situation was even more aggravated. The problem in this case was not created by invading Andean settlers, as had been the case in the Gran Pajonal. In Atalaya it was a problem with the well-established colonist and lumber patrons, descendants of the European rubber contractors who had taken possession of the Indian land and labor at the turn of the century. These patrons held hundreds of Ashéninka as their feudal serfs, who might be bought and sold and treated as the patrons saw fit to do. The trade in native individuals and families between patrons in the river area was common until very recently and is well documented (Sala 1897; Bodley 1972; Renard-Casevitz 1980; Gray and Hvalkof 1990b; Hvalkof 1998c). With a new influx of settlers and the beginning depletion of lumber resources, the overexploitation and abuse of indigenous labor reached new heights. After a series of grave incidents and denunciations, the national indigenous umbrella organization AIDESEP (Asociación Interétnica de la Selva Peruana) intervened in 1988 and succeeded in getting an intersectoral commission with official status under the Ministry of Justice appointed to investigate the allegations and complaints from the indigenous population and others (AIDESEP 1988a; 1988b; 1991a-c; IIP 1991; García 1998; Gray and Hvalkof 1990a; 1990b).

The commission's report is an appalling documentation of serious crimes ranging from multiple murder, disappearances, torture, assault and battery, slavery, abduction of children, rape, and other sexual abuses, to a series of infringements of labor laws and agrarian and forestry legislation. With few exceptions, all of the accused are local patrons involved in lumber extraction and their allied local authorities ranging from the forestry service over the police to the justice of the peace. Altogether seventeen of the local patrons and three major regional lumber bosses were accused of more than sixty criminal counts. Still the commission's investigation was only scratching the surface. Examples of Ashéninka testimonies were gathered by AIDESEP and presented in the denunciation to the Peruvian authorities, which led to the commission's investigation (García 1998, 20–25).

The Land Titling Process

Out of these initial attempts to intervene in the outrageous situation in Atalaya grew a new indigenous organization of Atalaya, the OIRA (Regional Indigenous Organization of Atalaya), which came to play a central role in the indigenous process. Inspired by the successful experiences in the neighboring district of Gran Pajonal, OIRA opted for land titling as a viable strategy for changing the situation. A large-scale demarcation and land titling project was set up. Agreements were signed with the authorities in charge in Lima and in the capital of the Ucayali Region, Pucallpa. Economic support was sought from the Danish Government's aid agency, DANIDA, through the indigenous support NGO, the Copenhagen-based International Work Group for Indigenous Affairs (IWGIA). The project was approved by DANIDA in 1989[11] and began operating from Pucallpa and Atalaya that same year.

The two indigenous organizations, the national AIDESEP and the regional OIRA, were responsible for implementing the project and carrying out all the technical and promotion work in the field. They set up a team of technicians, topographers, support field staff, and coordinators who for the following three years worked surveying, registering, and demarcating more than 160 native communities. It was an extremely complicated, difficult, and conflict-ridden task. They had to maneuver with extreme caution in a zone where the Colombian drug mafia, Sendero Luminoso, the MRTA, three different counterinsurgency corps, hostile patrons, contractors and logging companies, new settlers, officials, and bureaucrats opposed the project and where opportunistic political parties were all trying to set their own daily agenda. In addition to this, changing Peruvian governments were carrying through a series of radical neoliberal administrative reforms. Thus a policy of decentralization was being implemented in Peru that involved the establishment of regional governments with greater administrative autonomy, but without the necessary economic and legislative support from the central government in Lima. Later, things were centralized once more to some degree, but without eliminating the regional governments. The result was a total lack of continuity in public administration, including constant changes of officials and public sector workers.

Contrary to similar land legalization projects in neighboring countries (Brazil, Colombia, and Ecuador), the Ucayali project was devoid of indigenous "identity politics" and the inflated rhetoric which often accompanies this strategy (Conklin and Graham 1995; Jackson 1989; Veber 1998). AIDESEP and the project team opted for a practical and pragmatic approach and in general maintained a low profile in order to avoid a destructive politicization of the project. They worked their way from community to community and solved the problems that arose along the way.

Although we will not get into the intricacies of the technical and bureaucratic procedures of indigenous land titling in Peru in this chapter, we should mention that there are 26 technical and legal stages at the regional level alone from inscription over demarcation and classification to mapping and a series of confirmation and approval actions. Each stage has its own requirements and procedure circuits. When at last the paperwork and red tape is done within the regional bureaucracy, the title files are sent to Lima. In Lima another five stages have to be negotiated before the title is ready to be handed over to the new landowner—the indigenous community. The last five stages in the Lima bureaucracy alone may last eighteen months (Gray 1998). All this was carried out by the indigenous organizations and their technical staff. All fieldwork was done in co-staffed teams of mixed Ministry—OIRA personnel. Neither the funding agency, DANIDA, nor the supervising Danish non-governmental agency, IWGIA, set up offices or posted permanent representatives in Peru to monitor the project. It was supervised through recurrent reviews and interventions as well as political backup, but the daily work and the delicate negotiations were left entirely to the indigenous organizations themselves. This gradually generated a hitherto unknown respect for indigenous organizations within the public sphere, and this has been crucial to the subsequent political process in the region.

After five years of extremely conflictive and complicated work, the indigenous organizations involved had succeeded in demarcating close to 162 communities, restoring an enormous indigenous territory of approximately 1.5 million hectares of co-bordering community territories, and obtaining legal communal ownership with titles (deeds) for every native community in the project area. The project has later been followed-up by the establishment of four communal reserves (protected areas reserved as indigenous joint use areas for subsistence activities—pending approval), and some larger territorial demarcations for "uncontacted" groups (indigenous groups that have opted for withdrawal into remote rainforest areas and reject contact with the national society). The total effort has so far secured the indigenous population of the upper Ucayali a total land base of close to 4.4 million hectares (Ñaco et al. 1997). The effects of this project have been profound. Indeed, it changed the entire power structure in the region. Hundreds of former peons left their patrons to join and form new communities. Now the Indians were communal landowners and becoming a real autonomous political force. This altered their bargaining position in relation to the regional administration and to the colonist society. A new social reality was taking shape in the upper Ucayali.

The Indigenous Process

Democratic Post-Development

The land titling process itself turned out to be a catalyst for a drastic change in power relations encouraging indigenous self-organizing and participation in national political and civil life. In both Atalaya and the Gran Pajonal, the indigenous organizations had grown considerably in strength as a result of the whole process of territorial demarcation and legal procedures. This combination brought about a degree of organization and participation never before witnessed. The indigenous leadership was clear that to be in a position to defend their territorial integrity in the long term and ensure a long-term development based on specific indigenous needs and cultural qualities, it would be necessary to take hold of political power. That is, it would be necessary to participate in the civil democratic process on the premises set by the national society. As a result of the social mobilization and organizational consolidation generated, the indigenous organizations arranged for all community members to be registered to vote and to acquire their personal identification documents (quite a project on its own). At the following local elections in 1995 they ran for the political posts of mayor and councilors in the province of Atalaya, including the district and annex levels. To do so they established their own list of independent candidates in an attempt to avoid annexation and interference from the conventional political parties. This new political tool called MIAP (Movimiento Indígena de la Amazonía Peruana), which did not have much visibility in the town of Atalaya, took everybody by surprise by winning the majority of votes in four electoral districts, including the town of Atalaya itself in October 1995. They won the posts of mayor, vice mayor, and of all the councilors. The old colonist establishment went into shock with this first overwhelming indigenous electoral success. To colonists, this appeared as inconceivable as a natural disaster. But a few days after the result had been proclaimed, the local patrons and allies reacted by having almost every elected candidate from the winning MIAP arrested on accusations of ballot rigging, election fraud, and other irregularities.

Eventually, however, they had to relent as the national election commission confirmed the results. The indigenous organization moved into the town hall of this former center of rubber and slave trade, a situation that would have been absolutely unthinkable just a few years before. It is an almost surreal experience now to enter the town hall of the municipality of Atalaya and find the mayor's office full of assiduous Ashéninka in their striped brown or beige *cushmas* (cotton tunics) who no more than a few years ago were not even registered as Peruvian citizens and never appeared in Atalaya wearing their traditional dress fearing the spite of the colonist. It is quite an alteration to change status from commodified exotic labor to that of landowner and political decision maker. In October 1996, the London based Anti-Slavery International (ASI), honored the Regional Indigenous Organization of Atalaya (OIRA) with the Anti-Slavery Award.[12]

Two representatives from the organization were invited to London to receive the award. They also were received for tea in the House of Lords. The ASI gave the 1996 award to OIRA for "its work in freeing thousands of Asháninka, an indigenous people from the Peruvian Amazon, from debt bondage."

Many of the patrons are still there, in Gran Pajonal as well as in the Atalaya province, but their influence is significantly weakened. Illegal extraction permits are still being issued and peons are still being "habilitated," but the extent of such practices is much reduced, and the outrages that were part of daily life on the colonist ranches have stopped. Patrons, colonists, and Indians interact in daily political life and administrative decision making, and generally relate to each other on much more equal terms than ever before in the history of the Peruvian Amazon (and maybe in the history of all Peru).

The question now is what the indigenous population will do with this newly gained political power-potential, and most important, what kind of economic future the indigenous peoples are aspiring to and how this will be articulated. The situation has changed indeed and so have the strategies of the patrons. Although the lumber business is still in control of the regional economy and has the power of capital, there are few free areas left for indiscriminate lumber extraction. Communal Reserves are legally protected against any extractivist industry and furthermore controlled *in situ* by the indigenous population. The same goes for the special areas for "uncontacted" groups. The only potential areas for lumber extraction are parts of titled community territories, where extraction requires a subcontract and permission from the communities themselves (apart from a general extraction permit from the Ministry of Agriculture and environmental authorities). A good working relationship and rapport with the native communities is now a must for any contractor. So, today the lumber patrons basically rely on the convincing power of money and co-optation by the system. Increasingly they are attempting to influence indigenous decision making. Thus one of the most urgent challenges to the indigenous movement is now to identify and develop economic alternatives to a production system that for two centuries has been based on patron-peon relationships. Still, the bargaining position of the indigenous population and the general power relations in the province are considerably improved in favor of the former stigmatized indigenous majority.

Apart from the conspicuous political change in Atalaya, a series of other transformations and ventures emerged from the very same process. The Ashéninka populations of the Ucayali found out that they had certain rights, that there was a society outside of the province that could help enforce such rights, and that it in fact was possible to succeed. With these discoveries, the indigenous participation in local councils and other decision-making institutions grew remarkably. They were excited when things worked out in favor of the native communities, and they wanted more. They wanted their own politicians, their own schools, their own health system, and a new indigenous economy. The interest and enthusiasm in the communities, even in the most remote areas, were impressive. Julio Pacaya, a Yíne dirigente (leader) expressed it like this:

> Previously the *colonos* were our patrons and they exploited us. My grandparents and parents were exploited by the lumber barons. We were robbed, cheated, and poorly paid. This was in the past. Now it is as if the people have opened their eyes and have an understanding (Gray 1998, 171).

This general indigenous mobilization was the basis of their political success in the local 1995 elections. Presently they are developing their own bilingual inter-cultural education system, redirecting the bilingual education introduced decades ago by the protestant missionaries of the Summer Institute of Linguistics.[13] The latest of the new ventures is an alternative indigenous health program involving local shamans, healers, midwives, and other indigenous medical specialists in integrated teams with nurses trained in Western medical practices and representatives from the local indigenous organization. The program covers 75 indigenous communities in three provinces of the Ucayali region.[14] The project has been a tremendous success, not only in terms of health improvements, but also as an instrument to consolidate the indigenous social mobilization, participation, and self-confidence. It has drawn the attention of the medical establishment of Peru, and the public health system in the Ucayali region has signed cooperation agreements with the indigenous health program. As one indigenous representative from the land titling project staff explained during an international hearing in October 1998:

> Before we would never have access to offices of public institutions, not even the hospitals and health centers. We were nothing. But in fact now they invite us in and treat people politely, and not only that—they also take their time to listen to what we have to say. We definitely have an influence now.

Parameters for Success

During recent hearings on the international status of the indigenous movement worldwide, indigenous representatives from Peru were asked several times how it had been possible to break the power of well-established lumber businesses, challenge drug lords and guerrillas, and curb the expansionist settler society without being violently repressed. The question is understandable, especially if one knows recent Peruvian history, but the answer is complex. The evident success is not a simple result of indigenous ingenuity, self-sufficiency, or new ethnic nationalism. It is, rather, the outcome of unique conjunctures in the ongoing process of globalization and neoliberal reforms, in combination with specific political circumstances in Peru. A series of conditions favoring the results may be listed:

1. Global integration

- The coincidence of series of global discourses favoring indigenous self-determination in the Amazon, such as the discourses of human rights, sustainable development, bio-diversity, democracy, participation, and privatization.

- The increasing internationalization of decision making in normative issues as well as in economics and politics.

- The explosive growth in communication and communication technology.

- The privatization of conventional international development and massive transfer of fund to the NGO sphere.

This new development has made it possible for local indigenous organizations through new direct alliances with both national and foreign organizations and NGOs to reduce or circumvent the influence and significance of local power hierarchies, like that of the former patron regime in Atalaya. There is even a growing tendency to overrule normative decisions of the nation state. It is obvious, however, that these new international alliances also open up for new systems of co-optation, which in general can be seen in a growing NGO influence in social and popular movements.

2. National legislation and international law

- The existence in Peru of constitutional guarantees of indigenous land rights (recognized as early as in the 1920 and the 1933 constitutions) and rights to collective land titles.

- Corresponding legislation [*Ley de Comunidades Nativas* (D.L. 22175, 1978].

- ◆ Guaranteeing inalienable rights (with some modifications) to community territories, and supporting a certain degree of indigenous autonomy in the control of the titled areas.

- ◆ Legal norms as to the exclusion and compensation payment to third parties (colonists) inside community territory.

- ◆ Supportive civil code, laws of education, and other regulation in favoring indigenous self-management.

- ◆ International conventions and agreements, especially ILO convention 169, ratified by Peru.

Without the pre-existence of a solid legal basis for land titling, the project would never have been launched in the first place. An interesting aspect here is the fact that indigenous territory as such does not exist as a legal term in the existing legislation. The law specifically talks about collective right to land for individual communities. The prevailing concept of *comunidad* in Peru and other Andean countries is that of a "corporate peasant community," an organically integrated whole that operates economically, socially, and politically as a unit. This community form is basic to Andean indigenous peasant communities and is dominant in many peasant societies worldwide. The legislation on Native Communities in Peru (i.e., Amazonian Indian societies as depicted in Law on Native Communities # 22175) is a mimicked version of the law of Peasant Communities (i.e., Andean Indigenous and *mestizo* communities) which applies to the Andean region. This uncritical transfer of a legal and conceptual framework is based on the erroneous assumption than Indian communities are qualitatively alike whether in the Andean mountains or in the Amazonian forests. The idea that the values governing Andean indigenous communities apply to all indigenous societies is widespread in the Peruvian society as well as in neighboring countries. Through several decades this "andino-centrism" has contributed to the failure of many government and NGO projects in the Amazon as they build on assumptions of social and ecological functionality from the Andean highlands (Hvalkof 1989; 1998a).

However, indigenous societies in the Amazon have reinterpreted and redefined the Peruvian legislation on Native Communities, to fit their actual concepts and reality. As "the community" is the central feature in this legislation, they have adopted this notion, but it is primarily being seen as synonymous with a "territorial unit" owned and managed collectively by the dwellers inside this territory. Community members are free to move to another community if they prefer, and there are no collective constraints on such migrations. It is important to reiterate that "the community" does not exist as a collective unit of production but it does exist as a collective "representation" and a "control" institution in other spheres of social interaction. The community signifies collective control of land and resources, which have never been privately owned and which, due to ecological variations, must be accessible to everyone living in the micro-zone, alias "the community." Thus, the "community" guarantees economic access of the individual family. The "community" also takes care of representing the local dwellers (local family groups) to the public service system that in this case is limited to public education and public health. But the central importance of "a community" in our Amazonian context is that of an exclusive and delimited territory. By joining such demarcated "native communities" in large blocks of co-bordering communities the indigenous organizations *de facto* created large continuous indigenous territories. Paradoxically the alien "community" model originating in the very different Andean setting turned out to be instrumental to the participatory aspect of the titling process in the Peruvian Amazon. Larger indigenous territories may be a politically more stable form of tenure and technically easier to establish and title, but the smaller local units the community represents gave rise to direct involvement by local residence groups creating a patchwork of independent and actively involved local groups alias "communities" which increasingly participate in civil government (see item 5 below).

3. International funding and support

One of the crucial aspects of the process is the external funding for the project. Contrary to Western Europe and the United States, Latin American countries have no problem with passing laws for which they realistically have no economic means or will to enforce. The clauses on demarcation and titling of native communities in the law of native were of this nature. The legislature and the authorities administrating the law had no problem signing agreement with whatever indigenous organization on self-demarcation, as they knew that the public institutions would never have the budget, and their colonist idiosyncrasies prevented them from believing that indigenous people ever could succeed in obtaining international economic and political support of such magnitude. The fact that they did succeed with their organizational effort, initially created fear and confusion among settlers and in the colonist administration, but in the long run it also generated respect, particularly in the regional administration and government.

4. Indigenous project ownership

In the case of the Ucayali land titling process and succeeding initiatives, only one foreign NGO, IWGIA, has been directly involved in channeling funds, supervising, and acting as political backup on the international arena. IWGIA chose to supervise the project through frequent monitoring (visits that are called "recurrent intervention") rather than through a permanent presence in the project. This has many advantages. It lets the implementing counterpart solve its internal and external problems itself. It prevents the development of paternalistic attitudes on part of the sponsor, and it prevents the implementing organization from passing on the responsibility for errors and flaws to the foreign sponsor. It is of particular importance with indigenous projects that their own organizations negotiate directly with national authorities, breaking down racial and ethnic prejudices of the national society, while creating respect for their actions. The presence of any non-indigenous and external representative in such situations would merely confirm existing ethnic prejudices.

Thus, all of the project design, implementation, and day-to-day troubles of getting it going have been handled directly by the indigenous organizations. These organizations grew out of the very same process. The funds were channeled from the Danish government via the international NGO directly to the indigenous organizations involved. They administered the budgets themselves, and no money came from public institutions. This obviously gave AIDESEP and OIRA a very strong position in relation to the public administration and authorities in charge of the technical procedures. The indigenous organizations covered the travel and *per diem* expenses of the field staff of the Ministry, and all technical work and fieldwork was done with teams of mixed indigenous-public staffing. All drafts work and mapping were done by the indigenous organizations themselves and in their offices. All of this created a strong sense of project ownership and responsibility and valuable experience was accumulated in the indigenous organization itself, and not lost to anonymous external structures.

5. Community participation

Another important aspect of the high degree of participation and mobilization among the forest communities is indirectly a result of the "community" concept itself. The fact that each local group organized as a community has to be registered, demarcated, classified, and titled separately, implies that the whole indigenous territory is divided into a number of smaller "autonomous" territorial units. The members of each unit (community) will have to accompany the topographic team in the field during weeks, working, sleeping, and eating together. They will have to negotiate borders with neighbors and they will have to understand and discuss legal matters and negotiate with non-indigenous neighbors. They literally have to struggle for their lands. This kind of involvement creates a strong feeling of ownership and converts a deed and a map into a territory and a place (their own place). The paradox in this is that the imposed concept of "community" impeding the acceptance and establishment of larger indigenous territories has turned out to be beneficial for the creation of strong feelings of territorial identity, has generated a high degree of local participation, and subsequently has made the defense of territorial integrity a local concern. The strategy of co-bordering communities takes care of the problem of territorial continuity. The patchwork of smaller self-governing units guarantees active participation.[15]

The success of the Ashéninka in this case is also a result of their very pragmatic approach to the world that surrounds them, in which everything non-indigenous is regarded as a potential resource to be exploited.[16] The indigenous perspective is characterized by a pluralistic and multi-centered worldview, where all societies and cultures are viewed as separate and particular, each with its own self-centered universe. In the pluri-centered universe the most interesting and relevant of all worlds for the Ashéninka is obviously their own. The notion resembles our notion of "species," and the Ashéninka have no ideological, ethical, or moral preferences as to whom and to which world they may relate and with whom they might cooperate, as the symbolic and moral values they believe in apply to themselves only. In principle, their worldview is based on a non-essentialist and non-hierarchical episteme that allows the indigenous communities a remarkable maneuverability. The cultural content or essence of the non-Ashéninka is basically considered irrelevant and not a prerequisite for relating to it as a potential resource. From a western moralist point of view this may be judged as pragmatism or simply opportunism. But in a world where increasing global integration opens up the possibility of new institutional contacts and resources and where neoliberal policies debilitate the nation state as the integrating mechanism of society, the unrestrictedness and systemic openness of the indigenous seems to boost resource access as their sphere of interaction expands and possibilities multiply. They do not have to understand or know the larger system to be able to interact with it. Their own integrity in this process, however, is simultaneously being secured through international legislation guaranteeing their territorial and ethnic rights. The field of political and social articulation has moved from a national to an international context, in which their cosmology seems very fit (Hvalkof 1997).

Summary: Post-Development and Democracy

The highly dynamic and participatory process of titling indigenous territories in the Ucayali Region has itself become a new field of social interaction. Land titling has become a means of trans-cultural communication between the indigenous society and the colonist society, and between the indigenous society and the state. This interaction creates binding social relationships between the parties involved and redefines the position of the indigenous peoples in regional and national development. The process has created a non-ideologized sphere of cross-sector and inter-cultural communication. In this field of open values, indigenous rights are pragmatically expressed in specific actions related to common aspects of everyday rural Amazonian life. This new space of social interaction has had a significant impact on the peaceful development of a more democratic civil society in the Peruvian Amazon. Thus the process of identifying, demarcating, and titling indigenous territories has been imperative for the ongoing construction of an indigenous future defining a new role and identity for indigenous peoples within the national political process. The pattern of colonist society and modern development has been broken. If democracy consists of active participation in policy and decision making by a culturally mixed population creating common instruments for dealing with differences and conflicting interests, this has been achieved in this part of Peru's Amazon. The irreversibility of the process not only confronts the existing power structure in the region, it also challenges the very process and concept of development. New economic forms are emerging where the values of indigenous subsistence production, market economy, and extractivist industry will be balanced very differently than before, and merged with or coexist within a post-modern construction of culturally subjective and relative truths. It is however imperative for the continuous social stability in this situation that the international partners to the social movement take on the responsibility of persistent support, and that the social sciences connect to these processes as a resource of intellectual feedback and exchange. These exchanges are the building blocks of the post-development reality under construction.

Notes

1. Only a couple of years ago a doctor directing the provincial hospital in the Atalaya in the Peruvian Amazon told the author "that the only difference between the local indigenous Ashéninka and the animals, is that the Indians can speak."

2. Federación de los Centros Shuar. The initiative originally arose amongst the Salesian missionaries in Sucuá, who started a system of bilingual radio-schools (Shuar-Spanish)—a revolutionary approach at the time. The Shuar gradually took full control of the organization, which in the following decade became the exemplary model for other indigenous organizations to follow. However, the federation had promoted cattle raising as the legitimization of Shuar land claims and increasingly found itself caught in trap within this strategy which gradually appeared as a kind of "self-colonization," since extensive cattle raising in the Amazon demands continual clearing of new forest areas for pasture. Because of this, the Shuar Federation gradually lost its appeal as a role model for other indigenous organizations.

3. One conspicuous exception to this trend is the Inter-American Development Bank which until now has avoided explicit policies on indigenous issues.

4. The Montaña in general refers to the entire u-shaped montane forest area delimiting the Amazon basin toward the Andes running from today's Bolivia in the South through Peru, Ecuador, and into Colombia in the North.

5. These groups include the Asháninka, Ashéninka, Matsiguenga, Nomatsiguenga, Yánesha, Yíne (Piro), and the linguistically more distant Kakínte.

6. As the outmoded term *Campa* practically is out of use today, being encumbered with negative connotations, no generic term for this cluster of ethno-linguistic groups is in use. We will here refer to them as either Ashéninka or Asháninka dependent on the specific context.

7. *Hacienda* means a kind of large estate.

8. Simultaneously protestant missionaries mainly from the Summer Institute of Linguistics set up a bilingual education system that contributed to reorganization of indigenous communities constituting the basis for the political organization to come. Although fiercely criticized by anthropologists and other observers for its proselytizing agenda, the bilingual school system has been one of the keys to the organizational success of the indigenous movement (Hvalkof and Aaby 1981; Hvalkof 1997; Stoll 1982; Veber 1991).

9. Vaccination campaigns mainly carried out by protestant missionaries from the 1970s dramatically reduced indigenous mortality rates. The Asháninka population has subsequently become fast growing, increasingly claiming and reoccupying their old territories where possible.

10. Today the indigenous organization of Gran Pajonal, the OAGP has 34 associated communities, and is still consolidating its territory, filling in gaps in earlier demarcations, and adjusting community borders.

11. It was a historic moment that marked the beginning of a much wider acceptance of projects with indigenous peoples as relevant for "development" and requiring special attention and strategy development by the aid agencies involved.

12. The ASI is the modern continuation of the "Anti-Slavery and Aborigines Protection Society," which actively lobbied for British intervention to stop the atrocities of rubber extraction in the Congo and Peru at the beginning of this century (Gray 1990; 1997)

13. The national umbrella organization for the indigenous peoples of the Peruvian Amazon, AIDESEP, runs a bilingual and intercultural teacher training college in

Iquitos. It has now been operating for 10 years, and has developed a remarkable educational methodology for rural indigenous communities and indigenous teachers' in-service training.

14. The philosophy and principles of the indigenous health program has been developed by the AIDESEP's health secretariat, Programa de Salud Indígena (PSI), which is an all-indigenous initiative. To sucessfully run such an ambitious large-scale program, external funding is imperative. The PSI has received funding for this from a Danish endowment, the Karen Elise Jensen Foundation, normally sponsoring high-tech medical equipment for hospital research. The implementation has been supervised and reviewed by NORDECO, a professional Danish consultancy.

15. This is in contrast to large scale territorial allotments, given administratively top-down to a conglomerate of indigenous groups as common territories of large extensions, e.g., the "resguardos" of Vaupes and Amazonas in Colombia, which, to my knowledge, has not generated the same relationship to the territory and its integrity.

16. In many ways this practical view is similar to how the Maya, discussed in the chapters by Gudeman and Rivera-Gutiérrez, and by Pi-Sunyer, have survived and even taken advantage of the onslaught of tourism in Mexico and Guatemala.

References

AIDESEP (Asociación Interetnica de Desarrollo de la Selva Peruana). 1988a. *Informe Provisional Sobre la Problemática de la Zona de Influencia de la Ciudad de Atalaya Elaborado a Requerimiento de la Comisión de Alto Nivel Creada por Resolucion Ministerial No. 0083–88–PCM.* MS. Lima, Perú.

———. 1988b. *Informe de Infracciones Forestales Recopiladas en Atalaya y Presentadas ante la Dirección General de Forestal y Fauna.* AIDESEP. Lima. Perú.

———. 1991a. Esclavitud indígena en la región de Atalaya. *Amazonía Indígena*, Nos. 17 y 18, Año 11, Lima, Perú. 3–14.

———. 1991b. Aprovecha mi poco conocimiento de las leyes . . . *Amazonía Indígena*, Nos. 17 y 18, Año 11, Lima, Perú. 14–16.

———. 1991c. Nos dicen que somos indios y si nos matan nada pasa. *Amazonía Indígena*, Nos. 17 y 18, Año 11, Lima, Perú. 16–21.

Alavarez, Sonia E. and Arturo Escobar. 1992. Conclusion: theoretical and political horizons of change in contemporary Latin American social movements. In *The Making of Social Movements in Latin America. Identity, Strategy, and Democracy.* Boulder: Westview. 317–329.

Barclay, Frederica. 1989. *La Colonia del Perené: Capital Inglés y Economía Cafetalera en la Configuración de la Región de Chanchamayo.* Iquitos: CETA.

Bateson, Gregory. 1972. *Steps to an Ecology of Minds.* New York: Balantine.

Benavides, Margarita. 1992. Asháninka self defence in the central forest region. *IWGIA Newsleter* 2/92. Copenhagen: IWGIA. 36–45.

———. 1993. Los Asháninka, víctimas de la violencia y la guerra. *Ideele* 59–50, Dic 93, 116–118.

Bodley, John H. 1971. *Campa Socio-economic Adaptation.* Ph.D. Dissertation, University of Oregon.

———. 1972. *Tribal Survival in the Amazon: the Campa Case.* IWGIA Document 5. Copenhagen: IWGIA.

Brown, Michael F. and Eduardo Fernández. 1991. *War of Shadows: The Struggle for Utopia in the Peruvian Amazon*. Berkeley: University of California Press.

Conklin, Beth and Laura Graham. 1995. The shifting middle ground: Amazonian Indians and eco-politics. *American Anthropologist.* 97:695–710.

Davis, Shelton H. and Alaka Wali. 1994. Indigenous territories and tropical forest management in Latin America. *Indigenous Affairs.* No. 4. Copenhagen: IWGIA. 4–13.

Escobar, Arturo. 1995. *Encountering Development: The Making and the Unmaking of the Third World*. Princeton, N.J.: Princeton University Press.

García Hierro, Pedro. 1998. Atalaya: Caught in a time warp. In *Liberation Through Land Rights in the Peruvian Amazon*, edited by Alejandro Parellada and Søren Hvalkof. IWGIA Document No. 80, Copenhagen: IWGIA. 13–79

Gray, Andrew. 1990. *The Putumayo Atrocities Revisited*. Paper presented at Oxford University seminar on State, Boundaries, and Indians. Manuscript.

————. 1997. Peru. Freedom and Territory: Slavery in the Peruvian Amazon. In *Enslaved Peoples in the 1990s. Indigenous Peoples, Debt Bondage and Human Rights*, edited by Anti-Slavery International and IWGIA. Copenhagen. 183–215.

————. 1998. Demarcating development: titling indigenous territories in Peru. In *Liberation Through Land Rights in the Peruvian Amazon*. IWGIA Document No. 90. 165–216. Copenhagen: IWGIA.

Gray, Andrew and Søren Hvalkof. 1990a. *Supervision Report on Land Titling Pproject, Peruvian Amazon: Inscription and Titling of Native Communities in the Ucayali Department*. Report to IWGIA. Copenhagen, Denmark: IWGIA.

————. 1990b. Indigenous land titling in the Peruvian Amazon. *IWGIA Yearbook 1989*. Copenhagen: IWGIA. 230–243.

Hardenburg, Walter E. 1913. *The Putumayo. The Devil's Paradise: Travels in the Peruvian Amazon Region and an Account of the Atrocities Committed Upon the Indians Therein*. T. London and Leipsic: T. Fisher Unwin.

Hvalkof, Søren. 1986a. *Urgent Report on the Situation of the Ashéninka (Campa) Population of Gran Pajonal, Central Peruvian Amazon*. Research Report. Copenhagen: Danish International Development Agency and Danish Social Science Research Council.

————. 1986b. El drama actual del Gran Pajonal. Primer parte: Recursos, historia, Población y producción Ashéninka. In *Amazonía Indigena, Boletin de Analisis*. Vol. 6, no. 12, 22–30.

————. 1987. El drama actual del Gran Pajonal, Segunda parte: Colonización y violencia. *Amazonia Indigena, Boletin de Analisis*. Vol. 7, no. 13, 3–10.

————. 1989. The nature of development: native and settlers' views in Gran Pajonal, Peruvian Amazon. *Folk*. Vol. 31. Copenhagen: Danish Ethnographic Society. 125–150.

————. 1994a. The Asháninka disaster and struggle—the forgotten war in the Peruvian Amazon. *Indigenous Affairs.* No. 2/94. IWGIA. 20–32.

————. 1994b. Territorial organization and democracy in Peruvian Amazon: the current Asháninka struggle for land, autonomy, and recognition. Paper presented at symposium Sacred Land, Threatened Territories—Contested Landscapes in Native

South America—48th *International Congress of Americanists*. Stockholm/Uppsala. July 4–9, 1994.

———. 1997. From Curaca to president . . . indigenous leadership in Peruvian Amazon: the Ashéninka case. Paper presented at the session: "Contemporary indigenous leadership in the Amazon" *American Anthropological Association 96th Annual Meeting*. Nov. 19–23, 1997. Washington D.C.

———.1998a. Post-development, lumber business, and democracy: the case of the Upper Amazon in Peru. Paper prepared for the session: Political Ecology and Action Research in Forest Communities. *14th ICAES (International Congress of Anthropological and Ethnological Sciences)*. July 26–August 1, 1998. The College of Williams and Mary, Williamsburg, Virginia.

———. 2000. Outrage in rubber and oil: extractivism, indigenous peoples, and justice in the Upper Amazon. In *Peoples, Plants and Justice: Resource Extraction and Conservation in Tropical Developing Countries,* edited by Zerner, Charles. Rainforest Alliance, New York: Columbia University Press.

———. 1998c. From slavery to democracy: the indigenous process of Upper Ucayali and Gran Pajonal. In *Liberation Through Land Rights in The Peruvian Amazon,* edited by Parellada, Alejandro and Søren Hvalkof. IWGIA Document No. 80, Copenhagen. pp.83–162.

Hvalkof, Søren and Peter Aaby. 1981. *Is God an American? An anthropological perspective on the missionary work of the Summer Institute of Linguistics.* IWGIA Doc. 43. Copenhagen/London: IWGIA/Survival International.

———. 1989. *Informe final sobre las Medidas Referentes a los Derechos, al Bienestar y al Desarrollo de las Etnias Nativas de la Zona de Atalaya.* Documento elaborado por el Equipo Tecnico nominado por la Comisión Multisectorial conformada por la Resolución Ministerial No. 083–88–PCM. Lima: Instituto Indigenista Peruano.

Jackson, Jean. 1989. Is there a way to talk about making culture without making enemies? *Dialectical Anthropology.* 14:127–143.

Lehnertz, Jay F. 1972. Juan Santos primitive rebel on the campa frontier (1742–52). *Actas del XXXIX Congreso Internacional de Americanistas.* Vol. 4, Lima. 110–125.

Little, Paul. 1998. Beyond sovereignty and autonomy: political ecology research and contemporary Amazonian territorial struggles. Paper presented at the session "Political Ecology and Action Research in Forest Communities" at *14th ICAES (International Congress of Anthropological and Ethnological Sciences)*. July 26–Aug. 1. College of Williams and Mary, Williamsburg, Virginia.

Metraux, Alfred 1942. A Quechua Messiah in Eastern Peru. *American Anthropologist.* Vol. XLIV, 721–725.

Ñaco Rosa, Guillermo, Samuel Pérez Arbaiza, Beatriz Huertas, and Casiano Aguirre. 1997. Sira communal reserve, introduction. In *From Principle to Practice: Indigenous Peoples and Biodiversity Conservation in Latin America. Proceedings of the Pucallpa Conference.* IWGIA Document No. 87. Copenhagen: IWGIA. 20–42.

Renard-Casevitz, France-Marie. 1980. Contrast beween amerindian and colonist land use in the Southern Peruvian Amazon. In *Land, People, and Planning in Contemporary Amazonia,* edited by Barbira-Scazzocchio. F. Cambridge, UK: Cambridge University Centre of Latin American Studies.

Sala, Fray Gabriel A.P. 1897. Apuntes de viaje de R.P. Fray Gabriel Sala, exploración de los rios Pichis, Pachitea y Alto Ucayali, y de la Región del Gran Pajonal. In *Colección de Leyes, Decretos, Resoluciones y Otros Documentos Oficiales Referente al Departemento de Loreto*, edited by Larrabure y Correa, C. Vol. XII, 7–154.

Salazar, Ernesto. 1977. *An Indian Federation in Lowland Ecuador*. IWGIA Document 28. Copenhagen: IWGIA.

Santos Granero, Fernando. 1987. Epidemias y sublevaciones en el desarrollo demográfico de las misiones Amuesha del Cerro de la Sal, siglo XVIII, *Historica*. Vol. XI (1), Pontificia Universidad Católica del Perú, Lima.

———. 1992. *Etnohistoria de la Alta Amazonía*. Del siglo XV al XVIII, Editorial AbyaYala, Quito.

Schäfer, Manfred. 1988. *Ayompari, Amigos und die Peitsche: Die Verflechtung der ökonomische Tauschbeziehungen der Ashéninka in der Gesellschaft des Gran Pajonal/Ostperu*. Doctoral dissertation. Ludwig-Maximilians-Universtät zu München. Selbstverlag: Amorbach.

Steward, Julian H., ed. 1963/1945. *Handbook of South American Indians*. Vol. 3, *The Tropical Forest Tribes*. New York: Cooper Square Publishers, Inc.

Stoll, David. 1982. *Fishers of Men or Founders of Empire: The Wycliffe Bible Translators in Latin America*. London and Cambridge, Mass.: Zed Press and Cultural Survival.

Taussig, Michael. 1984. Culture of terror-space of death: Roger Casement's Putumayo report and the Explanation of Torture. *Comparative Studies in Society and History*. 26 (3). July.

———. 1985. *Shamanism, Colonialism, and the Wild Man: A Study of Terror and Healing*. Chicago and London: University of Chicago Press.

Touraine Alain. 1985. An introduction to the study of social movements. *Social Research*. 52(4):749–787

US Department of State. 1913. *Slavery in Peru: Message from the President of the United States. Transmitting Report of the Secretary of State, with Accompanying Papers, Concerning the Alleged Existence of Slavery in Peru*. February 7, 1913. 62D, 3rd Session. House of Representatives. Document No. 1366, Washington D.C.

Valcárcel, Carlos A. (juez). 1915. *El proceso del Putumayo y sus Secretos Inauditos*. Imprenta "Comercial" de Horacio La Rosa and Co., Lima.

Van Cott, Donna Lee. 1995. Indigenous peoples and democracy: Issues for policy-makers. In *Indigenous Peoples and Democracy in Latin America*, edited by Van Cott, Donna Lee. New York: The Inter American Dialogue.

Varese, Stefano.1973. *La Sal de los Cerros: Una Aproximación al Mundo Campa*. Lima, Perú: Retablo de Papel Ediciones.

Veber, Hanne M. 1991. Schools for the Ashéninka ethno-development in the making. Paper presented to the 47th International Congress of Americanists. New Orleans, July 7–11.

———. 1998. The salt of the Montaña: Interpreting indigenous activism in the rain forest. *Cultural Anthropology*. No. 13 (3). 382–413.

II

Private Lives and
Neoliberalism

5

Privatization and Private Lives: Gender, Reproduction, and Neoliberal Reforms in a Brazilian Company Town

Jacquelyn Chase

Introduction

In the early 1980s, the Brazilian government began to sell off many of its state enterprises to private investors (Lima 1997; Glade 1991). The most notorious of these privatizations occurred in April of 1997 when the gigantic mining conglomerate—the Companhia Vale do Rio Doce (CVRD)—was sold for 10 billion dollars to a consortium of Brazilian and foreign investors. Its privatization generated explosive reactions by unions, public employees, and other organized groups (Pinheiro 1996). One hundred and thirty lawsuits against this privatization helped to delay the auction. When the auction of the CVRD finally occurred at Rio de Janeiro's stock exchange, the governor called in an anti-riot force to disperse raging demonstrators ("Let the party begin" 1997). This opposition to privatization has been voiced primarily by political nationalists and labor unions, and pivots on the reduction of good, unionized jobs in the formal economy.[1]

But public demonstrations and national debates do not exhaust the social implications of privatization of state enterprises in Brazil or Latin America. Along with the loss of jobs for unionized public sector workers, we also see a shift of social costs of reproduction to families, and the growth in a flexible and weakly organized labor markets in which most new workers are women (Standing 1999; Tardanico 1997; Veltmeyer, Petras, and Vieux 1997). These public displays of rage and resistance are far removed from the private lives of people who must adjust to drastic changes in the way they live and work, and how they envision their children's lives in the future.

This chapter is about how families—and especially women—are able to cope with and prepare for life after the Companhia Vale do Rio Doce in the birthplace of this firm: Itabira. This is a town of about 70,000 people in the state of Minas Gerais that had become dependent on the jobs, steady wages for men, social services, and subsidized consumption provided by this firm over the last fifty years. I will argue that women have few means by which to become active labor market citizens in this town (see Schild 1998). However, they have become very good at controlling their fertility. It is through this bodily control that I argue women are going to actively participate in and try to reduce the uncertainty of the emerging post-privatization period in Itabira.

Analyses of privatization in Latin America rarely consider the regional and local impacts of this strategy, although many industrial regions grew under the influence of state firms and subsidies and are today especially vulnerable to state retraction and privatization. A state-region perspective would highlight the spatially uneven nature of this phase of capitalist development of Latin American economies, much like the regional and local studies of industrial restructuring in Great Britain and the United States did from the late 1970s to the 1990s (Cooke, 1989; Massey 1991; Allen, Massey, and Cochrane 1998; Bluestone and Harrison 1982).

Some Latin American scholars do cite very broad distinctions between city and countryside in the process of neoliberalism, and others have focused on metropolitan regions which have been hit especially hard by state downsizing and by the loss of services given their high concentration of state jobs (Tardanico 1997). New spatial configurations at the global scale under neoliberalism have brought certain Third World countries and regions such as the Caribbean and the United States-Mexican border onto center stage (Klak 1998; Conaghan and Malloy 1994). Sectoral analyses capture some of the diversity of enterprise privatization, but they usually evaluate the performance of privatized companies and sectors, with little interest in privatization in place, or in the human costs beyond the costs to consumers (Sánchez and Corona 1993; Baer and Birch 1994; OECD 1996; Glade 1991; Glade and Corona 1996).

I will argue further that previous locally-specific gender relations contextualize how regions are affected by neoliberalism in Latin America. Feminist geographers have placed gender as a central feature of the emerging regional and global geographies of the late twentieth century. Gender provides an opportunity to look outside the market for other sources of social interaction and meaning. According to Linda McDowell (1991, 77) for instance,

> Different schools of thought—from the flexible accumulation theorists, through the deindustrialization school, to the postindustrialists' emphasis on technological change—focus almost exclusively on economic consider-

ations, seldom expanding their analyses to include the concurrent changes in family life, social relations, and community involvement in a whole range of noneconomic struggles. Theorists focus on this sphere in contrast with, and in opposition to, the private world of emotion, obligations, love, and subjectivity, a feminine sphere that is the "natural" foundation of civil life requiring no theorization.

We have not seen a similar concern with gender in the reconstitution of Third World regions that are undergoing the effects of privatization or of neoliberalism more generally. Many studies of Latin American dynamic regions during "global restructuring" have highlighted the importance of gender and the household in supplying global capital with new sources of cheap female labor (Fernández-Kelly 1983; Safa 1995 and in this volume). Using the case of Itabira, I want to show that the way people cope when regional economies begin to unravel will depend on how labor, families, and consumption were articulated prior to the crisis. Regional and gendered identities are shaped by previous labor market and consumption strategies in particular places. These identities will in turn affect how women, men, and working families respond to privatization and other manifestations of state downsizing in Latin America (Allen, Massey, and Cochrane 1998).

Champions of neoliberalism have argued that labor markets in Latin America suffer from regulatory constraints that have shielded workers from competitive bidding or kept groups of potential workers such as women and peasants from the work force (Amadeo and Horton 1997). But a long-standing reliance on male wages and the peculiar cultural construction of households, gender relations, and class in Itabira when it was under a state-protected industry also make it unlikely that the town will be able to make the transition towards the kind of labor flexibility that the neoliberal doctrine proposes. The state-owned CVRD created a world of domestic security in Itabira, which included an enduring reliance on the male breadwinner, extraordinarily high levels of family consumption, and subsidies for school, medical care, and food. From the point of view of the firm, this provided a stable and compliant work force during its expansive phase that spanned more than thirty years, beginning in the early 1950s. Although domestication strategies worked well for families for some time, they also structured the local labor market and labor market institutions in ways that have made it difficult for working class families and especially for women to become "flexible" labor market citizens (Schild 1998). Women were highly educated, but were often kept from developing work skills by the historical construction of a "masculinized" (Allen, Massey, and Cochrane 1998) labor market and by upwardly mobile working class men who did not want their wives to work outside the home. When some women did begin to work, especially after 1970, they were stigmatized by being ancillary to the primary male-dominated activity of mining.[2] In terms of basic survival, women's wages alone are usually insufficient to live on.

This chapter has three main parts. I will first look at how the boom years of the CVRD in Itabira rested on gendered identities and household labor. The second part examines the corrosion of this pact as the company has been downsized, and looks at the limited ability of women and families to replace men in the labor market. I will end the chapter with an analysis of changing attitudes toward childbearing and child rearing in Itabira, arguing that the precipitous drop in fertility in Itabira can be explained by the peculiar gendered nature of its economic development. It is through reproductive change (taking further control of their bodies) that women have responded to their own restricted lives in this place during prosperity. They will probably continue to do so as the crisis of privatization removes access to economic security and social mobility for a once upwardly mobile working class population.

The Place: Labor Markets and Gendered Identities

Itabira was founded in 1720 as one of a constellation of towns in central Minas Gerais state that served to establish colonial domain over rich gold deposits found in local mountains. Strategic minerals such as iron ore were also in abundance in the region. The CVRD came to Itabira in 1942 as a result of Brazil's alliance with Great Britain and the United States early in World War II. This alliance culminated in the Washington Accords that were pieced together to ensure the wartime provisioning of iron ore and rubber, both abundant in Brazil and needed for wartime production. The Brazilian government under the populist President Getúlio Vargas formed the Companhia Vale do Rio Doce to undertake the massive task of starting iron ore exploration around Itabira. This moment coincided with the beginning of Brazil's ambitious import substitution industrialization program that supported the development of basic infrastructure, prime materials, and key manufacturing industries. Major Brazilian cities such as Rio de Janeiro and São Paulo had already emerged by the early part of the twentieth century as important sources of skilled and disciplined industrial labor (Weinstein 1997). But resource regions such as central Minas Gerais had neither the demographic nor social advantages of these urban centers. Local demographic, economic, and social conditions in Itabira on the eve of the birth of the CVRD help contextualize the challenges to the formation of a local labor market and the path the company chose to ensure itself a local supply of labor over the next two generations.

The Coming of the "Sweet Mother"

The town of Itabira was quite small in 1940, with 5,332 inhabitants. Roughly 17,000 lived in the municipality's countryside, and almost three-quarters of the 6,512 economically active people of Itabira were engaged in agriculture. In 1940, only 314 people worked in extractive industries in the municipality, 230 in commerce and 642 in services (Gontijo 1996, 60). Given the immense area in question—over 57 square miles, and the largest municipality in central Minas Gerais—we can surmise the rural population density was fairly low. Rural settlement was dispersed, a factor that challenged the recruitment and retention of the earliest generation of workers in the CVRD. Most rural Itabirans were descendants of the slave population brought to the region during the 18th century, who now worked the land as share-croppers on vast ranching properties, planting beans, cassava, rice, corn, and other short-cycle food crops for local consumption (Minayo 1986, 39). Money circulation was limited, and most transactions were done through barter and informal credit. The town also lacked basic services and housing. Makeshift camps eventually sprang up where men would offer themselves for work in the nascent company.

The way that people describe their lives in the shadow of the CVRD makes sense in the context of the changing technology, size, and market strategies of the company, as these factors affected how labor was recruited, disciplined, and domesticated. During the implantation phase of the company, which lasted about ten years, the CVRD did little to create the permanent, devoted work force that would later become its hallmark. Workers hacked away at trees and underbrush and began digging ore out of the mountainside with picks. Ore was hauled away by mules and men pushing wheelbarrows. Company foremen hired men on the basis of their physical appearance and kept them on the job on the basis of their endurance. Despite the apparently successful improvised character of labor recruitment, other allusions remember the challenges that a largely rural, scattered, agricultural population with little or no industrial work experience presented to labor recruiters for CVRD. The most important of these challenges were time discipline and immobilization of the work force, as the history of industrialization has shown more generally (Thompson 1963). These two concerns continued to drive the strategies of labor control, which eventually became embedded in the domestication of CVRD manual workers.

The precarious labor market that toiled to implant the company in Itabira eventually gave way to management's strategy to create a more skilled, stable, and committed work force out of the local populace. Although the vast majority of workers in the company have been men, the CVRD has relied on the compliance of men's wives, sons, and daughters to attain this goal. It has also benefited from a pervasive reference to itself as a "sweet mother" that created a regional cradle of well-being for people who had been treated as virtual slaves under the power of local landowners (Minayo 1986).

To ensure itself a compliant local labor force, the company in Itabira intervened in domestic life in a number of ways that are also common to mining towns in other settings (Gibson 1991; Klubock 1998; Gill 1990). This intervention included three sets of basic goods and services: housing, education, and medical care. In addition, the steady wages and subsidized company stores allowed workers and their families to greatly expand their consumption of industrialized goods that only a solid middle class could afford elsewhere in Brazil. In providing this material support, the company was able to achieve compliance and even deep loyalty of workers, without resorting to force or outright repression. But the stories told by men and women in Itabira cannot be reduced to complicity. People expose the sweet "mothering" project of the CVRD in its waning years by playfully bringing onto stage an "evil" woman well known in western culture: the stepmother.

The Stepmother Arrives

"People here like to say that the company used to be a sweet mother, but now it's a stepmother." One usually tires of a stale joke, but I only became more intrigued as I heard the stepmother line again and again. This metaphor had swept through Itabira in 1996, and by 1998 Itabirans had embellished it with ". . . and one who hits you really hard across the face," complete with the slapping motion and sound effects, *"tac, tac."* This is what the act of downsizing and privatization had come to in this town: the death of a protective mother and her substitution by an uncaring and even mean substitute. I believe this metaphor allowed local people to see themselves in this process as people in relationships, rather than as numbers (Chase 2001). But let us begin by looking at some of the numbers behind the stepmother anyway. First, the job loss associated with company downsizing and privatization that Itabira has experienced seems to coincide with larger trends in privatization of the mining sector in Brazil. Lima (1997, 39–41) shows that in the first ten years after privatization, the steel producer USIMINAS lost 18 percent of its work force. Overall, in his sample of ten major industries privatized in the 1990s, Lima found that job loss varied between 18 and 56 percent. Starting in 1985 at 4,745 (Gontijo 1996), the CVRD work force in Itabira fell to 2,900 workers in 1995 (Ferreira 1995, 11) and to an estimated 1,500 in 1998, a year after privatization. Much of the streamlining of the employment base had thus taken place in Itabira in anticipation of privatization, so post-privatization job stability is not the best gauge of the impact of privation on employment in this case (Petrazzini 1996).

When looked at in the context of Itabira's urban working population, these numbers gain fuller meaning. In 1991, for example, the total male working population of Itabira was almost 17,000. This means that over one-quarter of the male working population that year was employed by the company. Since the early 1990s, the company has been shedding labor, primarily through an early retirement package, known in Itabira as the "big soup" (sopão). This has been accompanied by a virtual hiring freeze and by greater expectations for individual productivity and worker citizenship. The big soup was a lump sum of money proportional to years an employee worked at the firm and offered to certain workers that agreed to quit or retire early. People close to retirement would have to pay into their fund for a certain number of years to be able to collect full retirement, whereas younger workers simply took the soup and cut their ties with the firm. The money was intended, at least officially, to help these workers adjust to the new neoliberal world, in which it was hoped many of them would make independent investments or put the money into a savings account for their children's education.

This fantasy of flexible and efficient adjustment by individuals pushed by neoliberalism is made transparent by the selective cuts the company has made since the early 1990s and by the inability of people to productively invest this money. First, these cuts targeted older and less-skilled men who were least likely to find employment elsewhere. These were also not the men who would be the most successful independent business owners with technical and refined administrative knowledge, or those with the best potential social networks with existing industries. Second, I heard numerous stories about how the big soup seemed like a windfall to many of the lower paid workers in the firm. Many of them spent the money on conspicuous consumption items like new cars or house remodeling, and have since had to sell their belongings to survive. Others had invested this money in small consumption-oriented businesses or services, but most city officials were skeptical that these would prove to be economically dynamic for the town or region. One woman I interviewed invested her husband's money in a home-based daycare center, which seemed to be doing fine, having remained open two years at the time of my research. But several families I knew of had set up neighborhood bars that had since closed.

There is also the sense among people connected to the company that it has become mean to those who stay on, using almost any pretext to fire or lay off employees. A woman I interviewed had left the company—where she had worked as an office worker—with the big soup, only to discover that the company still owed her more than she had received. Because her husband was still employed at the company, she asked me not to reveal her identity to anyone for fear of reprisals. Those who have remained feel the company becoming stricter about behavior and productivity, and less fair in its recruitment policies. One man worried that because he does not have a "godfather" in the company, he may be the next to fall. Skilled workers coming back from the Carajás complex in southern Amazônia are also being favored over local workers for advancement in the company.

The cuts extend beyond the work force to affect the children of company employees directly. More than any other group, Itabirans with school-age children are insecure about the future of Itabira. The government-run technical school that once served to graduate each new generation of manual and technical workers at CVRD is no longer preparing young people for this work. There is no expectation that the school will help them find good jobs in the company. Children have long stopped dreaming of a lifelong commitment to the CVRD. One fifteen-year-old boy said "No way!" when I asked him if he thought he might work for the company in the future. His preference was to go to medical school, and if that did not work out, he would try to get into law school.[3] Through its social support system and wage security in the past, the company helped create an ambitious but now embittered fourth generation of CVRD Itabirans, many of whom believe there is no hope but to leave town.

There are almost no areas of life in which severe cuts in social services have not been felt,[4] but the one most often mentioned by the women and men I interviewed were in the subsidies for their younger children's education. Once completely subsidized, the cost of private schooling that the company contributes will be 60 percent. In light of the wage squeeze that Itabirans and, in fact, all Brazilians have felt in the last decades, most families cannot afford what is left for them to pay. Most young families I spoke with had taken one or more of their children out of private schools. City government offices are no longer absorbing the highly educated sons, daughters, and wives of CVRD employees. The mayoral election of 1996 in Itabira helped stir up resistance to the incumbent on the basis that he was giving preference to early retirees, closing off an important local route of professionalization for neophyte workers.[5] Parents are finding they have to send their sons and daughters away to the state capital, Belo Horizonte, to high school and college, as the educational specializations in Itabira have been too narrowly prescribed in the interest of the company.[6] Ironically, in a country where children were once expected to help their parents at all stages in the life cycle, company retirees are now helping their children and their grandchildren far into adulthood.

The wives of CVRD employees told me they were making other cuts in their basic consumption that would have been unimaginable a generation ago. One family eats fruit only twice a month, for example. The yearly get-away has long disappeared for young families with children. Although the company has eliminated subsidized family vacations, men have not curtailed their own leisure, but shifted it to activities in which their wives and children do not normally participate.

Moving away from Itabira is a dream that I heard expressed by several young women whose husbands still held onto their company jobs. What is likely to continue is the seepage of population through the out-migration of young unmarried adults who leave to study or work elsewhere. But it is unlikely that the city will see an immediate exodus, as people are heavily invested in homes and connected to large kin groups. Families worry about house payments and the housing market, knowing that selling out and leaving will be difficult if the company fires even more of its workers. The worker neighborhoods where many of them live have few amenities. Ironically, the neighborhood built at the foot of the Cauê mine with all the social infrastructure described earlier is now extremely undesirable as a result of the heavy dose of particulates it has received from the mine over the years.[7]

The impact of job loss or wage cuts on families must be looked at in the context of families' previous financial commitments and expectations. Itabira is a notoriously "consumption-oriented" town. I have described how some of the high expectations for good schools, medical care, and leisure became part of families' everyday life, but people also became tied into easy credit markets for big ticket items such as cars, telephones,[8] domestic appliances, and computers, most of which are not widely available to working class Brazilians. According to census information, 3,544 households out of a total of 15,210 in Itabira (23 percent) owned telephones in 1991, slightly above the average 19 percent for Brazil in 1989. However, this number might surely be higher among CVRD employees' families. The majority of the population of the town of Itabira in fact earned very little in 1991: almost 7,000 people earned less than one minimum wage per month, out of a total active labor force of over 25,000 people. Although I do not have company figures on wages, the demographic census of 1991 showed that workers in the state sector in Itabira, the great majority of whom would be CVRD employees, had on average higher wages. About 200 people out of about 4,500 in this sector earned less than one minimum wage, but these could not be full-time employees. Those earning three minimum wages or above accounted for 75 percent of all workers in state companies, as opposed to about 27 percent for all other sectors. In comparison, 27 percent of the Brazilian working population as a whole also earned over three minimum wages in 1988, according to the Brazilian statistics bureau, IBGE (1990, 95).

Nonetheless, we see an especially frightening situation for people who have been raised to expect security and whose ability to adjust to economic hard times and the demands of flexibility has not been honed in the last three generations. The company, it seems, takes some responsibility for creating this situation, and is concerned with the impacts of indebtedness on its workers. Recently it has offered courses for its employees on how to manage their finances in tight circumstances. Correcting runaway consumption, however, is unlikely to bridge the gap between lost income and household survival if men lose their jobs.

One classic response to shrinking wages and insecure labor markets in Latin America and elsewhere has been an ever-increasing number of women going into the workplace for the first time (González de la Rocha 1994; Standing 1999; Safa 1995 and this volume). How and under what conditions will women enter the fragile new economy of Itabira after privatization? Many women declared their enthusiasm to work to support their families, but women's turn toward a more active public, economic life has not been easy or very gratifying. One of the great ironies of life in this company town for women was that they grew up with high educational expectations and resources, but with few opportunities for good-paying jobs. The growth in the local public sector added many jobs to the economy that women were most likely to fill, and the result has been a fairly robust female job market for women, especially for those with at least a high school education. In 1991, almost 9,000 women worked in the city of Itabira, compared to about 17,000 men. This represented about one-third of all women of working age. Of these women 1,882 work in administrative jobs, 3,600 work in service occupations, 950 in commercial occupations, and 602 in construction and industry.[9] None worked in mining, although mining companies such as CVRD employ female office work. Economic dependence of women on their husbands, however, was a badge of honor for many company men who considered themselves well paid and able to support a family, with its middle class lifestyle and financial commitments. Many women, despite high educational and job aspirations, have stayed out of the market, and have only now begun to respond to their families' impending crises by working in home-based crafts and food preparation. Pay for both groups of women is very low, although public workers benefit from a regular income.[10] A college-educated social worker for example earned less than half what her high-school educated husband earned at the company. Nearly twice as many working women in Itabira were college educated (1,029) as men (652); but only 108 of these college-educated women, compared to 300 college-educated men, made over ten times the minimum wage per month (roughly 1,000 dollars in 1996). In fact, there are five times as many men earning more than twenty minimum wages (103) with only a *grade school* education, as there are women in that earning category with *college* degrees (20).[11]

The Changing Meaning of Family, Children, and Reproduction

The most dramatic changes to occur in Brazil in the last two decades have been in the private lives of working people as they have adjusted to the dual stress of economic modernization and crisis. Household coping strategies are widely documented in the Latin American literature, and attest to the resiliency and creativity of the poor in getting by (González de la Rocha 1994; Escobar Latapí and González de la Rocha, this volume; Safa, this volume; Roberts 1991). Roberts (1991, 141–2) sums up these strategies as follows:

> a. reducing household expenditures by cutting consumption or ejecting non-productive members; b. intensifying the exploitation of internal household resources through self-provisioning and reciprocity with kin and friends; c. adopting market-oriented strategies, which in the urban context are usually labor market strategies, but not exclusively so as the flourishing of an informal economy indicates; and d. seeking aid from powerful external agents, such as the state, as of right or in return for political support.

The literature on household coping strategies has rarely recognized fertility decline as one of the most profound changes to take place within the household.[12] An unprecedented decline in fertility since the 1960s has brought Brazilian family structure and size close to patterns of industrialized countries (Carvalho and Wong 1996; Potter 1996). Such a widespread decline could only have taken place had it been adopted by poor women as well as middle and upper class Brazilians, and it deserves recognition as one of the main strategies by which poor households—and especially women—cope with uncertainty.

Polarized Explanations

The tools we have to work with to understand the relationship between the economy and fertility are vast, but tend to come out of the single tradition of classic demographic transition theory, with its roots in ideas of western economic and cultural modernization. Susan Greenhalgh (1995, 5) summarizes this heritage:

Classic transition theory was a version of modernization theory, the paradigm of third-world development that dominated social-scientific research on Asia, Africa, and Latin America from the early post-World War II years until roughly the late 1960s. The modernization school, which embraced many disciplines and diverse points of view, created universal theories that were beyond time and place, and that focused on social and economic forces for change, to the exclusion of political and cultural ones.

This view of modernization has become increasingly problematic and challenging over time for economists and demographers alike. The recognition of the persistence of third world poverty, believed to be heightened by global competition and technological change, questioned such a convergence of modern economic systems across space and time cite. In addition, demographers and reproductive rights advocates (Hartmann 1995; Carvalho and Wong 1996; Cosío 1996) have argued that the decline in fertility in Latin America is less a sign of convergence toward a modern norm than an indicator of failed mobility and stress among women. The convergence that we can see between social groups and regions toward lower fertility is really a mirage that hides the contradictions inherent for poor women living in a rich country, constantly inundated with messages of prosperity and social mobility.

Data from Itabira confounds the explanations that we could draw directly from the coping strategy literature on urban poverty that would lead us to associate lower fertility with impoverishment, because people there are not "poor" in the sense of deprivation of basic needs. But neither does the case of Itabira fit easily into a frame of modernization, which has been used to explain falling fertility in wealthier countries. Instead, its rapid and continued decline suggests a combination of both models. Itabira has greatly preceded and exceeded this more general decline in Brazilian fertility. In 1970, when Brazil's total fertility rate was still almost five children per woman, the municipality of Itabira had a total fertility rate of 2.6. In other words, the fertility of Itabira in 1970 was slightly above the rate that Brazil had, twenty years later. This difference persisted as Itabira's fertility dropped to below replacement by 1991. This makes Itabira's fertility comparable to that of countries with the lowest known fertility rates in the world, such as Cuba, Spain, and Italy. What is most curious about this trend is that Itabira began experiencing a much lower fertility than on average in Brazil precisely at a moment when local working class households were doing quite well in terms of job creation for men and rising consumption. In the next section I will suggest a way that we might combine gender and economic analysis to understand this anomaly.

Gender and the Family: Patriarchy without the Patriarch

A central feature of social modernization in classic demographic transition theory is the emergence of a more democratic, non-patriarchal household. Gary Becker (1981) defined the altruistic household as one in which all members shared equally in resources and power, in contrast to patriarchal systems which repress or bypass the needs of women and children. In Becker's formulation, which also predicted smaller families, women and men were increasingly able to discuss their reproductive preferences and goals in an open and democratic fashion. The division of labor that would become paradigmatic of the modern family did not typically include a working wife, but instead a "natural" division of labor based on increased investment in children's well-being. Being an altruistic operation, the nuclear family would automatically reward women and children through a family wage.

Among the company families in Itabira there is only superficial compliance with this model. This is not because, as most feminists would argue, that women indeed work outside the home in great numbers. In fact, they didn't in Itabira until after the 1970s. When women did go into the work force, it was very much in the shadow of their men and to this day highly prepared women are grossly under-remunerated next to men of much lower educational status. Recall that the company did much to enhance the nuclear, stable, home-owning family dependent on one male breadwinner and was fairly successful in doing so, even with women working outside the home. But if we look a bit deeper we see an extremely contradictory and tense coexistence of patriarchal privilege, middle class consumption standards, and women's constrained economic opportunities, that together have probably reinforced a plunging fertility.

The company created a world in which working men were put on a pedestal by women and the community. The uniform, the job, the camaraderie, and privilege were extremely attractive to young women, according to informants. In exchange for this status, men were expected to never say no to the company's demands. As the company expanded in the 1960s and 1970s, these demands were intense, and men's devotion to the company left women alone and lonely. Women I interviewed expressed this as gaining the status of being married to a company man, in exchange for the benefit they might otherwise have of having a man in the house (Chase 2001). Daughters of CVRD employees complained their fathers were never home, and some women have compared the CVRD to an "other woman" (Chase 2001). This was not unique to Itabira, as other studies on time and family life abundantly show in the world of male—and increasingly female—workaholics (Aitken 1998; Hochschild 1997). As Allen, Massey, and Cochrane (1998) point out in the case of high tech workers in England, the intensification of highly regarded work tends to pull men away from their homes, deepens the split between private and public spheres, and promotes the colonization of the former by the latter.

What made life for Itabiran women most difficult under these conditions was that their independence was restricted by the extremely low valuation of other paid work in Itabira in the shadow of the mining company. Ironically, women were neither blatantly restricted from meaningful public work, nor from meaningful public life. Indeed, they spent many years in excellent schools and have increased their participation in the labor market. However, both activities have been clearly demarcated as adding to the status of company families rather than as critical for their survival and development.

Education and Economic Participation of Women

Almost all reproductive studies today recognize the importance of educational opportunities for girls and women. Almost universally, as the level of education for females improves, fertility drops. The mechanisms behind this association are not well understood. Is it through better-educated women's greater access to good jobs and higher pay that this association works? As I showed earlier, the advances made by women in Itabira in education and work did little to ensure them a rewarding place in the local labor market at least in terms of their wages. Can education influence fertility independently of its direct effects on women in the job market? Other studies suggest that it might. Sri Lanka and Kerala provide some examples of poor societies where women are highly educated, where women are not entering employment at rapid rates nor benefiting from the jobs they are able to secure, and yet where fertility has declined dramatically nonetheless (Yapa and Siddhisena 1998; Nieuwenhuys 1994). In a similar way, Cuban women also moved very quickly to lower their fertility after the Revolution. Although their educational achievements did not produce notable individual wealth for women, they have increased women's participation in the public arena through work and political participation (Cervera 1996).

In Itabira, the daughters of company men attended good elementary and junior high schools, and many of them finished high school. But because they have had little access to jobs, as individuals these women gained little from their advanced schooling besides frustrated ambitions. This is particularly true of women who are married to men of lower rank within the CVRD who often restrict their wives' access to work outside the home. It is the context of this long-standing frustration, along with more recent fears for their families' well-being, that we can understand another facet of women's desire for much smaller families. In interviews, women usually inscribed their reproductive strategies within a desire to transfer their own unfinished and frustrated ambitions to their children.

Education and the Future

As I have mentioned already, the level of consumption for CVRD workers and their families was exceptional in the context of Brazil. Buffeted by subsidies and stable wages, families were able to accumulate a number of consumer items and services of which most working class Brazilians could only dream. One of these services was subsidized education for children. This is now greatly reduced by the downsizing and privatization of CVRD.

The education of children is a key theme stated by women as they face the future after privatization. The cost of educating children effectively has risen for two reasons. First and most obviously, the cost of education for families has increased because the CVRD has withdrawn its subsidies by 40 percent, as I described earlier. Secondly, this picture suggests other contradictions to sustainable inter-generational economic growth in Itabira. Education and social mobility are still highly valued and supported by local institutions, but education is no longer providing young adults with access to jobs in the company or even in the city. This leads many families to send their teenagers to other cities for high school and college, although the whole family rarely moves. So for education to remain an effective means for advancement in the context of local economic downsizing, we can assume its cost for families has risen more quickly than subsidies have declined.

Family Planning and Reproductive Agency

This story would be incomplete if we did not take into account the availability of family planning technologies for women in Itabira. According to many demographers, the most powerful direct or "proximate" determinant of fertility decline in developing nations has been access to and use of modern contraceptive technologies such as the birth control pill, sterilization, and intra-uterine devices (Yapa and Siddhisena 1998). Reproductive care in Itabira has a reputation for being exceptionally good by Brazilian standards. The standard of medical treatment as a result of the presence of the CVRD has benefited the public sector where many low income people seek treatment in ten neighborhood clinics. In 1993, a study of public health in the city of Itabira found that the number of general practitioners working in public clinics and hospitals exceeded recommended standards by 50 percent (Município de Itabira 1993, Table XXIII).[13] In these clinics, doctors and nurses distribute free IUDs, pills, injectables, and condoms.

Nonetheless, I hesitate to attribute the low fertility of Itabira solely to the availability of clinics and modern birth control methods. High levels of abortion and sterilization are indicators in most societies that women have poor access to information and are unhappy with their choices of reversible methods. The number of curettages in public hospitals points to a high number of abortions in Itabira, also confirmed by interviews with doctors and nurses in Itabira. According to municipal records, the second and third most common type of surgery in the city's two hospitals in 1992 was curettage (Município de Itabira 1993, Tables XXIII and XXV).[14] Many women with children talked about their inability to find a secure and dependable birth control method. Over half the women I interviewed had experienced contraceptive failure while on the pill or believed they would if they took it. The lack of confidence in existing reversible methods led them increasingly towards the decision to undergo sterilization. Sterilization operations have never been difficult for CVRD women to secure, and indeed most women eventually opted for this method and had the operation paid for by the CVRD. Non-company women however were in a constant battle in 1996, when I first visited Itabira, to find the right method for them, and were being pushed to accept the IUD almost indiscriminately as an alternative to the sterilization operation.

I predict that this bifurcated system of contraceptive delivery will begin to affect local company women as they lose access to company subsidies. According to public health personnel, as the CVRD has begun to pull back resources for family health, these families are beginning to crowd into free municipal clinics, which are also losing funds.[15] Other resources are seriously lacking in the public health sector of Itabira,[16] which will only be aggravated as CVRD employees begin to visit these public clinics in greater number. Given the dependence of the municipality on the company, it is likely that these public resources will continue to be scaled back in response to shrinking revenue just as women are made more vulnerable by economic change.

Not only will overall care diminish, the array of reproductive choices (especially access to sterilization) that more privileged company women expect may also change. Although considered of high quality, the public clinics produce a much more restricted set of contraceptive choices for women than private clinics and doctors subcontracted by the CVRD. The most visible difference is that public sector doctors in Itabira follow a much stricter code of ethics that restricts access to sterilization of men and women. The different treatment by public and private doctors led to a double standard for women. Those connected to the private doctors of the CVRD could negotiate their sterilization operations more easily, either on demand or as the solution to a medical condition. Women seeking public assistance have recently found it almost impossible to have an operation, as doctors applied the strict medical code of ethics that described sterilization as mutilation (*lesão corporal*). This separate and unequal access to health care has begun to affect the families of company employees who have seen their co-payment rise in their health plans and are increasingly reliant on the public system.

As support for families disappears in Itabira with the downsizing of the CVRD, as discussed above, women have become more adamant about finding a completely foolproof contraceptive method as a way to manage the uncertainty they are facing in the local economy (see Gudeman and Rivera-Gutiérrez, this volume, for a discussion of uncertainty). The extraordinary demand for sterilization and clandestine abortions that are so much a part of the Brazilian reproductive scenario will no doubt continue at an even more intense pace in Itabira. It is quite likely that the demand for sterilization will rise in Itabira just as the supply will diminish with further cutbacks in health spending. This will occur even though national policy has become more permissive about who can legally have a sterilization operation today in public hospitals.[17]

Conclusion

The discourses surrounding privatization and neoliberalism are contentious, in Itabira as they are elsewhere. Some people in Itabira see the death of the "sweet mother" as the deliverance of individualism, hard work, and independence (Schild 1998). For others, the substitution of the mother by a more dangerous female spells the death of love and caring in public life. These contradictory feelings mirror debates elsewhere about the future of the welfare state and the role that families and women, in particular, should take on to ensure themselves access to resources for survival. The liberal state has come under attack as the "nanny state" in Australia and the United Kingdom, and gendered images in the United States about welfare queens and unwed teenage mothers abound (Sawer 1996; McDowell 1991). Public discourse in Latin America and the Caribbean about single mothers is beginning to mimic the moralistic tone of similar discussions in the United States. Shifting the burden of economic and social support to families and women suggests two contradictory principles. One is that economies must be modernized in countries where free labor markets have been hindered by a strong interventionist and paternalistic state. The other is that the traditional roles of families as caring associations must be reinforced in order to ensure the reproduction of this labor (Schild 1998). This appeal to the modernization of capitalism through the traditionalism of private institutions suggests numerous ways in which the neoliberal project rests on an oversimplified separation of public and private lives. In this chapter I have looked at how one aspect of neoliberal reform, the privatization of a state-run enterprise, is creating tensions and preliminary responses by families and women in Itabira. Privatization, and neoliberal reforms more generally, occur in space and time. It is thus impossible to generalize about this strategy without understanding the unique social and cultural base of production that is being dismantled today by privatization in many regions and towns.

Women in Itabira on the whole have brought their fertility to extremely low levels. I have argued that this determination to have smaller families will probably become even more intense in the post-privatization lifestyle taking shape in Itabira. If patriarchy drove down levels in the 1970s, women now have even greater motivations to lower their fertility as their standard of living is substantially threatened, state supported services are in decline, and they are having no choice other than go into a precarious labor market. I finished this chapter with examples of how women use their own fertility as a means to ensure their children remain middle class citizens during neoliberal restructuring. This strategy underscores the intersections between production, class, place, and gender that feminist geographers have been working toward.

Notes

1. The loss of fundamental natural resources, many of which are not well inventoried, to foreign owners, and the undemocratic process by which the privatization program has been carried out in Brazil have also been sharply critiqued. Many argue that state resources are being sold well beneath their true market value and in ways that are not being sufficiently debated in public (Pinheiro 1996; Veltmeyer, Petras, and Vieux 1997).
2. Women's labor market participation may not have given them economic security or independence, but it did openly challenge men's control over their time and space. Women I spoke with in Itabira talked of how defying their husbands was a learning process for their husbands, who ended up accepting their wives' greater independence and benefiting from the additional family income as well.
3. In Brazil, law school and medical school are five-year courses that begin as soon as a student begins college.
4. Free neighborhood medical clinics, the pride of Itabira's wealthy city government, have recently become over taxed with requests for care by CVRD employees who cannot afford to pay the new co-payments and pharmacy costs which have come about as part of the company's rationalization of social costs.
5. A local newspaper reported the suicide of a young man whose parents attributed his anguish to not finding a job in Itabira after high school graduation.

6. Interview with mining expert and labor activist Lourival Araújo de Andrade, Belo Horizonte, July 1998.
7. Pulmonary problems such as asthma and bronchitis are chronic in Itabira (Ferreira 1995). In customary irony, one of my informants said "The air here is pure. It's pure minerals!"
8. Until recently, telephones in Brazil were purchased or rented by private individuals, and monthly bills and connection fees were paid to state-run phone companies. The cost of a phone line in Brazil has hovered around $2,000.
9. Construction and industry would include all manner of manufacturing, including artesanal manufactures, dressmaking, and food preparation.
10. Even that is no longer guaranteed, as the municipality, as in many Brazilian towns, often misses payroll.
11. The minimum wage in 1991 was roughly $100 per month. Of those college graduates that earned over twenty times the minimum wage, there were 201 men and only twenty women. These data are from the 1991 data set of the Brazilian Demographic Census.
12. Helen Safa (1995, 119) is an exception, although fertility change is not central to her work. She sees the drop in fertility in the Dominican Republic as "one area where . . . Dominican women . . . are clearly challenging male authority." In addition, Safa notes that since the 1980s Dominican women have been seeking sterilization in huge numbers as a result of the pressures placed on them to join the work force as the men in their lives become less able or willing to support them and their children. Her work exemplifies the multiple paths to lower fertility in poor populations.
13. The number of general practitioners was thirty in 1993.
14. For some reason the data on surgeries do not include cesarean sections, which are included under "delivery" in hospital admissions data. The numbers of hospital curettages—140 in 1992—are obviously not representative of total abortions in Itabira.
15. Between 1990 and 1993, the distribution of funds to health dropped from 15 percent to 10 percent of the municipal budget (Município de Itabira 1993, Graph V).
16. The Municipality estimates that only 46 percent of the ideal number of publicly funded medical examinations took place in 1992 (Município de Itabira 1993, Table XLI).
17. In 1997, the Brazilian Congress passed a law that changed some of the restrictions on sterilization. This included the reduction in the minimum age from 35 to 25 years, and parity was reduced from three to two children. However, a waiting period of six months between their last birth and the operation has been imposed.

References

Aitken, Stuart. 1998. *Family Fantasies and Community Space*. New Brunswick, N.J.: Rutgers University Press.

Allen, John, Doreen Massey, and Allan Cochrane. 1998. *Rethinking the Region*. London and New York: Routledge.

Amadeo, Edward and Susan Horton, ed. 1997. *Labour Productivity and Flexibility*. New York: St. Martin's Press.

Becker, Gary. 1981. *A Treatise on the Family*. Cambridge and London: Harvard University Press.

Baer, Werner and Melissa H. Birch, ed. 1994. *Privatization in Latin America: New Roles for the Public and Private Sectors*. Westport: Praeger.

Bluestone, Barry and Bennett Harrison. 1982. *The Deindustrialization of America: Plant Closings, Community Abandonment, and the Dismantling of Basic Industry*. New York: Basic Books.

Carvalho, José Alberto Magno de and Wong, Laura Rodríguez. 1996. The Fertility transition in Brazil: causes and consequences. In *The Fertility Transition in Latin America*, edited by José Miguel Guzmán, Susheela Singh, Germán Rodríguez, and Edith A. Pantelides. 373–96. Oxford: Clarendon.

Cervera, Sonia I. Catasus. 1996. The sociodemographic and reproductive characteristics of Cuban women. *Latin American Perspectives*. 23:87–98.

Chase, Jacquelyn. 1997. Controlling labor commitment in Brazil's global agriculture the crisis of competing flexibilites. *Environment and Planning D: Society and Space*. 15:587–610.

———. 2001. In the valley of the sweet mother: gendered metaphors and domestic lives under a Brazilian state mining company. *Gender, Place, and Culture*. 8(2):169–187.

Conaghan, Catherine M. and James M. Malloy. 1994. *Unsettling Statecraft: Democracy and Neoliberalism in the Central Andes*. Pittsburgh and London: University of Pittsburgh.

Cooke, Phillip, ed. 1989. *Localities*. London: Unwin Hyman.

Cosío, María Eugenia Zavala De. 1996. The demographic transition in Latin America and Europe. In *The Fertility Transition in Latin America*, edited by José Miguel Guzmán, Susheela Singh, Germán Rodríguez, and Edith A. Pantelides. 95–112. Oxford: Clarendon.

Fernández-Kelly, María Patricia. 1983. *For We Are Sold, I and My People: Women and Industry in Mexico's Frontier*. Albany: State University of New York Press.

Ferreira, Vanja Abdallah.1995. *Desenvolvimento municipal, mineração e meio ambiente: o caso da CVRD em Itabira*. Senior essay in economics. Belo Horizonte: Federal University of Minas Gerais, Department of Economics.

Gibson, Katherine. 1991. Company towns and class processes: a study of the coal towns of Central Queensland. *Environment and Planning D: Society and Space*. 9:285–308.

Gill, Alison. 1990. Women in isolated resource towns: an examination of gender differences in cognitive structures. *Geoforum*. 1:347–358.

Glade, William, ed. 1991. *Privatization of Public Enterprises in Latin America*. La Jolla: Center for U.S.-Mexican Studies.

Glade, William with Rossana Corona, ed. 1996. *Bigger Economies, Smaller Governments: Privatization in Latin America*. Boulder: Westview.

Gontijo, Claúdio. 1996. *Levantamento das perdas econômicas, financeiras e ambientais de Itabira por efeito da atuação da Companhia Vale do Rio Doce*. Unpublished Document. Belo Horizonte.

González de la Rocha, Mercedes. 1994. *The Resources of Poverty: Women and Survival in a Mexican City*. Oxford, UK; Cambridge, USA: Blackwell.

Greenhalgh, Susan, ed. 1995. *Situating Fertility: Anthropology and Demographic Inquiry*. Cambridge, UK; New York, USA: Cambridge University Press.

Hartmann, Betsy. 1995. *Reproductive Rights and Wrongs: The Global Politics of Population Control*. Boston: South End Press.

Hochschild, Arlie Russell. 1997. *The Time Bind: When Work Becomes Home and Home Becomes Work*. New York: Metropolitan Books.

IBGE (Instituto Brasileiro de Geografia e Estatística). 1990. *Anuário Estatístico do Brasil*. Vol. 50.

Klak, Thomas, ed. 1998. *Globalization and Neoliberalism: The Caribbean Context*. New York: Roman and Littlefield.

Klubock, Thomas Miller. 1998. From welfare capitalism to the free market in Chile: gender, culture and politics in the copper mines. In *Close Encounters of Empire: Writing the Cultural History of U.S.-Latin American Relations*, edited by Gilbert Joseph, Catherine C. Legrand, and Ricardo D. Salvatore. Durham, Duke University Press. 369–399.

Let the party begin. 1997. *The Economist*. 26 April: 57–59.

Lima, Edilberto Carlos Pontes. 1997. Privatização e desempenho econômico: teoria e evidência empírica. Brasilia and Rio de Janeiro: IPEA (Instituto de Pesquisa Econômica Aplicada). Discussion paper number 532.

Massey, Doreen. 1991. The political place of locality studies. *Environment and Planning A*, 23:267–81.

McDowell, Linda. 1991. Restructuring production and reproduction: some theoretical and empirical issues relating to gender, or women in Britain. In *Urban Life in Transition*, edited by M. Gottdiener and Chris G. Pickvance. 77–105. Newbury Park, London and New Delhi: Sage Publications.

Minayo, Maria Cecília. 1986. *Os homens de ferro: estudo sobre os trabalhadores da Vale do Rio Doce em Itabira*. Rio de Janeiro: Dois Pontos.

Município de Itabira. Secretaria Municipal de Saúde de Itabira. 1993. *Análise da situação saúde em Itabira. Anexo I: relatório das fontes secundárias*. Itabira: Município de Itabira.

Nieuwenhuys, Olga. 1994. *Children's Lifeworlds: Gender, Welfare, and Labour in the Developing World*. London: Routledge.

OECD. 1996. *Privatisation in Asia, Europe, and Latin America*. Paris: OECD.

Petrazzini, Ben A. 1996. The labor sector: a post-privatization assessment. In *Bigger Economies, Smaller Governments: Privatization in Latin America*, edited by William Glade with Rossana Corona. 347–68. Boulder: Westview.

Pinheiro, João César de Freitas. 1996. *Companhia Vale do Rio Doce: o engasgo dos neoliberais*. Belo Horizonte: self-published.

Potter, Joseph. 1996. The social consequences of rapid fertility decline during a period of economic crisis. In *The Fertility Transition in Latin America*, edited by José Miguel Guzmán, Susheela Singh, Germán Rodríguez, and Edith A. Pantelides. 275–88. Oxford: Clarendon.

Radding, Cynthia. 1997. *Wandering Peoples: Colonialism, Ethnic Spaces, and Ecological Frontiers in Northwestern Mexico, 1700–1850*. Durham and London: Duke University Press.

Roberts, Bryan R. 1991. Household coping strategies and urban poverty in a comparative perspective. In *Urban Life in Transition*, edited by M. Gottdiener and Chris G. Pickvance. 35–68. Newbury Park, London, and New Delhi: Sage Publications.

Safa, Helen. 1995. *The Myth of the Male Breadwinner: Women and Industrialization in the Caribbean*. Boulder, San Francisco, and Oxford: Westview Press.

Sánchez, Manuel and Rossana Corona, ed. 1993. *Privatization in Latin America*. New York: Inter-American Development Bank.

Sawer, Marian. 1996. Gender, metaphor and the state. *Feminist Review*, 52:118–134.

Schild, Verónica. 1998. *Neoliberalism's New Gendered Market Citizens: The "Civilizing" Dimension of Social Programs in Chile*. Paper presented to conference Space, Place, and Nation: Reconstructing Neoliberalism in the Americas. November 1998. University of Massachusetts, Amherst.

Standing, Guy. 1999. *Global Labour Flexibility: Seeking Distributive Justice*. New York: St. Martin's Press.

Tardanico, Richard. 1997. From crisis to restructuring: Latin American transformations and urban employment in world perspective. In *Global Restructuring, Employment, and Social Inequality in Urban Latin America*, edited by Richard Tardanico and Rafael Menjívar Larín. 1–46. Miami: North-South Center.

Thompson, E.P. 1963. *The Making of the English Working Class*. New York: Pantheon Books.

Veltmeyer, Henry, James Petras, and Steve Vieux. 1997. *Neoliberalism and Class Conflict in Latin America: A Comparative Perspective on the Political Economy of Structural Adjustment*. New York: St. Martin's.

Weinstein, Barbara. 1997. Unskilled worker, skilled housewife: constructing the working-class woman in São Paulo, Brazil. In *The Gendered Worlds of Latin American Women Workers: From Household and Factory to the Union Hall and Ballot Box*, edited by John D. French, and Daniel James. 72–99. Durham and London: Duke University Press.

Yapa, Lakshman and Padmasiri Siddhisena. 1998. Locational specificities of fertility transition in Sri Lanka. *GeoJournal*. 45:177–88.

6

Women and Globalization: Lessons from the Dominican Republic

Helen I. Safa

Economic globalization still generates enthusiasm among some neoliberal scholars. It is also true that globalization has helped to bring unprecedented prosperity to the United States, and to some middle class women who have risen to leadership positions in the government and private business. Globalization has produced greater equality between educated middle-class women and men while creating greater inequality between women. Globalization reinforced the increasing participation of women throughout the world in the paid, non-agricultural labor force, but most of these women are confined to low-paying jobs, often in the informal sector, without protection, security, or hope of mobility. For example, in Japan 70 percent of the 2.5 million part-time workers who have joined the labor force since 1995 are women, and one-fourth of these women are the main breadwinner (Kamo 2000). So, despite its promise of greater economic prosperity for all, globalization has produced greater class, gender, and regional inequality.

Globalization is based on ". . . a movement toward a world economy characterized by free trade, free mobility of both financial and real capital, and rapid diffusion of products, technologies, information, and consumption patterns" (United Nations 1999, xv). The internationalization and fragmentation of production produce fierce competitiveness among developing countries seeking foreign investment by maintaining a low level of wages and non-wage labor costs and high productivity. While purporting to be a universal economic model, the principles of globalization have been applied selectively. Capital flows from developed countries have been primarily to selected countries in East Asia (principally China), Central America, and the Caribbean, with a disciplined, highly productive but cheap labor force.

Cheap labor thus becomes a comparative advantage in specific world areas, and women provide much of this cheap labor.

This feminization of labor characterized by flexible, casual, and informal work has led to a decline in full-time, permanent wage employment, among men as well as women, with lower rates of male labor force participation, lower real wages, and higher rates of unemployment (Standing 1999). Some decline in occupational segregation and in the male-female wage gap in developed countries such as the United States may be as much a product of a deterioration in male employment as the result of women's advances (United Nations 1999, 16).

This chapter cannot deal adequately with all the aspects of women and globalization, which also include positive achievements such as the growth of an international women's movement and the recognition of women's rights as human rights. Because of time, and my own area of expertise, I shall confine myself to an analysis of gender and the globalization of work, using the Dominican Republic as the backdrop to this analysis. However, I shall not deal only with the workplace, but examine the implications of women's increased labor force participation on gender relations and family structure. A previous book of mine (1995) analyzed women industrial workers in Cuba, Puerto Rico, and the Dominican Republic. I argued that the male breadwinner model, where the man is considered the principal provider in the household and women are at best supplementary wage earners, is being eroded with economic structuring resulting from globalization. As women bear increasing responsibility for basic household expenses, they acquire greater control over the household budget and basic decisions. At the same time, marital bonds have grown more fragile, often resulting in the formation of female-headed households. This chapter presents additional data from a recent study in a Dominican community to the northwest of the capital city Santo Domingo, Villa Altagracia. This community had undergone a rapid change from sugar production to garment export processing, producing dramatic changes in the gender and age composition of the labor force, and consequent gender relations. In an addition, I will look at debates surrounding the regulation of labor by the international labor movement.

Export-led Industrialization in Villa Altagracia

The Caribbean has long depended on exports for economic growth. The plantations established during the colonial period grew sugar, coffee, tobacco, and fruits for export to their mother countries. The long period of colonialism, which in the Hispanic Caribbean lasted until the 19th century (and that is still prevalent in Puerto Rico), weakened the sense of autonomy and the development of a national bourgeoisie. In addition, these were small states lacking great mineral wealth or other natural resources. They were also sharply divided by race and ethnicity, brought on by years of slavery and indentured labor. Many of the characteristics today associated with globalization can be found in the Caribbean historically. Even so, Caribbean economies have entered a new phase of globalization, in which multinational corporations and international lending agencies like the World Bank and the International Monetary Fund now play a hegemonic role.

The Dominican Republic has moved rapidly since 1960 from an agricultural economy based on sugar exports and import substitution industrialization to a service economy dependent on tourism, export manufacturing, and agribusiness. The country remained dependent on sugar exports until the early 1980s, when the United States drastically cut its sugar quota. The emphasis shifted to export manufacturing, and during the 1980s, the Dominican Republic became the leading garment manufacturer in the Caribbean Basin, producing mostly for the U.S. market.

Strong state incentives combined with tariff initiatives offered by the United States under the Caribbean Basin Initiative (CBI) and other programs led to an employment boom in export manufacturing, where the mostly female labor force expanded from 20,000 workers in 1980 to 182,000 in 1997, when this study was conducted (Consejo Nacional de Zonas Francas de Exportación [CNZFE] 1998). Labor costs were also lowered during this period, due principally to currency devaluations mandated by structural adjustment. As a result, the real hourly minimum wage declined 62 percent between 1984 and 1990 (Fundapec 1992, 32). The hourly wage of U.S. $0.56 an hour in 1990 was one of the lowest in the Caribbean.

Though export manufacturing generated jobs for women, it had a dampening effect on male employment, due not only to a decline in sugar production, but in import substitution industries, where men predominated. Domestic manufacturing has actually suffered a loss in employment and investment since 1980 (Itzigsohn 1997, 51). In the 1980s, female labor force participation rates grew at a higher rate than those of men (Itzigsohn 1997, 51). Nationally, however, unemployment continues to be higher for women than for men, and men's average wage is still much higher than that of women. In addition, as I will show in greater detail later, men's participation in free zone employment in the Dominican Republic has been increasingly rapidly, especially in the more desirable and higher paying jobs. Desite the efforts at collective bargaining, labor organizing has left women with little sense that their lives are going to improve within the export sector. The convergence of patriarchy, continued low wages, and an unresponsive institutional environment has led many women in the export processing zones of the Dominican Republic to turn to international migration.

In Villa Altagracia, a town 30 kilometers north of the capital of Santo Domingo, the changes in the gender composition of the labor force have been even more dramatic. The town's economy had been dominated for 40 years by a large, state-owned sugar mill that closed in 1986 due to low prices, low productivity, and a cut in the U.S. sugar quota. A free trade zone took over the existing buildings, including a large, Korean-owned garment plant employing about 2,500 workers (most of whom were women) and two smaller plants. Villa Altagracia thus presents in microcosm the changes from sugar production to export manufacturing that have taken place in the Dominican Republic more generally since 1980. In Villa Altagracia, unemployment is much higher among men than among women, particularly among older, unskilled workers who could not find new jobs in the city. According to one former mill worker, "Before the father worked and maintained his family, but now it is the children who work," implying a change in the age as well as the gender composition of the labor force.

Our study included interviews with former sugar mill workers, many of whom continue to reside in Villa Altagracia in the single family frame houses ceded to them by the mill after it closed. Many of these former workers are over 60 and receive a modest pension of about U.S. $85 a month from the mill, which combined with informal work such as vendors and carpenters provides them with an average monthly household income of about U.S. $284. Younger members of the household, especially daughters employed in the free trade zone, also contribute to this household income, but as long as they are living in the paternal home, they defer to the father's authority. Ninety percent of these men claim that they are the head of the household, although they often live with children and grandchildren. Some of these older men are very resentful of the independence which paid employment has conferred on women working in the free trade zone. Tomás at 72 has had seven children with three women, and is now raising his two youngest. He claims that women working in the free trade zones are a ". . . disaster. They have to dress pretty, they have to go clean everyday, they cannot even be touched (*si ni que las toquen*)." Men accuse the women of "having fun with men," of spending their money in bars and beauty salons, and contributing little to the household economy. This stereotype appears to reflect men's resentment at the erosion of their authority and the shattering of a gender hierarchy in which men were in authority as principal breadwinners and women were, at best, supplemental wage earners.

Though it has been more than a decade since the closing of the sugar mill, Villa Altagracia never recovered from this blow. The mill was not only the town's principal employer. It also supported many social services such as sports clubs, health clinics, a pharmacy, schools, bus transportation to the capital for university students, and even caskets for impoverished residents. With declining budgets, municipal authorities have been unable to fill the gap, and public services are deteriorating. Villa Altagracia has severe shortages of electricity and potable water, and the sewage system has deteriorated as the mill no longer maintains it. There is no garbage collection, and most streets are unpaved and in poor condition. With the continuing influx of people from surrounding rural areas, housing is at a premium. In 1997, 20 families had been occupying a school after their own houses burned. Health problems abound, including child malnutrition and a high incidence of AIDS. Though they had been approached by municipal authorities, the Korean-owned factory refused to provide funds for town improvement, even for a street light at the factory exit. The Korean management mingles little with town residents, and resides apart in the better housing once reserved for the mill's administrative elite, replicating the class hierarchy of sugar production.

Women Workers and Gender Relations

The Korean-owned garment plant has replaced the paternalism of the sugar mill with rigid factory rules emphasizing high productivity, tight discipline, and total obedience. They know they are by far the most important employer in town. The two smaller plants employ fewer workers, and pay less. The minimum weekly wage in 1997 was RD 447 per week, close to the national minimum wage, but with incentives and overtime, most workers make about RD 600 (U.S. $50) per week. Incentives are paid for high productivity and perfect attendance. Absenteeism is severely penalized and more than two unexcused absences can lead to dismissal. Turnover is a major problem, because workers become exhausted from 10-hour workdays, and many women work nights if required. Workers complain that they are fired if they refuse to work overtime, which is especially difficult for young mothers who have not seen their children all day.

The young mothers we interviewed, all of whom are under 30 and employed primarily at the large plant and at one of the smaller garment factories, completely reject the image of the irresponsible, promiscuous women that men in Villa Altagracia have painted of them. Many have children they support on their own with little or no assistance from the children's fathers. Maritza at 24 has been working in the free trade zone for 9 years, and has a three-year-old child. The father works and lives in the capital, and provides some money for schools and medicine, but Maritza lives with her parents. Single mothers who live with their parents or other relatives normally pay them a basic stipend to cover rent and food, while paying other expenses themselves, but this is still much cheaper than living on their own. Maritza also studies at night and just managed to finish her high school degree. Maritza claims most women in the free trade zone are working to support their children, but that it was more difficult for women when the sugar mill was in operation. In the past, Maritza says, men ". . . worked and earned money for the home and did what they pleased, but now the woman works; she must support herself, clothe herself, buy shoes for herself; it cannot be the same (*Eran los que trabajaban y llevaban el peso a la casa y hacia lo que le daban la gana, pero ahora la mujer se va a trabajar, ella misma se mantiene, se viste, se calza, no puede ser igual*)."

Paid work has given women a new sense of autonomy, as Glenda, a married women with a one-year-old child, notes: "When one works, one feels more liberated, to manage one's own money . . . One feels more free to do anything because it is your own money. But when you are supported or they give you something, you have to be beneath the person who supports you." Her husband works in the free trade zone, but they cannot afford a home of their own, so they live with his parents.

Extended families play a critical role in supporting women workers, especially single mothers. They provide not only housing and other forms of financial support, but childcare for those who are employed. In extended households, there is an expectation that every adult will contribute in some way, but financial responsibility is flexible, adjusting to changing circumstances. Thus, Maria moved in with her parents and three brothers when the youngest of her three children became sick and she had to take care of him. Her husband is unemployed and does not live with Maria and her children. Maria had worked previously in the free trade zone and as a domestic servant in the capital. She claims her brothers do not complain about supporting her because she does the cooking and the housework (her mother is employed as a domestic worker in the city and only returns on weekends). She says: "When I worked, they didn't work, and I gave money to them." Now apparently it is her turn.

Mothers and daughters are especially flexible at exchanging roles, and reflect the strength of the mother-daughter tie in most Dominican families. Dominica at 47 has been in three consensual unions, and "raised her children (while) working in the factories." At her age, it would be difficult to find a factory job, so she stays home and watches her daughter's two young children while her daughter works in the zone and attends night school. Her daughter says she is lucky to have her mother's support, and Dominica claims: "I take care of her children and she studies at night. She is already in the second year of high school. If she really achieves something, then I also gain. I have to sit and take care of her children so that she can get ahead."

The flexibility of these complex, fluid household arrangements allows low-income households to survive and strengthens ties among consanguineal kin, often at the expense of the conjugal bond. An analysis of the 1991 nation-wide Demographic and Health Survey in the Dominican Republic revealed that though female heads of household earn less than male heads and have a much higher rate of unemployment, overall, family incomes for the two types are nearly equal (Duarte and Tejada 1995). Apparently female-headed households are able to raise their income level through the contributions of other family members, including remittances. Extended households include all relatives living under the same roof. Many of these are three generational. In the 1991 survey, extended families comprised 40 percent of all Domini-can households, and were more prevalent in urban than in rural areas. Extended households nationwide are found in 53 percent of the households headed by women, compared to 35 percent of those headed by men. They are even more prevalent among the middle strata than among the poor. This suggests that the incorporation of additional wage earners into extended households is a strategy used not only by the poor but also by the middle class to combat the economic crisis and the high cost of living.

The importance of extended families should not be seen simply as a response to economic crisis, but as a manifestation of the importance of consanguineal kin in low-income households in the Caribbean. Even in male-headed households, the strongest bond is often between mother and child and consanguineal kin, rather than the conjugal tie which is emphasized in the nuclear family (Fonseca 1991; Safa 1974; 1995). Our Eurocentric emphasis on the nuclear family as the norm and the embodi-ment of modernity and progress leads us to view female-headed households, and particularly single mothers, as pathological, rather than as an alterna-tive form of family with its own legitimacy. The assumption is that the family is centered on marriage or the conjugal bond, whereas in the Caribbean conjugal bonds are weak and unstable in comparison with consanguineal relationships, particularly among female kin (Safa 1999a; 1999b). Marital bonds have been weakened further by the decline in employment for men. This has eroded the man's authority as chief breadwinner. Raquel has two small children, aged one and three, and left her partner to return to live with her family when he could not find a job. She claims: "All Dominican men are bad . . . our grandmothers tell us." But unemployment has made men worse, because ". . . if he doesn't get work, then he can't help out. If you pressure him, he is resentful because he has no place to turn, to work." Raquel also claimed some men don't try hard enough to find a job and are supported by their partners working in the zone. Even unemployed men, however, rarely look after children or do household chores.

Labor Rights and Working Conditions in the Free Trade Zone

Globalization is also reflected in recent changes in labor conditions in the Dominican free trade zones, such as the growing percentage of men employed, the growing number of factories owned by Dominicans, and the new Labor Code of 1992. Since the early 1980's, the percentage of men employed nationally in the Dominican free trade zones has more than doubled to over 40 percent, and in technical jobs, they now outnumber women (CNZFE 1997, 25). Men predominate in the higher paid managerial, professional, or supervisory positions in the Dominican free trade zones (Fundapec 1992, 28), which helps account for the salary differential between men and women. In 1996 the average monthly salary in the free trade zones for women was U.S. $179 versus U.S. $250 for men. As Chase, in this volume, shows in her case study of a Brazilian company town, the occupational segmentation between men and women cannot be explained by educational levels, which in the Dominican free trade zones, as well as nationally, are now higher for women than for men. In 1991, 63 percent of women in the free trade zones had completed secondary school compared with 47 percent of men (Fundapec 1992).

This trend toward increasing male employment in export manufacturing has also been noted globally and is explained by the diversification of the export product towards higher value added, and the increasing capital intensity of production technology (United Nations 1999, 10). Diversification is evident in the Dominican Republic, where more men are employed in plants producing trousers, coats, and other heavier garments. However, men often perceive this as the deterioration of employment, as they are forced to seek jobs as operators in garment plants, which they formerly identified as women's work. One man who had been working in La Romana, another Dominican free trade zone, for 8 years, described his desperation at the conditions of this employment: "Work in the free trade zone is no good . . . You work because you have to and because there is no other source of income. The policies of managers are always to suppress, to squeeze you dry, when you want to demand your rights. Especially in this country, the laws are not carried out. The big fish eats the little fish."

Increased male employment in Dominican export manufacturing also reflects added protection for women resulting from a new Labor Code issued in 1992. Under this code, pregnant women are entitled to three months of maternity leave at half pay, and neither they nor women with infants can be fired. Given the high rate of pregnancy among young women workers, the Korean-owned plant in Villa Altagracia has insisted on a pregnancy test given to every female job applicant and to women workers monthly. This practice violates national and international labor rights, but it is difficult to identify and punish perpetrators. The new Labor Code passed in 1992 under pressure from organized labor in the Dominican Republic and the U.S. was designed to modernize a labor code passed by the dictator Trujillo, and to insure the right to collective bargaining for all workers. Since export manufacturing began in 1969, there was an informal prohibition on union activity in the free trade zones, and workers who were active in union activity lost their jobs, and were blacklisted from employment with other firms in the zones (Safa 1995).

Women workers are still reluctant to speak of their participation in union activity and, until recently, were not well represented in the leadership of the union movement, a traditionally male preserve. Workers are particularly happy at receiving an annual severance pay from the plants, which they mistakenly think is part of the Labor Code. Actually, employers introduced the annual severance pay as a way of reducing the costs of paying seniority on severance and other worker benefits, and as a way of getting rid of "undesirable" workers. By terminating all workers each December, workers who are suspected of labor union activity or other "irregularities" will not be rehired.

The new Labor Code stimulated the emergence of about 100 new unions, organized by the newly formed National Federation of Free Trade Zone Workers (FENETRAZONAS). FENETRAZONAS is affiliated with the National Confederation of Dominican Workers (CNTD), the largest of the three major Dominican labor confederations. The CNTD has the support of the American Institute for Free Labor Development (AIFLD), which petitioned the U.S. government to retract the tariff benefits the Dominican Republic received under the Generalized System of Preferences because of violation of worker rights. Two export licenses were canceled, both in Asian firms. The Dominican Ministry of Labor also brought sanctions against several firms for code violations, which is unusual because in the past, worker complaints of mistreatment or unjust dismissal had generally been rejected in favor of management (Safa 1995). However, government sanctions led to attacks of bias in favor of organized labor on the Ministry by an official of ADOZONA, the Dominican free trade company association, and they were later withdrawn (United States Department of Labor 1994–95). After protracted struggles in which several hundred workers lost their jobs, out of 114 unions registered in the free trade zones in 1995, only eleven had finally signed collective bargaining agreements with management by 1997 (United States Department of Labor 1998). The AIFLD withdrew its petition to the U.S. government, but UNITE (Unions of Needletrades, Industrial and Textile Employees of the United States and Canada) continues to support labor organizing in Dominican free trade zones.

In the Nicaraguan free trade zones, recent labor struggles have resulted in the firing of more then 150 union members, chiefly at a large Taiwanese garment plant. Nicaraguan salaries are even lower than in the Dominican Republic, and unemployment reaches 60 percent, while workers suffer from the same forced overtime and lack of union recognition taking place in the Dominican Republic. Taiwan, unlike Korea, has given hundreds of millions of dollars in aid to Nicaragua, chiefly to build government offices, and other Central American nations that support its readmission to the United Nations.

Globalization has forced U.S. labor unions to become more international and to abandon the protectionist stance they supported earlier. In the Spring of 1998, UNITE organized a tour of U.S. universities for three Dominican free trade zone workers, including two from the Korean-owned plant studied here. The purpose of this trip was to convince students and administrators at several Ivy League universities to adopt codes of conduct that would prohibit the purchase of products made under unfair labor conditions. (Kim 1998). This campaign has been quite successful and spread to many U.S. universities. Most large U.S. apparel companies operating in the Dominican Republic have implemented codes of conduct in recent years, but they generally rely on self-monitoring for enforcement, and firms still harass and fire workers who try to form unions (United States Department of Labor 1998, 7).

Two male union leaders I interviewed in 1997 in Villa Altagracia had not returned to work in the free trade zone since 1992. Despite several meetings with the Secretary of Labor and court hearings, their case had not yet been settled, and they had refused to accept the severance pay that the plant offered them to terminate their employment. The principal leader feels they were not given enough support by the labor confederation, two of which now vie to organize free trade zone workers. Competing labor confederations claim the pacts signed by FENETRAZONAS have not improved worker conditions, but it remains the only federation to have achieved a free zone collective bargaining agreement. The four chief labor confederations are characterized by intense rivalry and remain fragmented, chiefly because of ties to political parties (Espinal 1991).

In an interview with Jacobo Ramos, the Secretary-General of FENE-TRAZONAS, he explained that codes of conduct are a new strategy of targeting U.S. consumers to boycott products produced in overseas plants that violate labor laws and offer poor working conditions. However, Ramos warns that codes of conduct should not be seen as a substitute for collective bargaining contracts, and fears that monitoring of compliance with the codes by NGOs could create "conflicts of interest" and a vehicle for accommodation. Although Asian firms like the Korean-owned plant are the worst offenders, it is interesting that they have been singled out for condemnation, when there are many U.S. firms in the free trade zones of the Dominican Republic who also violate workers rights (Safa 1995). Undoubtedly, UNITE and AIFLD receive more support from U.S. multinationals in their attack on Asian companies in the Caribbean, who are resented for taking advantage of tariff provisions designed to benefit U.S. manufacturers.

Parity is another issue where a conflict of national interests may hinder efforts to organize workers across national lines. The apparel industry in the Caribbean has been hurt by not being included in the trade benefits provided under the Caribbean Basin Initiative (CBI). Although some apparel from the Dominican Republic and other countries in the Caribbean Basin enter the United States duty-free, they are limited to garments made entirely from U.S. made and cut fabric (Deere and Meléndez 1992). Competition with Mexico has increased as a result of the duty-free trade benefits the apparel sector enjoys under NAFTA. Government and business leaders in the Dominican Republic and other countries covered by the CBI have sought a parity proposal that would give their apparel sector equivalent trade benefits. U.S. retailers such as J.C. Penney also favor such a proposal, because it would make their products cheaper to buy. However, this parity proposal is opposed by both the U.S. textile industry and the very U.S. unions that have assisted in labor organizing in the Dominican free trade zones, because of the threat parity poses to U.S. workers. An effort in Congress to pass such a parity proposal for the Caribbean and Central America was defeated in November of 1999 (Bloomberg News 1999a; 1999b), but finally passed in October 2000 (although still limited to garments made from U.S.-made and cut fabric). Here we see how conflicting interests of U.S. labor, retailers, manufacturers, and now U.S. NGOs like the National Labor Committee, which has supported unionization in the free trade zones abroad and anti-sweatshop campaigns, forestall a concerted effort to improve labor conditions among the region's workers.

Ramos argues that business leaders have exaggerated the importance of parity for the Dominican market, and that parity must include a social clause that guarantees the rights of workers to organize and have a decent living, a provision which the AFL-CIO also supports. Ramos, who is also Vice-President of the International Federation of Free Trade Zones, speaks eloquently of the need for labor to internationalize in order to prevent conflicts between workers from the United States, the Dominican Republic, and Central America. He admitted he has been attacked in the Dominican Republic for siding too closely with U.S. unions, who some argue wish to close Dominican factories and return them to the United States. Though Ramos agrees that labor conditions and wages in the Dominican Republic and the United States can never be equal, he points to the inadequacy of a neoliberal model supported by international organizations like the World Bank, and the International Monetary Fund, which is accelerating poverty in the Dominican Republic. Ramos adds: "Because when the labor force is sick, when the labor force is badly paid, when the labor force has no type of work conditions, no country can develop on this basis, no country." As this case eloquently documents, the internationalization of labor is much weaker than the internationalization of capital, and cannot adequately protect workers from the exploitation of multinational corporations.

Dominican investment in the free trade zones is increasing since 1990. In 1992, Dominican plants represented one-fourth of all plants, especially in the apparel sector (CNZFE 1993). All of these Dominican-owned plants subcontract to United States and other foreign producers, who prefer to let them deal with labor problems and other troublesome issues on their own. Subcontracting or joint ventures is again part of a global trend to reduce the visibility of multinational corporations and to meet increasing competition. However, in the Dominican Republic, labor costs are so low and labor regulation so weak that multinationals have not had to resort to the informal sector or home-based work to further reduce labor costs. The inability to achieve parity with NAFTA and the growing importance of the apparel sector in Central America, where wages are still cheaper and labor discipline more severe, undermines the efforts of Dominican labor and the state to improve the labor rights and working conditions of workers in export manufacturing.

The Reassertion of Patriarchy and Women's Migration

As we can see from the above discussion, even the gains Dominican women have made in terms of increased labor force participation under globalization may be short-lived. In the free trade zones, men still predominate in the better paid technical and managerial jobs, and are increasing their numbers as operators as well. Attempts to address women's concerns, such as paid maternity leave, may result in women losing their preferential status over men in some apparel sectors.

What we are witnessing is a reassertion of patriarchy, and more specifically the male breadwinner model, at the institutional level by employers, labor unions, and political parties. The male breadwinner model, has been substantially eroded at the household level, as our female informants testify, but in my 1995 book, I maintained that this ideology still prevails at the level of the workplace and the state. It can be seen in the resentment men in Villa Altagracia feel toward women working in the free trade zones, accusing them of being frivolous and even promiscuous. It can be seen in employers' preference for men in supervisory positions and in the reluctance of labor unions to support women's leadership. Unions offer little relief from these abuses of women, as they only represent 10 percent of the labor force in the Dominican Republic, and are marked by corruption and fragmentation. These traits have begun to penetrate the recently created labor federation in the free trade zones.

Female workers have grown increasingly cynical, and prefer to pin their hopes for improvement on emigration, legally or illegally to the United States, Puerto Rico, Spain, and other areas. One earlier informant, who had previously been fired from her job in the free trade zone of La Romana for labor union activity, and now has left to work in St. Thomas as a hotel housekeeper, observed: "People are ready to risk their lives in order to leave the country. Everything is too expensive . . . imagine, here in the zone, where the majority depend on the zone and the sugar mill. A family cannot survive on 1,000 pesos."

Poor people risk their lives chiefly crossing the Mona Straits on 20-foot rafts to Puerto Rico, where lax border patrols have led to sharp declines in detainees since 1994. It is estimated that 5,000 people went to Puerto Rico from 1997 to 1999, joining a total Dominican population in Puerto Rico of approximately 100,000 (Anderson 1999). In Puerto Rico, migrants from the Dominican Republic are discriminated against as black and uneducated, much as they are in New York City, where the principal Dominican diaspora resides (Duany, Hernandez and Rey 1995; Duany 1994). Remittances from Dominican residents in the United States are estimated to exceed U.S. $1 billion annually, and along with tourism and the free trade zones, represent an important source of hard currency. Several of our respondents in Villa Alt-agracia received remittances from the United States, and one man even collected social security for the 10 years he had worked in New York City.

Why should people be leaving a booming economy that has been dubbed "the hottest in the Americas," with growth rates of 7 to 8 percent a year since 1996? Leonel Fernández, the North American-educated Dominican who assumed the Presidency in that year, made foreign investment a key concern. But as in many economies booming under globalization, inequality has also increased. Foreign investment in the free trade zones is based on cheap labor, and if wages rise, it will go elsewhere, like Central America. Under pressure from Adozona, the lobby of the free trade associations, the National Salaries Committee in 1997 set a minimum wage for large companies in free zones at 29 percent below the national minimum wage, which is already low (United States Department of Labor 1998, 7). Unemployment in 1997 still stood at 15.9 percent, a slight decrease over 1996.

As we have seen in Villa Altagracia, extended households where members pool resources from several sources are a major survival strategy, particularly for single mothers raising young children on their own. However, household strategies have their limits, as González de la Rocha (n.d.) demonstrates in a recent article analyzing the effects of the deepening of the economic crisis in Mexico in the 1990s. The exclusion of a large segment of the adult popula-tion from the formal labor market also reduces the possibilities of informal sector employment and other self-provisioning activities because people need money to engage in these activities. In Villa Altagracia, in particular the most affected people are older, unskilled men who had been displaced from traditional sources of employment in agriculture and heavy industry. Even mutual aid among kin is predicated upon a minimal amount of resources, so that González de la Rocha argues that her former "resources of poverty" model (González de la Rocha 1994), which she developed from household studies in the 1980s, has now been transformed into the "poverty of resources" model of the 1990s. The response, both in Mexico and the Dominican Republic, has been massive migration to the United States, which accelerated markedly in both countries in the 1990s. The Caribbean has long lived on the export of its labor, but now under the effects of globalization, larger, more diversified economies such as Mexico's, are being forced to do the same.

Conclusion: Inequality and the Global Labor Force

Women's migration out of the free trade zones of the Dominican Republic must be understood within the frames of a persistent and reinvigorated patriarchy, and the income inequality created by globalization. Globalization has increased inequality both between and within countries because it has benefited capital far more than labor. The Asian financial crisis swept through countries that were once considered the success stories of globalization. This paradox points to the enormous costs of globalization to domestic economies and workers when this model is fully applied. Even in developed countries, increasing numbers of workers have become part of the informal sector. Far from being archaic, this sector has become an integral strategy for lowering wages in the formal sector. Thousands of women, the majority of whom are Latin American and Asian immigrants, have lost their jobs in the garment industry in New York City and other parts of the United States and have been pushed into sweatshops or homework. In Europe, the proportion of women among homeworkers—most of whom are married women with young children—varies between 90 to 95 percent in Germany to 75 percent in Spain (United Nations 1999, 28). Wage polarization is growing in the United States and the United Kingdom between college-educated skilled workers (particularly those schooled in informatics) and unskilled, low wage jobs. Developing nations have become too weak to mediate between capital and labor, since the revenues of multinational corporations often exceed national budgets, and many are strapped by debt burdens and structural adjustment programs. But the governments of the G7 industrial countries could do more, and are increasingly being called upon to relieve growing world poverty, even by the leaders of the World Bank and the International Monetary Fund. American foreign aid declined an average of 8 percent annually in the 1990s and is the lowest of all rich countries. Rather than free trade and capitalism, the new consensus for fighting poverty calls on rich countries to provide more and debt relief, while reducing tariff restrictions on products produced by the poor, such as apparel in the case of the Dominican Republic.

Notes

A similar piece appears in the *Journal of Developing Societies*, Spring 2002, under the title "Women, Globalization and Inequality: Lessons from the Dominican Republic." Willowdale, Ontario: de Sitter Publications.

Some of the material used in this chapter was drawn from a piece published by the North-South Center at the University of Miami, with the title "Women coping with crisis: social consequences of export-led industrialization in the Dominican Republic" (Agenda paper #36, April 1999). I want to thank the North-South Center for funding this research project, and Jeffrey Lizardo of INTEC in the Dominican Republic for his able assistance.

References

Anderson, James. 1999. Dominicans risk Caribbean passage. *Associated Press*. October 24.

Bloomberg News. 1999a. U.S. bills for Africa, Caribbean imperiled by backers' demands. October 27.

———. 1999b. Senate passes Africa, Caribbean Free-trade measure. November 3.

Consejo Nacional de Zonas Francas de Exportación (CNZFE), Secretaría de Estado de Industria y Comercio. 1993. *Informe Estadístico 1992*, Sector de Zonas Francas. Santo Domingo, D.R.

Consejo Nacional de Zonas Francas de Exportación (CNZFE), Secretaría de Estado de Industria y Comercio. 1998. *Informe Estadístico 1997*, Sector de Zonas Francas. Santo Domingo, D.R.

Deere, Carmen Diana and Edwin Meléndez. 1992. When export growth is not enough: U.S. trade policy and Caribbean basin economic recovery. *Caribbean Affairs* 5:61–70.

Duany, Jorge, Luisa Hernandez, and César Rey. 1995. *El Barrio Gandul: economía subterránea y migración indocumentada en Puerto Rico*. Caracas: Nueva Sociedad.

Duany, Jorge. 1994. *Quisqueya on the Hudson: The Transnational Identity of Dominicans in Washington Heights*. New York: Dominican Studies Institute, City University of New York.

Duarte, Isis and Ramón Tejada Holguín. 1995. *Los hogares dominicanos: el mito de la familia ideal y los tipos de jefaturas de hogar*. Santo Domingo: Instituto de Estudios de Población y Desarrollo.

Espinal, Rosario. 1991. Between authoritarianism and crisis-prone democracy: the Dominican Republic after Trujillo. In *Society and Politics in the Caribbean*, edited by Colin Clarke. 145–165. Oxford: Macmillan.

Fonseca C. 1991. Spouses, siblings, and sex-linked bonding: a look at kinship organization in a Brazilian slum. In *Family, Household and Gender Relations in Latin America*, edited by Elizabeth Jelin. 133–160. UNESCO, Paris.

Fundapec (Fundación APEC de Crédito Educativo, Inc.). 1992. *Encuesta nacional de mano de obra*. Santo Domingo, Dominican Republic. Report prepared for Inter-American Development Bank.

González de la Rocha, Mercedes. n.d. The erosion of a survival model: urban household responses to persistent poverty. Unpublished manuscript.

―――. 1994. *The Resources of Poverty: Women and Survival in a Mexican City*. Oxford: Blackwell.

Itzigsohn, José. 1997. The Dominican Republic: politico-economic transformation, employment and poverty. In *Global Restructuring, Employment, and Social Inequality in Urban Latin America*, edited by R. Tardanico and R. Menjívar Larín. 47–77. Miami: North-South Center Press, University of Miami.

Kamo, Momoyo. 2000. Feminism and globalization: women 2000. *Proceedings of the Beijing Plus Five Global Feminism Symposia*. New York City, June 5–8. Co-sponsored by the Center for the Study of Women and Society, CUNY Graduate Center; National Center for Research on Women; and the Japan Preparatory Committee, Year 2000 Project.

Kim, Carrie. 1998. Caps for sale. *UNITE* 4:2425.

McClenaghan, Sharon Olivia. 1997. *Factory Work, Gender Relations, and Political Identity in the 1990s: Villa Altagracia, the Dominican Republic*. Ph.D. diss., University of Portsmouth, United Kingdom.

Safa, Helen I. 1974. *The Urban Poor of Puerto Rico: A Study of Development and Inequality*. New York: Harcourt Brace.

―――. 1995. *The Myth of the Male Breadwinner: Women and Industrialization in the Caribbean*. Boulder: Westview Press.

―――. 1998. Free markets and the marriage market: structural adjustment, gender relations, and working conditions among Dominican women workers. *Environment and Planning A* (30). 291–304.

―――. 1999a. Women coping with crisis: Social consequences of export-led industrialization in the Dominican Republic. Agenda paper 36, the North-South Center. Miami: University of Miami.

―――. 1999b. Female-headed households in the Caribbean: sign of pathology or alternative form of family organization? *Latino(a) Research Review*, 4:16–26.

Shaiken, Harley with Stephen Herzenberg. 1987. *Automation and Global Production: Automobile Engine Production in Mexico, the United States, and Canada*. La Jolla, California: Center for U.S.-Mexican Studies, University of California, San Diego.

Standing, Guy. 1989. Global feminization through flexible labor. *World Development*. 17:1077–1096.

―――. 1999. Global Feminization through flexible labor: a theme revisited. *World Development*, 27:583–602.

United States Department of Labor. 1994–95. Foreign Labor Trends: *Dominican Republic*. Washington, D.C.

―――. 1998. *Foreign Labor Trends: Dominican Republic*. Washington, D.C.

United Nations. 1999. 1999 *World Survey on the Role of Women in Development: Globalization, Gender, and Work*. Division for the Advancement of Women, Department of Economic and Social Affairs. New York: United Nations.

III

On the Edge
of Neoliberalism

7

Neither Duck Nor Rabbit: Sustainability, Political Economy, and the Dialectics of Economy

Stephen Gudeman and Alberto Rivera-Gutiérrez

Over the past decade and more, neoliberalism has swept through many parts of Latin America, influencing state practices, market forms, and ideological proclamations. As recently as the 1970s, structural policies such as limited protectionism with an emphasis on import substitution and focused state investment were important tools for achieving economic growth and a more equitable distribution of income. With the advent of neoliberalism and its emphasis on financial regulation, national markets have been increasingly "opened" to competitive forces and to privatization: state control has become more limited, subsidies on national goods and restrictions on imports are lowered, foreign capital is allowed greater entry, goods and services are removed from production and distribution in the public sector, and larger parts of material life are commoditized. Neoliberalism meshes well with economic globalization and the increased mobility of capital as an investment vehicle across national borders.

The impacts of neoliberalism, especially in relation to physical and conceptual spaces, are complex and finely interwoven, as Chase points out in her introduction to this book. For one thing, neoliberal policies and ideology offer little space for alternative practices and discourses on economy. The dismantling of state economic policies is tied closely to the presumption that the economy constitutes a separate, independent sector made up of atomic and bounded units of production and consumption that interact through markets. These units, underwritten as private property, "precede" state forms, though they also require legal backing through the state.

This neoliberal or classic picture of economy, however, represents a considerable simplification of real practices and institutions, especially in

Latin America, and in Guatemala more specifically. Economies have never consisted only of markets, nor is the market form their teleology. Considerable economic work is carried out in local realms—a factor not recognized in neoliberal ideology. In this essay, we shall look at economic practices at the local level. We want to bring into focus connections among globalization, neoliberalism, communities, and the environment. We hold that communities are local places in the economy but also may be important economic spaces that offer a very different way of relating to the environment—not as a separate object but as mediator between humans in community.

How we model the environment in conjunction with economy has become increasingly important, for evidence of environmental degradation is mounting. Global warming, desertification, water pollution, and depletion of the earth's resources attest to the planet's fragility. Latin America alone has witnessed its share of devastating environmental losses—water pollution, soil degradation, deforestation—and their impact on local groups. We shall propose that this process, heightened by market activities that are fostered by neoliberal policies, can be resisted and slowed by strengthening and expanding the community realm of economy. Market practices are not the only source of severe environmental change. Population growth and the workings of other economic formations, including socialist systems, have also taken their toll. But we argue for strengthening the role of human association in economy and the morality it offers in managing the world's physical heritage and countering some of the dynamics of market systems. We thus focus on the impact of the market realm of economy, influenced by neoliberalism, as it increasingly affects local places, and we argue for recognizing, representing, and understanding a second realm, community, without which any economy is incomplete.

In the spring of 1994, and earlier years, we carried out fieldwork in various locales of Guatemala, exploring the ways different communities manage their space and environment. The communities we examined ranged from relatively isolated Indian crops in highland regions to seacoast villages, collections of small scale agriculturalists, urban groups, and private organizations. Each community is organized around enduring social relationships and holds something in common, although they differ widely. Some represent a precolonial, colonial, or postcolonial heritage; others are informed by the ideal of market transactions or the language of ecological movements. As Pi-Sunyer also demonstrates in his chapter on the Maya of Quintana Roo, Mexico, all communities studied by us demonstrate how humans make and remake communities in relation to market practices. In approaching the problem of environment in this way, and by starting with practices, we are suggesting that one set of solutions to contemporary environmental problems needs to come from "outside" the realm of the market and private property, and that "the economy," as described and delimited by much contemporary discourse, does not encompass all forms of material behavior.

The Two Spheres of Material Life

All economies are built on the interacting realms of communal and commercial value. Material life is double-sided, for humans harbor feelings of both "mutuality" and "self-interest." For simplicity, we label these two realms, *community* and *market* (or trade). A communal value is a common or shared interest that may or may not have a material form. Market value is represented by price in money, although by an older terminology *value* (the underlying measure) and *price* (its financial expression) were distinguished. The first, communal realm, placing each of us within a matrix of social relationships that mediate material life in which communal projects take precedence over self-interest, offers a degree of predictability and provides one bulwark against material uncertainty. The second—the trade realm—situates individuals and groups as separate actors in material life, and represents an opening to the world of fortune, although ways of managing contingency are developed in this realm, too. In the market, the self-interest of the unit—whether an individual, family, or corporation—is a primary motivation for action and an underlying value of its practice. In reality, most institutions and actions are mixtures of the two modes, but they are constructed of just these two.

The market realm consists of short-term material relationships that are undertaken *for the sake of* achieving a project or securing a good. In the community realm, material goods are exchanged through relationships that are kept *for their own sake*. Sometimes the two spheres are separated in acts, institutions, and sectors. Sometimes they complement and join one another in unpredictable ways, but with one or the other being dominant; sometimes the realms envelop or interpenetrate each other so that features of one are categorized as if they were part of the other.

Each realm is partial. Neither is a total system. For example, material life based on the regime of social value can lead to self-sufficiency or autarky, but even in small house economies—as in Latin America—the complementary sphere of trade is part of material life. Conversely, no pure trade or market system exists without the support of communal agreements, such as shared languages, mutual ways of interacting, and implicit understandings. Communities are inside markets, as households, corporations, unions, guilds, and oligopolies, and contain them as nation-states that provide a legal structure for contracts and material infrastructure.

Many combined patterns have been recorded. There are dualistic or parallel systems as in the case of colonial regimes when a cross-national corporation makes use of a local, community economy through political power. Likewise, ports-of-trade—such as Portobello in old Panama—are international marketplaces that have been given a special time and quarantined place in a local economy (Boeke 1942; Geertz 1963; Polanyi, Arensberg, and Pearson 1957). There exist inner and outer relationships when a house economy is contained within a market economy as in rural Panama or in our own lives (although we now increasingly marketize transactions within the domestic family: both the affluent and less wealthy may pay for childcare providers, use premarital contracts, or employ low paid migrants to provide domestic services). Sometimes a market draws a surplus from a community economy, when subsistence farming supports cash cropping or when people undertake piecework or telemarketing from their homes at very low rates of remuneration. In the western world this long-term shift from community to market is often described as modernization, progress, and the triumph of rationality.

The two spheres may be institutionally and tactically interwoven, as in a "trade partnership," found in many parts of the world, in which two members of different groups located in different areas maintain an enduring relationship (communal), yet each aims to secure a monetary profit from the other (commercial).[1] Similarly, in the "trader's dilemma" (Evers 1994), a local merchant is caught between the aims of maximizing profit in selling and maintaining relationships with customers with whom he shares kinship, residential, or social ties. Likewise, the house-business in Latin America that combines the two modes is neither transitional nor on the road to modernization, but is enduring under certain conditions.

Most of us use both strategies every day. Some days we buy at an impersonal superstore that has no clerks and uses automatic checkouts, taking pleasure in anonymity, not having to talk with others, and securing a low price. Other days we buy at a small, nearby store so that we can support a business community or chat for a moment with a clerk or cashier, though at the cost of paying higher prices. Sometimes we go to both stores within the same hour, as if to seek a psychic balance; and some of us—ill-mannered or confused by this realm of social tactics—seek social contact in the anonymous store or avoid it in the communal one, thus producing quizzical if not curt responses in both. Material life is thus always double: communities generate anonymous exchanges inside themselves and at their borders; impersonal interactions presuppose and may nourish mutuality. The interplay is continual, and the relative importance of the two realms varies widely.

Humans also invent, make sense of, and interpret many micro-behaviors by projecting these building blocks onto practical action. Consider opening a door. Sometimes one does it for oneself: this is individual self-sufficiency. But sometimes one does it for another as an act of communality or social connection. Here the complications start. The communal courtesy can be an act of friendship, but until recently it was for males a gendered act indicating dominance, although one sometimes opens a door for a banker, businessman, or president, as an expression of submission. Nonetheless, all are acts within community, indicating social connection.

Conversely, a doorman at a hotel or restaurant may open doors. That is a market act, especially since the prices of the establishment will be raised to cover the doorman's pay. This act may be seen as a projection of communal relations, for the restaurant or hotel sells itself as an establishment of community, although the doorman may depend on communal tips for survival. Are the tips a market repayment for a service, a communal act of friendship that converts a market gain to community, a mystification of community relationships—or does their interpretation depend on the local context?

Women today are suing to be able to practice this male profession. This is an apt illustration of the way the realm of community helps structure market participation. Because part of the significance of the doorman's act is its gendered nature, contestation against this power and the closed labor market must originate in shifting communal expectations. From gender, to tips, to the projected sense of mutuality, the significance of the doorperson's act depends on its place as a material service within community and market that interact in shifting ways.

In contrast to this actual intertwining of trade and mutuality in everyday life, the two usually are separated by our knowledge systems or discourses, a feature that has become further endorsed by neoliberal ideologies of development. Throughout Western history various discourses about these two domains have been constructed from Aristotle (1984) on the polis or purely communal economy to contemporary neoclassical economics on the market. Most of these discourses segment the linked domains and highlight one while marginalizing and obscuring the presence of the other. For example, neoclassical economics, although it makes claims to universality, focuses on the commercial dimension only, thereby equating economy with market and defining material life in community as noneconomic. Today the language of neoclassical economics is dominant especially because it promises "efficiency" in the allocation of product, distribution of resources, and production of goods and services through markets. Communal transactions may achieve equity, but they cannot assure efficiency (which is most valued by the market). In contrast to such pure discourses that dominate our thinking about economies, we hold that most material practices are combinations of things. Economies are complex mixes, separations, and negotiations of the two realms of community and market.

Both dimensions of material life have their attractions, though today the market sphere dominates for the freedom and life-style it offers as well for its potential for accumulating wealth and dominating others through competition. Our purpose in exploring the diverse and multiple community side of the economy is not to propose a specific alternative to market life but to provide a language for and examples of this other realm. We want to point to its changing presence and forms so that a wider range of choices in managing the environment may be considered.

Commons and Capital

Social and natural relationships have a very different cast and temporality in the market and in the community. Communities, as we use the term, may be face-to-face, as in the case of the household, or imagined as in the nation state (Anderson 1991). They rarely encompass a person's total life or make up complete entities themselves. Often communities are organized around specific activities, and people participate in many different kinds of activities in their daily living. Communities may be hierarchically arranged, embedded, or overlapping. For example, cities comprise many communities, variously based on ethnicity, religion, school districts, wealth, recreational zones, and commerce. Each one of these communities is linked to a different social identity. The same principle holds in so-called small-scale societies. A "matrilineal" group in northern Colombia, for example, is made up of cross-cutting matricentral units, homesteads, uterine kin, females who garden together, males who herd together, and trekking groups (Rivera-Gutiérrez 1986). The composition of communities also shifts as affiliations are changed in authorized ways or by manipulating qualifications of membership, based on genealogy, marital status, language spoken, and place of birth. In modern times especially, "racial" purity has been invoked to constrict membership in private clubs, nation states, and the human race. The rules of inclusion also may be contested and altered as in the case of political struggles in the United States over which age groups and citizens qualify for community-supported welfare and health care. In the contemporary world, communities cross national borders sometimes with the goal of resisting market forces. As examples, animal rights groups, drawing on membership from around the world, slice the nets of fishing boats from one or another nation; money and help from different countries flow to victims of floods in the Midwest of the United States or in South Asia. Such acts depend on an imagined commonality between people in different places.

The community realm of the economy has several distinctive features: (1) a base or *commons*, and ways of maintaining that base through time; (2) the circulation of goods through processes of *allotment* that encode and ensure enduring moralities; (3) reliance on *situated*, contextual, or local *reasoning*; (4) a degree of *self-sufficiency* that becomes part of its identity; (5) an emphasis on "living well" or flourishing by maintaining social relationships; and (6) the use and control of external trade.

A community economy, above all, makes and shares a commons. We also term this feature the *base* or *foundation*, adapting some terms from Latin America. The base is a shared interest or value. It is the patrimony or legacy of a community and refers to anything that contributes to the material and social sustenance of a people with a shared identity: land, buildings, seed stock, knowledge of practices, a transportation network, an educational system, or rituals. As the lasting core, though changeable over time, the base represents temporality and continuity. Without a commons, there is no community; without a community, there is no commons.

Most modern economists—after Galileo, Descartes, and Locke—interpret the material commons of a people as an independent, objective entity that can be properly managed only by having expressly stated rights of access (Ostrom 1990). They re-read the commons as something separate from a human community, perhaps as a symbol of community but not the community itself. This market and modernist reading separates objects from subjects.

In our view, the commons is the material thing or knowledge a people have in common, what they share, so that what happens to a commons is not a physical incident, but a social event. Taking away the commons destroys community, and destroying a complex of relationships demolishes a commons. Likewise, denying others access to the commons denies community with them, which is exactly what the assertion of private property rights does. The so-called "tragedy of the commons" (Hardin 1968), that refers to destruction of a resource through unlimited use by individuals, is a tragedy not of a physical commons but of a human community, because of the failure of its members to treat one another as communicants and its transformation to a competitive situation.

Our use of the term *commons* is different in another way from that used by most contemporary economists and political scientists. For them, a commons is real property used by market agents and contained within a market. A commons is either an open access resource, freely available to all, or a common-pool resource, regulated by rules of use (Ostrom 1990). These theorists would show how control of certain scarce resources through social rules rather than competitive exchange supports market ends and the achievement of efficiency. Thus, they argue, market actors sometimes agree for reasons of self-interest to form limited economic communities with a commons. We think this formulation represents a misunderstanding of the social sphere of value, reduces the social to self-interest, and conflates community and market through the misapplication or imperialist use of the language of trade. Communities of the form we describe are not devised to serve market life. Irreducibly social, they operate for themselves as they relate to the world of trade.

Often a community economy does not despoil the environment as rapidly as a market economy does, because in doing so it despoils itself. A commons is regulated through moral obligations that have the backing of powerful sanctions. But communities are hardly homes of equality and altruism, and they provide ample space for the assertion of power and exploitation from patriarchy to feudal servitude. As expressed in European writing from Locke through Mill, one attraction of arranging society through exchanges born of private property and individual contract, and liberated of persisting social claims and ties, lies in the freedom it offers to all members to engage in economic and political transactions that are advantageous to them as individuals.

The substance of the base or commons varies widely, comprising more than real and productive property. For example, by communicating and sharing knowledge, scholars make a community. They hold and enjoy knowledge in common which sustains both community and individual goals. The base may be composed of land, natural resources such as water or minerals, or of a fishing or hunting domain. The commons may be a stand of trees, kept from human entry, held for recreational enjoyment, or maintained for long-term use. In Latin American cities, squatter settlements may form around a water supply, and then local associations begin to demand sewage and electricity services which become their commons. When Indian communities on Guatemala's Lake Atitlán reserve forest land from individual use, in order to preserve their water sources and keep wood for communal use, they add to their material commons and to their community. Communities are made thus around a commons that can be land, trees, animals, saints, dolphins, organic foods, ancestors, or the refusal to buy green grapes or redwood hot tubs.

The distinction between market and community is well captured by the contrast and similarity of capital and commons. If a key feature of market capitalism is making profits and their accumulation as capital, a central characteristic of community is making and sustaining its commons. Measured in money, profit arises through market transactions. But it is created by innovations that, in Schumpeter's expression, constitute "creative destruction." An innovation destroys the accepted or traditional—that which is common—as it creates the new (Schumpeter 1934[1926]). In this process, as new goods are introduced, value is created, and the heritage or legacy of market participants is expanded. On the Schumpeterian argument, the increment of new value created is initially embodied in a surplus of money secured by the "innovator" or entrepreneur. Money profit constitutes the return for the creative, accepted, and purchased addition to the commonweal. It is also private property as well as capital.

But like profit and capital, a base is also made and remade through innovations. For a community, innovations also expand the heritage or patrimony. These tokens at the margin, however, are not held by individuals, but are shared. Yet, what begins as profit in a market system eventually does become the "commons," for when a profitable innovation is broadly produced and held, it becomes a component of the general welfare or well-being through the new consumer goods, higher wages, and lower prices it brings. Conversely, as we shall suggest later, innovations for profit depend on the existence of a cultural legacy. Capital and commons are thus closely connected.

But what are the environmental or spatial implications of innovations and the expansion of value as capital or commons? In general, an innovation may or may not have a direct effect on the use of resources: sometimes a particular innovation saves, sometimes it maintains, and sometimes it increases the use of material resources. But spurred by global competition and neoliberal policies, the quest for innovations has become perpetual in the contemporary economy. When innovations themselves spread and become common coin, the use of the living and inanimate worlds is heightened. Certainly, innovations may be labor or land saving, but their elaboration and dispersion, stimulated by competition and the search for profits, and manifested as the desire for increased living standards and heightened consumption, almost always lead to greater use of the environment.

We are suggesting that the market economy affects community and environment in a triple way. First, innovation for profit often draws upon and "creatively destroys" a cultural heritage. Second, profit-making may draw upon human effort previously directed to creating community, bringing it to account. Third, profit-making may help turn a physical resource from a potential or current use in the commons to a private holding.

But communities within or without the market also contest and circumscribe market activity. People everywhere, now and in the past, have drawn on their communities to create and support, to set boundaries upon, to resist, and to dissent from the market. Zoning laws, architectural stipulations, and the rejection of shopping malls or mass retailers are some examples of the latter. Similarly, when an association of people turns land or another resource into a commons, they are not just acting on "nature" as an object but changing its context of use and meaning from being an objective and separate input for the market to being part of a seamless community of a people in a place. A community economy is built upon the commitment to care for, maintain, and hold together an association of humans and their commons, which is a different project from individual acquisition and accumulation.

Our suggestion, then, is that a principal way people have managed "nature" is not only by using the tools of the market system. Rather than valuing the "objective" resources of nature by extending market calculations (Repetto 1992), calculating externalities and converting them to a property rights system (Demsetz 1964; 1967), or figuring the entropic costs and effects of economic behavior (Daly and Townsend 1993; Georgescu-Roegen 1971), human groups also manage environmental problems through community and its morality, and by judiciously mixing market and community economies. It is the existence and potential of this complementary discourse and set of practices that we want to explore in the next sections of this chapter related to our Guatemalan research.

Two Communities and Market Containment

Guatemala is an extraordinarily varied nation. With 21 Mayan languages (plus Garifuna and Spanish), tense ethnic divisions, a colonial past, archaeological riches, and a highly varied topography, it provides a context for the development of many different types of community and their interactions with markets. Some communities are known for their activist intellectuals and some for their native groups; some preserve the environment as an end in and of itself, and some maintain resources basically to meet human needs. To illustrate several ways profit-making affects community life, we provide a selection from the stories we heard in different parts of the country during our research.

An initial tale of two urban communities that has nothing to do with material resources illustrates how a people may struggle to maintain their heritage or patrimony, their identity and commons in the face of increasing market forces. In each of these cases the patrimonies are expensive to maintain and so each community has had to make its adjustments with the market. The different adaptations illustrate how communities both resist and use the market to maintain themselves.

Each community we discuss here is actually a collection of *cofradías* or religious brotherhoods. Both are located in large cities, one about an hour from Guatemala City itself, the other some three to four hours away. Every *cofradía* possesses a saint's idol in whose honor it mounts a procession on the saint's day and other feast days. A common practice in the past, processions today are usually found only in small communities. The festivities, which feature bands, dancers, and a well-appointed float for the saint, are expensive to produce. Male members of a *cofradía* take turns organizing and collecting funds for each year's festivities. The work, unpaid, is regarded as a "service" for the saint and the community, and an honor, just as its performance is considered an end itself. In both of the urban areas, the costs of the processions have risen dramatically in recent years, and the *cofradías* are in danger of financial collapse. The performances are well attended, however, and they draw tourists whose presence benefits local businesses. This financial gain has opened up new possibilities of support for the *cofradías*, but their responses have been cautious and divergent.

In one city, the municipal authorities—at the urging of local businesses—offered financial support for the processions; but they asked the *cofradías* to play music and perform on nonreligious days for tourists who would be charged for the entertainment. In response, the *cofradías* suggested that for religious processions they would collect less than their expenses, because these performances were a service and a community "commitment." However, for tourist performances, they would charge the city a higher rate. The *cofradías* obviously distinguished between community commitment and market performance. Both practices maintain the patrimony, but the *cofradías* used the market, via local businesses, to earn a profit for their heritage. They perpetuated their community by both limiting and drawing on the market, making their own complex working agreement with it.

The events and patterns in the second town were different. Religious processions there also are drawing tourists. The owners of hotels, restaurants, and shops who benefit from the processions agreed to pay the *cofradías* for the performances. The *cofradías* responded that they were not charging for their service to the saints and the community. They proposed that the businesses offer them alms (*limosna*), though not specifying the amount. The people's response again differentiated between community and market economy. A community is supported by alms, donations, gifts, and services, and not by the "purchase" of its performances with "payments." What a person offers is determined by commitment rather than by competition. As the people say, a donation is given "in accordance with one's heart." In this second case, the *cofradías* drew the hotels and others into their way of life and they asked the market actors to transform their behavior from market to community. In so doing they incorporated the wealth of the market into the community but in a way deemed appropriate to their cultural practices and worldviews.

In both cities, the *cofradías* provide a service, hold onto their material base, and add to the greater well-being through a self-fulfilling activity. Because participants must feed and clothe themselves, pay for their musical instruments, and purchase market goods, each community must incorporate the market in some way. Both however have refused to sell their community foundation outright. In one case, the people separate unpaid community and paid market performance, and in the other, they ask market actors to transform their behavior by offering alms instead of wages. Market and community are separated yet combined. Neither community response indicates ignorance of the "market value" of religious performances, but they signal commitment to resist, circumscribe, and use the market.

Support of the Commons

For our third example we turn to a small Indian village, located on relatively marginal land in a highland area to the west of Guatemala City. Many men of the community seek wage labor outside its borders, at least part of the year, and most people are only partly dependent on local resources. The case illustrates the way a community within a town manages, holds and defends a commons. In this instance, a *cofradía* sustains both a religious patrimony and a material resource that together compose its shared commons.

In the larger town, most agricultural land is possessed as private property, but some is owned in commons by one or another *cofradía*, a legacy from the prior century. Each brotherhood consists of member households that used the land, and composes a community within the town. A *cofradía* requires member participation in its festivities and donations to its saint. In the people's formulation, the productivity of community land and crops is a divine blessing that depends on honoring the saint, because humans, the saint, and God are co-owners of the earth in community. Soil fertility signifies the divine presence. By this metaphoric or analogical construction productivity is made meaningful and seen through divine grace (Gudeman 1986; Mirowski 1989).

The brotherhood we studied has both a highland commons, consisting of a forest, and a lowland commons used for agriculture. Members' families cannot fully sustain themselves from either region or in combination, and most hold private land as well. Both commons are divided into plots to which individual families have exclusive access. On the lowland commons, the people make *milpa*, meaning they grow maize, beans, and other crops for home consumption. Members also grow coffee as a cash crop, but they use the market returns to buy goods for "maintaining the house" and "meeting its needs." The highland forest is carefully managed and may be cut only to meet the "needs" of a house for firewood or construction materials. Effectively, both commons are used to meet domestic "necessities" or to maintain the base of the household.

Cofradía control of the commons is illustrated by the story the people tell when a mayor of the larger town, without consultation or warning, tried to sell 72 trees from their stand to an outside contractor. Upon seeing the marked timber and learning of his plans, the people marched to the forest and physically stopped the process. In recounting the story, they stated that the trees were for use and not sale, that the *cofradía* had not been consulted, that the mayor did not have the right to sell its commons, that they did not know how money from the sale would be used, and that plots of trees were held for use by families, anyway. Effectively, the mayor acted as if the stand of trees were town capital and not a commons and integral part of the *cofradía*. In the telling, the people added that when the town church needed timber for a new roof a few years prior, several families of the *cofradía* offered trees from their plots.

In these examples, *cofradía* members were not only protecting material goods but their social interactions. The rights to shares in their patrimony, realized as plots in the forest and farmland, are passed from father to child. But the *cofradía* holds title, and inheritance and retention of plots are not automatic. This transmission depends on providing *cofradía* service. For example, on the saint's day the *cofradía* sponsors a procession, ritual, and celebration. The ritual leader of this service, known as the principal, keeps the saint's idol in his house and offers food to *cofradía* members on the fiesta day. When the saint is at his house, the people say that the saint, together with the human owner, is the "owner" of the principal's house. Both are "patrons" just as the saint is co-owner of the land. The position of principal, which is very costly, rotates yearly, and everyone must take a turn. Even so, the people have little difficulty recruiting leaders. This is because if a man refuses to serve and offer time, goods, and money that honor the saint, he loses the right to use the commons and to pass his usufruct rights to his children. If a man moves away and cannot participate in the *cofradía's* work, his rights in the commons also lapse. In such cases, the *cofradía* reallots the resources to new members. The commons, thus, helps to support community members just as they support the saint and community.

This case shows how a community defends its commons. A community economy represents a form of life in which humans achieve "well-being" (*bienestar*) not by continuously acquiring goods but participating with others. Managing a *cofradía* requires time—there is a transaction cost—but the people do not count this as an expense. Serving the saint is said to be a "pleasure" and leads to reinforcing social, political, and economic ties with others while preserving these bonds for one's offspring. A community of this form operates with a longer time perspective than a competitive market unit: it hoards or saves (*hacer economías*) land and trees for future use, and not as "investments" designed to secure a financial return. The example illustrates how communities may be embedded in larger communities, and in markets, yet at the same time defend important spheres of life from the latter. The material and ideological are here welded in a way that is hardly understandable through a discourse that separates rational subjects from material objects.

Community Struggles

The expression, "Life is a struggle," heard frequently in many regions of Latin America, is well illustrated by accounts from two villages in Guatemala that have struggled to defend their commons. The shared resource, in these cases, is held at the municipal level, but flows from these resources are devoted to everyday maintenance, especially for one of these communities.

One village held title to a stand of trees. Rights to cut timber were occasionally sold to outsiders with the revenues flowing to the municipality. Recently, two roads were built near the forest, which allowed for the easy, illegal stealing of wood, often by the truckload. Municipal police caught some invaders, but enforcement proved to be costly, and the forest was rapidly depleted. This loss of the commons was not simply a function of the high cost of guarding and the low cost of stealing. No community actually shared the commons. That is, they did not mediate social relationships through it. Instead, the trees were a town resource. They were separate from the people, whose occasional use yielded a revenue disbursed by the mayor. The benefit never flowed to a collectivity. We might say that the trees were never actually a commons or that the community, which the commons serves, consists only of those who cut the trees! The forest was an "open access" resource.

The commons of the neighboring community presents a very different story. This municipality of more than 2,000 persons holds six *caballerías* of land (one *caballería* equals about 41 hectares). One-half of this land is forest and the other half is farmland. The entirety is used by 200 renters who are the poorest folk in town. The renters say that the land is blessed, because its productivity constitutes their only source of maintenance. These people have formed a committee, led by seven men, to protect the commons.

One afternoon, when we met the renters' group, consisting of males, they recounted their struggles. The committee of seven consists of several elders plus some young men, including one who is unmarried. They reach decisions through consensus after everyone has given voice. The men explained that each renter made *milpa* and was permitted to sell the produce, hold it for domestic consumption, or do both in combination. Disposal of the product was no concern of the community, but holding the patrimony was. Long in the telling, the story of their fights to keep the land can be separated into several stages. The struggles began some years ago when the town's mayor tried to sell some of the trees on the reserved land to a contractor in order to raise money for the municipality. A few trees in wetlands and around springs were cut. The renters' community immediately complained, however, that much of the forest also protected the municipality's water sources and that the woods were meant for household use. The mayor canceled the contract but then tried to sell some of the agricultural plots to an outsider. Instantly, the struggle between the renters and the mayor intensified, armed fights broke out, and several renters lost their lives. Eventually, the mayor backed down. Following this conflict, he offered to sell the land to the renters, with the capital value to be paid to the municipality over time. The offer seemed attractive, because individuals would hold personal title to the land they used. The renters discussed the offer at length and then refused, because—as one after another explained—whereas each might gain access to sufficient land, when they had children and their children had children, there would not be enough land for everyone. They needed to think of the "future" and "the children."

On the face of it, their argument against privatization of the land was hardly convincing, for the same demographic pressures affect a commons. But the leaders explained that a community would not let its commons be divided into ever smaller plots, because its purpose is to maintain people sufficiently for their well-being. They knew also that if privatized, the land might be sold to complete outsiders. In their explanations the leaders pitted community against market, and commons against capital. Kept as a community holding, the land would not be used to secure short-term gains.

The people's refusal to convert the land into a commodity produced another response from the mayor. He decided to raise the land rent. Many years ago, the charge was 50 cents per *cuerda* but this had risen to 5 *quetzals*, or 10 times the first amount. (One *cuerda* equals approximately 1/10 hectare; 400 *cuerdas* equal one *caballería*.) By his latest offer, the mayor would increase the rent 15 times to 75 *quetzals* per *cuerda*. The renters' community complained, but not for the reason one might expect. They were willing to pay a higher rent but wanted to see a plan for use of the money; and the rental receipts had to be used for the "benefit" of the municipality, such as improving its water supply or repairing the streets. Community members suspected that the mayor would use some of the returns personally, but their main desire was that any rents they paid for use of the commons be expended for the benefit of the larger municipality. To underline their convictions, nearly half the renters marched on the mayor's office, and he agreed to keep the rent at its current level.

After hearing that the community was willing to pay an increased land rent, we wondered what level they considered to be appropriate. Drawing on our experience in the uplands of Colombia—where local folk speak of the "just price"—we asked the Guatemalan renters what they thought a just rent would be. They understood the meaning. A just rent had nothing to with a market price or an "honest" price as it once meant to the Schoolmen. The people also were not concerned with finding out what the rents were for comparable pieces of land. A just rent was the return needed to "meet the necessities" of a community. In the highlands of Colombia, a "just price" is one that meets the needs of both parties to the exchange. Anything charged above or below the just price signals the taking of a gain or profit by one and the rejection of mutuality. In Guatemala, a just rent for individual use of the commons may be any amount as long as it is used to meet the needs of the receiving community. The level of the just rent has nothing to do with market forces and the equilibration of supply and demand, but with community maintenance.

In these four successive struggles, the community placed boundaries on the market, that is, on the commodification of pieces of land and of trees. The agent against whom the renters' community struggled was an elected official. Although he was selected by the broader municipality, he did not represent the renters, and seemed to be using his political position to seek rents for himself. Adopting a market perspective, he valued the land, forest, and water as if each had a monetary price determined by its potential market uses. In response to the mayor's incursions, the people drew on a different economic discourse. Certainly, the resisting renters had an interest in not purchasing the land and in keeping the rent low, but they also were saying that the land was not for sale, even by them. It constituted their "base," the foundation by which they lived, and thus fell outside market evaluation. In opposing the initial sale of forest products, then the sale of land to outsiders, subsequently the sale of land to themselves, and finally a rise in rents, the renters voiced a community model that legitimated their practices to themselves as well as the larger market and polity.

This sequence of struggles also raised a question about community legitimacy in the larger legal or state framework. Since their last struggle with the mayor, the renters' group has been trying to secure title to the agricultural land. The process has been stalled by political impediments, and a new fact has now emerged. The forest land, consisting of three *caballerías* is owned by the municipality, but the three *caballerías* of farm land have no official owner, and so are possessed by the state. Yet, the municipality has been acting as owner of this state land and collecting rents for years, and the people have been transmitting their use rights to their offspring. This complicated situation, which has its origins in the conquest and colonial times, raises the question of what makes a land claim legitimate? The case suggests that a community's holding of a commons, its moral claim to a part of the environment, is partly a matter of persuasion and possession made through actions, such as demonstrating in front of a mayor's office. Communities make themselves. Increasingly today they are doing this through struggles with market forces.

Who is Subsidizing Whom?

Community formation is often hard to achieve, especially when a material commons providing immediate sustenance is not possessed. We saw this problem in relation to environmental protection. In an attempt to help preserve the biosphere and for other reasons, Guatemala has created a number of national park reserves. We visited one, located in a wetlands area adjacent to a Pacific coast village. This town has grown dramatically in the last decade due to population increase and the search for subsistence resources by people from other parts of the nation. Environmental problems in the area are many, including loss of timber, wetlands, and the sand beach. Due to extensive fishing, marine life—from sharks to corvina and turtles—is being seriously depleted as well. Underfunded and struggling against overpowering forces, the park staff focuses its efforts on a few problems. For example, the park keeps tanks and cages for reproducing some of the endangered animals, and it carries out educational functions in the town and at its visitors' center.

Officials at the park are concerned about the disappearance of large sea turtles. Hunted for their meat and fed as bait to sharks that also are prized, the turtles are doubly in danger because their eggs are considered a delicacy and an aphrodisiac. The turtles lay eggs on the town's beach, but residential and hotel expansion has narrowed the sand strip. Night lights also confuse the turtles who sometimes lose their way and turn back to the ocean without laying. Egg collectors, who sell their booty, are the major danger. National laws prohibit taking eggs and killing turtles, but enforcement problems, including understaffed and underpaid police, are many. One of the park employees lamented that many in the local village had become "predators," because they did not think of the effects their practices would have on their children. Despite the bleak prospect, he often spoke with the villagers about the turtle problem and requested that they contribute one-tenth of their collected eggs to the reserve so that it might hatch them, raise the baby turtles in its tanks, and release grown ones in the ocean. The park employee tried to persuade his neighbors by saying this payment would be a donation or alms, and in fact the amount he requested equaled the tithe. Some villagers refused, saying they would not donate because others would not, but many responded positively, and the park has been able to stock its tanks. A member of the village himself, the park worker appealed, as he explained, to the people's *consciencia*—roughly, to their community sentiment or social consciousness. He used a community lexicon to help persuade them to make a commons of turtle eggs.

The story is hardly straightforward, however, for this small enactment of community economy is set within a larger market and global economy. The turtle commons and park, sponsored by the local village and the state, subsidize market actors by reproducing turtles whose meat will be hunted and eggs will be scavenged for profit. Still, in the midst of the predation, a few of the collectors with a social consciousness are willing to set aside (*guardar*) a tithe for the commons, even if their own behavior, shifting from market to commons to market, is double-sided and dialogic in its contradictory nature.

We learned about other ways of rescuing turtle eggs when we talked with a young man involved in plant and animal conservation projects. In our conversation with him, we came to understand even more clearly the dual and divided economic life that everyone leads. This energetic organizer works saving species and developing educational programs on conservation. Protecting species, he says, is impossible without involving local communities and demonstrating the benefits of conservation. He adds that successful programs meet the *needs* of the people involved—his language draws heavily on the community lexicon. But he voices a different side as well. He recounted how he served as consultant to a leather factory whose waste materials were polluting a town's river. The problem was that the factory provided about 90 percent of the jobs in the area. If it were shut down, he said, who would lose but the community? And who really lost, he added, by the unsafe discharge? He claimed to have solved the problem by explaining to the owners of the factory, whose main customers are in the United States, that there is a demand for environmentally safe products in the North. If the factory were to clean up its waste, it could advertise that it sold green products only, and the subsequent increase in demand would cover the clean up costs.

The young man then spoke of other ways to attack environmental pollution. All his explanations involved market solutions and employed the concepts of externalities, opportunity costs, and demand. He turned to the turtle problem, saying that the national law against the taking of eggs should be strictly applied in the area we visited and that the local reserve officials "lacked the balls" to enforce the law. Furthermore, their practices, relying on community sentiment, were "half-assed." He told about a different way of solving the problem. Elsewhere along the beach, a small store—affiliated with a reserve—bartered used clothing from the United States for turtle eggs. Local people were enthusiastically responding, and the store was providing many more eggs to its park reserve than the one we visited. Here, said he, was an ingenious market solution to problems of the environment.

But his market story omitted discussion of the source of the used clothing, which in fact further involves the dialogical relation of market and community. Much used clothing in Guatemala comes from organizations in the United States, such as Goodwill Industries. Donations to Goodwill and other charitable agencies are leftovers of the household economy that procures them in the market. Frequently, Goodwill sells these gifts at auction, and entrepreneurs purchase large quantities that they transport south and sell to others, such as marketeers in Guatemala and nonprofit organizations that operate beach stores. Establishing a commons of turtle eggs through the barter of clothes thus has a complicated placement in the global economy. First, clothing is produced (sometimes in Guatemala itself) for sale in the United States. After a period of use, it becomes a donation (and a tax deduction) to a community organization. The recipient or charitable organization returns the clothing to the market realm by selling it at a low rate. The purchased clothing then is transported to Guatemala by entrepreneurs where it is bought with community funds to trade it, at below market rates, for turtle eggs which then are removed from the market sphere but ultimately returned to it free of charge. In this sequence that cycles from market to community and back, community economy subsidizes the market. It can only do this because people seem easily to shift their practices and discourse between the two domains.

Double Lives and Uncertainty

The commons, as a holding or savings, constitutes one defense against uncertainty. This seems clear by the frequency with which people talk about holding land or other resources "for the future." Given this propensity to hoard in community, we sought situations in which people were preserving a resource to find out how they imagined and verbalized their actions, especially in relation to the uncertainty of living through the market.

One Saturday we made our way to a remote Indian village to learn about the large forest the inhabitants were preserving in the mountains above the town. We found over a hundred people building a new church in the village center. Men were digging trenches, women were carting water, and children were involved in tasks everywhere. As the people explained, in a language now familiar to us, they were performing a *service* in which one *collaborated*. No one was paid money, so the community had no financial costs (*costos*), although the work was a personal expenditure (*un gasto*) of effort. The organizers, who were members of Catholic Action, had sought and received permission from the mayor to cut designated trees in the community's forest for use in building the church.

We found the mayor sick in bed. He explained that the forest, which was inaccessible by road and half a day's walk from the village, constituted a "fund" (*fondo*) for the community. Before anyone could cut a tree, she had to ask the mayor and he in turn consulted with town elders. If permission was given, ten new trees had to be planted for each one cut in order to preserve both the timber and the watershed. The mayor, proud of the forest and a commons land kept for domestic crops, talked at length about several communal groups that were run by unpaid collaboration and cooperation.

He then switched topics and said that young men in the community were earning cash by winding string balls used in a kicking game popular in the United States. He had encouraged the young men to undertake this wage work but suggested that they keep "making *milpa*" in case the work stopped. The mayor continued that he was spending considerable time urging government agencies to complete the building of a new road to the village. With a proper road, he thought, maize could be brought in and sold to people in the town, even though the villagers raised it in their *milpas*. He surmised that tourists would also visit, and so stimulate local arts, trade, and more cash work. The mayor did not express concern about a conflict between maintaining community—such as building a church on Saturdays, caring for the communal forest, and holding a commons for farming—and augmenting market interactions through tourism, wage work, and greater dependence on purchased commodities. Like the Ashéninkas in Hvalkof's chapter, who maintained relations with the Peruvian nation state in order to defend their own cultures and protect themselves, the mayor of this town lived a double life. His economic duality was signaled by his shifting use of community and market discourses, and he visualized no clash of the two.

Several days later we had another double-sided conversation that was different from the mayor's. This one illustrated more sharply the limits of market rationality in coping with uncertainty. When we met the head of a wildlife foundation, he talked at length about Guatemala's bleak ecological situation. The Petén jungle was a frontier zone subject to the usual wave of destruction. First, contractors cut wood for sale. *Colonos* then burned the remainder in order to seed subsistence crops. Ranchers took over the land

and the *colonos* moved further into the jungle. Finally, the land was planted in export crops. The destructive and irreversible process was hard to stop given the land and economic pressures in the nation that were erupting in political struggles. In parts of the country, he continued, cadastral surveys were inadequate and the land titling system was a mess. Typically, one plot title had been granted on top of another. Regardless of production system or tenure rules, the loss of topsoil continued.

He then told about his foundation's attempt to convince political authorities to protect one forest region in Guatemala. The foundation had undertaken studies comparing the revenues produced by sale of the timber with the costs of cutting and damage to the watershed. The research showed that cutting down the forest was not profitable. His group had found some success in convincing the government to protect the region, because the study, drawing on numerical calculations, accounting techniques, and modern economics, had been stated in a language the officials understood.[2]

With a smile, our conversant then simply added, "This is not all." He was conscious of using a cost-benefit discourse to persuade others of the value of preserving the forest, however he recognized there were limits to this language. He knew that one could never be certain of selecting the right discount rate to evaluate the future flow of timber or water, and his forestry study could always be improved and made more accurate. But in stating, "This is not all," he was also saying something about the discourse he had employed. The market model had limits. It was incomplete and there was a nonquantifiable element he had not included. Explaining that alternative ways of constructing the environment must always exist, our discussant concluded that he did not see "the environment" as something separate from humans, as an object characterized by mechanical laws and consisting of discrete elements such as water, wood, and leaves. Yet, he was not totally clear in what he was trying to say. Did he believe that his discourse itself created a realm of uncertainty, or did he think that a domain of uncertainty remained outside any discourse? Perhaps he expected that his knowledge system would itself change in time. Certainly, he lacked an alternative or supplementary discourse. Then, as an afterthought, he produced another study his group had commissioned. This study described the practices and ideas of the people who had for centuries been living in the region his foundation had studied. Filled with local metaphors and imagery, this second study set forth the multiple and divergent local perspectives on the forest and environment. Our conversationalist did not know what to do with this study and had not presented it to the government.

How should we appreciate and understand his partly split, partly incomplete, discourse? We suggest that his statement, "This is not all," marks the boundary between the market discourse, which uses notions of risk and constructs probabilistic outcomes, and what we will call uncertainty (Dewey 1929; Knight 1971[1921]). Risk refers to sets of outcomes to which probabilities may be attached, however imprecise, given historical information. Roulette or coin flips are risky ventures. In contrast, uncertainty refers to the zone outside risk to which we cannot attach probabilities. Uncertainty, in our view, concerns our lack of knowledge (1) about the future; (2) about what is "really there;" (3) about the knowledge formulations we may someday use; and (4) about where the limits of our knowledge lie. This undetermined space cannot be quantified and tamed through the construction and projection of probability distributions and risk calculations. The tool of rational choice may not be capable of dealing with uncertainty. Our thesis is that we cope with uncertainty by drawing on the security of community, by adjusting and being pragmatic as events unfold, and by preserving a commons as a space for experimentation. We cannot manage the environment simply through market practices, supported by neoliberal policies, and figured by risk probabilities. Nor, ironically is market-derived profit itself made by calculating risk, for it represents a plunge into uncertainty, which was precisely Schumpeter's and Knight's argument.

Profits and Community

The small, independent house-business in Latin America, straddling community and market, illustrates how profits, built by innovation in conditions of uncertainty, draw on community and its base, and so underlines the importance of conserving them. Consider the case of a successful woman potter outside Guatemala City, who was crafting new figurines for sale when we visited her. She worked in a corner of her kitchen but had a separate store that was stocked with finished pieces. Buyers came from the city to purchase in quantity, her husband spent much of his time overseeing the practical arrangements, and the woman had accumulated enough money to make other small investments in her village. The woman's items were selling well, but she liked to make new pieces and was experimenting with figures of angels. Each figurine emerged from the potter's hands with a slightly different form as the woman made adjustments to achieve greater balance or more stability. Looking at earlier angel figures, one could also see that the overall design had been evolving. The figures had taken well to the firing, and the results were generally good. As the potter explained, all her work was done by touch and testing (*tantear*) or contextual reason.

Feeling one's way also characterized the potter's pricing. For a batch of figures, she knew what quantity of clay was used and the time she spent. Each new figurine had a real cost basis derived from the cost of the raw materials and labor return the potter had been receiving. (Unlike some household workers, this potter considered her labor to be a monetary "cost" and not an unpriced "expense of the house" that supported production of the market commodity through the use of "unaccounted" housework.) Still, the sum of her material costs and labor, a calculation the potter made with a high degree of precision, was not the price she charged. For pricing, the ceramist would also feel her way. Depending on what the market would bear she raised or lowered her price, and would or would not make a profit above costs. Her expenditures were calculable and predictable for every angel figure, but her profit was not. Her profit was always uncertain, depending on the market.

The ceramist's profit also was temporary and uncertain for a double reason. If her product continued to sell well, eventually she would recalculate the gain as an augmentation to the "value of her work." She increased the figured return to her own labor, and this could have a long-term effect on what she charged for her other pieces. But other potters in the community would also see what she had done, how the figure was made, and whether it drew buyers. They were adept artisans, too, and would quickly copy her figurine if it became popular. Still, the potter said that even with competition the eventual sale price of a new figure usually did not fall to its original cost of production (and she added that as she made more angel figures she would find ways to produce them better and more quickly). Although the price of new ceramic pieces might decline through competition, the remuneration for her own labor almost always increased because even with competition, she was able to absorb some of the initial profit as a return to her labor. Over time, the value of all her work efforts had in fact been rising. She had observed, for example, that although she had learned her craft directly from her mother at home, her standard of living was appreciably higher than that of her parent.

In miniature, the potter's case neatly displays the foundation, course, and effects of profit making. The new product, as well the price she charged for it, were established by trial and error. The angel figure as a material creation in the household of the woman initially was an uncertain product. Then, its price was uncertain, as was its profit. Even so, profit on the innovation was temporary. But as it disappeared it was distributed as a higher imputed wage to the original maker, lower prices to consumers, and increased returns to other potters. What had been profit became higher wages and lower prices. The woman potter fits Schumpeter's classic model whereby the entrepreneur invents a new process, introduces it to the market, and holds a short-term monopoly. Eventually, the improvement is distributed one way or another within the system and alters economic development.

The potter's example also shows how market practices rely on community. The figurines themselves were suggested by the media and other sources. As products, they varied with the batches of clay, the characteristics of the oven, and the skills of the potter in relation to these. But the woman learned her skills by watching and working in her mother's kitchen, just as she continued to work in her own kitchen and her offspring learned from her. In addition, she added to this legacy—or commons—because her neighbors who were also "competitors" would visit, watch, and copy her work just as she could benefit from their innovations. The series of innovations that emerged from and circulated among all the potters added to the village heritage. Artisanship was sustained by house and village communities, as were the practices of trial-and-error in conditions of uncertainty. The innovations lay in the entire communal situation, including practiced hands, clay, and other people. The potter's case suggests how innovation—that engages uncertainty, alters a heritage, draws a profit, and raises the standard of living—depends on and flourishes in the communal dimension of economy, and so rests on preserving a base in the broadest sense.

Telling Tales

In Guatemala, we talked with many people who spoke in terms of risks and probabilities, and of neoliberal policies. For them, solutions to the problems of the environment had to be found within the market and market theory. For example, most contemporary economists agree that if people desire "green products," demand them, and pay for them, this preference will lead suppliers to change their ways. On this view, community morality influences the market through demand. But if a product supplied by two vendors appears the same to sensory experience and one is less expensive than the other, most market participants will choose the cheaper to preserve capital. The ordinary argument leaves out the quest for profit and the power of capital as well as the pervasiveness of imperfect information and the fact that almost no market is perfectly competitive. Some might also argue that if we priced all environmental expenditures in production and took into account the full cost of waste, then even in market terms corporations could never make a profit or the standard of living would drop. They might suggest that we live on borrowed time because the world's stocks of resources are being turned into flows for the market (Daly and Townsend 1993).

We invoke a different story. The market may be a competition, a game of winning and losing as the Spanish word for profit (*ganar*) suggests. But who shall be the umpire, who shall set the rules of the game? Players cannot also be referee (*juez y parte*). The market has never been "self-regulating" (Polanyi 1944). The rules about what can and cannot enter the market game, and what the exits must look like, are set externally. Communities situate a market, and support it by yielding their leftovers as uncosted gains and accepting its garbage as uncosted waste. Communities define what place the market shall occupy, and they struggle with the market over this space. To phrase this in a language from Latin America, the market deals with numerical costs (*costos*) determined in *exchange*, and the community copes with incommensurate *expenditures* (*gastos*) of materials and work. Entries to and exits from the market support profit making and have to do with using community *expenditures* in place of market *costs*, and with converting market costs to community *expenditures*. This access is determined by a community placing boundaries on the market.

Our Guatemalan cases suggest that such assertions of community are made and remade, by acts such as demonstrating in front of a mayor's office. But communities, such as those protecting turtles, need not be locally based or face-to-face (Anderson 1991). In today's global market, communities cross national borders, assume new forms, and place new limits on transnational actors.

The "environmental problem" can refer to using up limited resources, generating excessive waste, degrading the planet's environment and living conditions, or all three. Certainly, demographic growth may increase environmental pressures, and human life and the making of social agreements are entropic activities. But we view the environmental problem through the lens of the dual model of economy, as part of the struggle between market and community, or capital and base. Let us return to the central market act of making a profit by innovation.

Some innovations are thrifty or have a negligible effect on the use of materials. A smaller computer chip is thrifty; the potter who made angel figurines sold new ones in place of others; automobiles may be made with lighter materials or designed to use less gasoline; tires may be manufactured to last longer. Innovations also may revolve about recycling, a common practice in less capitalized sectors. In many parts of Latin America, used tires are first mended and remade, then fashioned into sandals or used for cushioning boats at docks and piers.

But profit making through innovations and their diffusion can have the reverse effect. What had been used to sustain community by its base may be diverted to the market. This debasement process is part of the environmental problem not because a community conserves resources better than market participants but because a commons or base is part of a market's environment. The physical environment is our shared heritage, even though it is sometimes unseen. Transforming this patrimony changes a people's identity by altering the base of its community and the possibilities it affords for future practices.

For this reason, although economists and others "factor in" environmental effects through cost/benefit analyses, they may be part of the problem they would eradicate. With heroic assumptions, we may price the value of an unused forest by figuring the monetary value of all its previously uncounted benefits, arranging these as a stream of wealth that accrues over time, and discounting this flow to capture its current capital value which can then be weighed against alternative uses. But this impeccable technique uses the logic of market activity to save the environment from that same activity!

Making things commensurate through the market is an exercise in eradicating unpredictability and denying the human desire to innovate and encounter uncertainty. A community's commons, even if fuzzy-edged, offers a base and space for exploration and discovery. We can never know how the environment will be used in 1,000 or even 50 years. To price a forest, river, air, or lake implies that its long-term value is determinant now and not subject to future discovery. By pricing the environment and assigning it a capital value—even for the sake of preserving it—we limit the legacy for our successors while contradicting our status as legatees of a base, not capital.

The environment is in part a realm of uncertainty. How should we act in the face of such true uncertainty? Should we act to support systems of growth and claims that our knowledge system can encompass this uncertainty? Or should we maintain communities and the commons on which they depend? In the latter, "nature" is not divided from human society, and humans are not seen as holding a position superordinate to a purely rule-governed environment. People cannot destroy "the externality" except at peril to themselves. The commons is the holding space for the incommensurate, castoffs, and unused materials. In these places, humans cope by trial-and-error. We can value the environment also by making it part of community.

The environmental issue, therefore, has to be discussed partly within a language of community. We do not presume that the spread of the market is bad or good, or that a community will manage the environment well. We preserve our environment for the future, however, because we cannot predict the meanings, values, and uses that may be supported by a base. Times to come are incalculable and potential uses of our shared base must be addressed in light of the economy's totality or two sides.

Tomorrow's struggles over the use of the environment and human labor—or tomorrow's political economy—we surmise, will take the form of community versus market. Perhaps this negotiation will supersede both the neoliberal discussion and the class struggle. This struggle itself may now be reread as one between communities and global market interests.

Notes

A similar piece appears in *Land, Property, and the Environment*, edited by John Richards, with the title "Sustaining the community, resisting the market: Guatemalan perspectives." Oakland, Calif.: Institute for Contemporary Studies Press, 2001.

1. One example is the *pratique* relationship in Haiti, as described by Mintz (1961).
2. For a discussion of the evaluation of forest products using local or ethnographic information see Godoy and Lubowski 1992.

References

Anderson, Benedict. 1991. *Imagined Communities*. London: Verso.

Aristotle. 1984. *The Politics*. Cambridge: Cambridge University Press.

Boeke, J.H. 1942. *The Structure of Netherlands Indian Economy*. New York: Institute of Pacific Relations.

Daly, Herman, and Kenneth Townsend. 1993. *Valuing the Earth*. Cambridge: MIT Press.

Dewey, John. 1929. *The Quest for Certainty*. New York: Minton, Balch, and Co.

Demsetz, Harold. 1964. The exchange and enforcement of property rights. *Journal of Law and Economics*. 7:11–26.

Demsetz, Harold. 1967. Toward a theory of property rights. *American Economic Review*. LVII: 347–359.

Evers, Hans-Dieter. 1994. The trader's dilemma. In *The Moral Economy of Trade*, edited by Hans-Dieter Evers and Heiko Schrader. 7–14. London: Routledge.

Geertz, Clifford. 1963. *Agricultural Involution*. Berkeley: University of California Press.

Georgescu-Roegen, Nicholas. 1971. *The Entropy Law and the Economic Process*. Cambridge: Harvard University Press.

Godoy, Ricardo, and Ruben Lubowski. 1992. Guidelines for the economic valuation of nontimber tropical-forest products. *Current Anthropology*. 33:423–433.

Gudeman, Stephen. 1986. *Economics as Culture*. London: Routledge.

Hardin, G. 1968. The tragedy of the commons. *Science*. 162:1243–48.

Knight, Frank H. 1971[1921]. *Risk, Uncertainty, and Profit*. Chicago: University of Chicago Press.

Mintz, Sidney W. 1961. Pratik: Haitian personal economic relationships. *Annals of the Symposium Patterns of Land Utilization and Other Papers*. 54–63. Seattle: American Ethnological Society.

Mirowski, Philip. 1989. *More Heat Than Light*. Cambridge: Cambridge University Press.

Ostrom, Elinor. 1990. *Governing the Commons*. Cambridge: Cambridge University Press.

Polanyi, Karl. 1944. *The Great Transformation*. Boston: Beacon Press.

Polanyi, Karl, Conrad Arensberg, and Harry Pearson, eds. 1957. *Trade and Market in the Early Empires*. Glencoe: Free Press.

Repetto, Robert. 1992. Accounting for environmental assets. *Scientific American*. June: 94–100.

Rivera-Gutiérrez, Alberto. 1986. *Material Life and Social Metaphor*. Ph.D. diss., University of Minnesota.

Schumpeter, Joseph. 1934 [1926]. *The Theory of Economic Development*. Cambridge: Harvard University Press.

8

The Restructuring of Labor Markets, International Migration, and Household Economies in Urban Mexico

Agustín Escobar Latapí and
Mercedes González de la Rocha

Introduction

What is the nature of poverty in Mexico today? What social institutions and actions support the daily struggle of people for survival? Are these elements producing a new profile of Mexican migration to the United States? The increase in international migration during Mexico's period of crisis and neoliberal restructuring in the 1980s was accompanied by increasing employment instability in cities. Mexican cities suffered from a shortage of jobs and income sources and the increasing precariousness of employment. While broad changes in political economy can explain the evolution of employment and wage levels, international migration is one among several means by which urban households are expanding and extending their members' job opportunities. Thus, labor market transnationalization is a tool that urban residents are adding to their rather worn set of assets to cope with increasing poverty.

The Mexican crisis of the 1980s became a depressing but appropriate social laboratory in which to evaluate the operation of the social mechanisms which urban popular sectors use on a daily basis to deal with low wages and diminishing levels of state support. Restructuring took place not only at the macroeconomic and political level, but also, and most importantly, at the household level and in the workplace, with decreasing real wages and increasing unemployment.[1] In fact, in Mexico, as elsewhere in Latin America,[2] most of the social responses to austerity and economic policies took place within the household. By focusing mostly on Guadalajara, this chapter shares an interest with the previous chapter on community and market.

Like the people in Gudeman and Rivera-Gutiérrez's study, the households we came to know in Guadalajara accessed markets by invoking the community economies of family, house, and kin (González de la Rocha 1991; Benería 1992). But uneven development in Mexico, and the place that Guadalajara inhabits in it, has made access to the formal market exceedingly difficult. Like the Maya in Pi-Sunyer's study in the next chapter, the people of Guadalajara are watching the neoliberal action from the sidelines.

Antecedents: Social Change and Poverty During Import Substitution Industrialization

During the period of Import Substitution Industrialization (ISI) from 1940 to 1980, Mexico's economy grew an average of 6 percent a year and succeeded in creating two new social classes: the urban middle class and a new working class (Escobar Latapí and Roberts 1991). The latter was part of the "urban popular sector." Its members moved frequently from one firm, economic sector, or occupation to another, and families had workers in different jobs and types of employment arrangements. People from this group intermarried and shared many common challenges for survival, living in new, under-equipped urban environments.[3] Nonetheless, by 1978, at least half of the new Mexican working class in manufacturing had reached or surpassed wage levels which enabled a single worker to support a family (Escobar Latapí and Roberts 1991, based on Boltvinik 1987 and Reyes Heroles 1983), and had basic social security, including health care and retirement benefits.

The urban middle class also expanded rapidly, and derived substantially greater benefits from the ISI model of development. Subsidies in goods and services under ISI, apparently designed to alleviate the conditions of the urban poor, to a large extent served the middle class.[4] Thus, the urbanization, modernization, and industrialization that Mexico underwent from 1940 to 1980 created substantial new class sectors and income groups, and the middle range of the income distribution grew. The growth in these urban sectors occurred at the expense of the rural poor. The poorest 10 percent, comprised mostly of rural laborers, were marginalized. Their real income stagnated and lost significant ground as a proportion of national income (Tello 1991). The working class experienced relative gains, with modest but perceptible 3 to 5 percent growth in real income per year. Contrary to a widely held perception, the shifts in income distribution substantially reduced the top 10 percent's share of national income, bringing it closer to the new urban middle class (Escobar Latapí and Roberts 1991, based on Reyes Heroles 1985). In fact, by 1980, the top 10 percent was made up largely of professionals, managers, and small entrepreneurs. Because of rapid economic growth, the changes in the distribution of income meant that the real income of all remained stable or rose, despite losses in relative shares of national income. As a result of this, the percentage of poor households decreased substantially during the sixties and seventies, from 80.7 in 1963 to 52.5 in 1981 (Tuirán Gutiérrez 1993).

The relative success of Mexican development in these terms should not obscure the fact that survival remained very difficult for the poor. Only half of those employed enjoyed job security and social security. Access to urban infrastructure remained deficient. The non-existence or lack of access to goods and services for the working poor[5] meant that their schooling, housing, malnutrition, and mortality rates were still considerably worse than those of the middle class in this period. Thus, while the small rise in the working classes' share of GDP from 1950 to 1977 entailed a doubling of their real incomes thanks to rapid growth, this added income was spent on a more monetized, urban economy and therefore had a less positive impact on their quality of life. For example, in the city housing involves substantial expenses, while in traditional rural areas housing required using natural resources and activating community mutual help.

During the "Mexican Miracle" the poor drew on and expanded household organizational resources. Most of the mechanisms or strategies to deal with the new economic demands of urban life were implemented at the household level. The household has been, indeed, the social unit where poverty is "solved," as the poor cannot survive individually with such low wages. Analyses conducted in Mexico (as elsewhere) show the importance of the collective nature of survival strategies, and the important role which the household plays in the achievement of survival and reproduction of the working poor (González de la Rocha 1986; 1994a; Chant 1994; Morris 1990; Selby, Murphy, and Lorenzen 1990). Thus, while the crisis and restructuring of the 1980s and early 1990s substantially altered the trends of the previous forty years, the household remained at the center of the diverse actions the poor undertook to survive amidst their increasing hardships. As we shall see later in this chapter, and as Safa shows in hers, this has included an increasing reliance on transnational resources through migration.

Crisis and Restructuring in Latin America

Economic crisis erupted in Mexico and most Latin American countries between the end of the 1970s and the beginning of the 1980s. Economic growth halted, reversing the trends of previous years. The impact of the economic crisis on the structure of employment and the prices of consumption goods made the livelihoods of the urban masses even more difficult. The urban poor were hit particularly hard by shrinking wages, growing unemployment, stagnation of formal employment, and decreasing public budgets for social expenditures and subsidies previously aimed at basic foodstuffs and urban services.

The international capital crisis drove Mexico and most of Latin America to restructure their economies along neoliberal lines (Benería 1992; Cordera and González Tiburcio 1991; Safa and Antrobus 1992; McFarren 1992; Pérez-Alemán 1992). Most countries took drastic steps to open their economies, attempting to resume growth on the basis of export industries (whether agricultural or manufacturing). Low wages became crucial to the new scheme because they formed a more or less prominent part of the cost of exports, not because they influenced the behavior of consumption, as previously was the case. The drive to export became a push to lower wages and to make work more flexible (or precarious). As Feldman (1992) points out, there was a transition from high levels of employment and rates of growth of national income and trade to higher levels of unemployment and higher prices, but declining wages and standards of living.

Debt service and policies aimed at lowering the prices of Latin American products have been based on deteriorating living conditions for a growing number of people. Structural adjustment policies reorganized production on a global scale, restructured local labor markets, and reduced public sector employment, food subsidies, and public expenditures (Feldman 1992; Benería 1992; Cordera and González Tiburcio 1991). Poverty increased as a result of the crisis and neoliberal economic policies,[6] and the economic crisis had a stronger impact on urban populations than on rural ones.[7] However, in Mexico the social impacts of restructuring spread to the rural areas, destabilizing existing crops, work patterns and previous circulatory migration circuits, thereby adding another sector to this process.

In 1983, the average minimum wage in Mexico had dropped to 72.5 percent of its 1978 value; by 1990 it was down to only 39.4 percent (Tuirán Gutiérrez 1993). Minimum wages, however, lost importance as basic reference wages (see below). The cost of food and of what has been called the "basic food basket" rose systematically from 1980 to 1987 as inflation increased (Cordera and González Tiburcio 1991) and many previously comfortable households sank into poverty. With the exception of the in-bond export industries, new jobs were to be found or created only in small enterprises, the informal sector, or through self-employment.[8] Women's participation in the labor market increased, and households were forced to restructure their division of labor and budgets in order to cope with the new conditions imposed by neoliberal economic policies.

The 1980s in Mexico: From Crisis and Adjustment to Restructuring

The social and economic changes of the 1980s can be understood in terms of three fairly discrete periods, each affecting the nature and extent of poverty in different ways. The first, the only one that can strictly be called "crisis and adjustment," began with the Mexican debt crisis of 1982 and ended sometime in 1986 or 1987. During this first period, wage and income levels fell drastically. This period was marked by drastic economic oscillations, a drop in official and actual real wages, several acute devaluations of the peso, capital flight, and fiscal austerity. All this had an especially sharp effect on social spending. During this period, however, the general framework of Mexican economic policy did not change. Government union relations remained mostly unaltered, ISI remained at the basis of policy, and the state was still perceived as responsible for Mexican development via a "strategic" sector of public and private enterprises. The *maquiladora* or export processing manufacturing industry was unusually prosperous due to the double cheapening of Mexican labor (through an undervaluation of the peso and a lowering of real wages). It too was viewed as a valuable source of foreign currency, but remained marginal to the general thrust of Mexican economic development.

During the second period, starting in 1986 and ending near 1988, profound neoliberal restructuring began to take place. Wages continued to fall, inflation remained high (reaching a peak of 159 percent in 1987), the government began privatizing many of its enterprises, and social expenditure kept falling.[9] Mexico signed the General Agreement on Trade and Tariffs (GATT) in 1986, taking additional unilateral steps to open local markets to foreign goods, partly to allow local exporters to benefit from lower prices of imported parts and raw materials. By 1988, imports began to impact the domestic market while domestic (non-*maquiladora*) industry was scarcely able to export its products. Clothing, footwear, and textile industries were the hardest hit. The Mexican economy was seriously destabilized towards the end of 1987, with new devaluations and a new surge of capital flight. *Maquiladora* employment kept growing and U.S. auto industry multinationals became the largest exporters after the state-owned oil firm PEMEX. Growth in the *maquiladora* sector was spurred during this second period not only by cheap Mexican labor, but also by increased access to the Mexican market, which before had been off-limits to export processing plants. The *maquiladora* industry enjoyed a significant advantage over national industries, since *maquiladoras* paid much lower wages. This, together with the reform of the role of the public sector in the Mexican economy, began to pose the question of the competitiveness of previously protected, better paying Mexican industries. Both multinational and national firms began their drive to equalize *maquiladora* and other wages. The same multinationals, for example, paid workers in their new plants in northern Mexico wages that were 60 percent below those of workers in their older plants in and around Mexico City (Shaiken 1987). Concerted efforts were made to either keep strong unions away from the new plants, or to make them agree to lower pay and higher productivity packages. Public sector and private firm employment remained stagnant or fell. Between 1980 and 1987, informal employment in Mexico grew 80 percent. As a proportion of the total economically active population (EAP) it rose from 24 to 33 percent (ECLAC 1989). Social expenditure remained at roughly half its 1980 level, although in some specific areas it was even lower. This was due in part to lower public sector wages (in education and health services), but lack of investment in infrastructure, material, and equipment also lowered the quality of services. Doctors had to see more patients, surgical materials were often missing, classes had to be held outdoors with virtually no teaching aids, and so on.

The third period, from 1988, began with the renegotiation of Mexico's foreign debt under the Brady Plan (which reduced both total debt and interest payments), and the first of a series of "social pacts" aimed at reducing inflation and stabilizing the Mexican economy. These pacts were more successful in Mexico than elsewhere, partly because the government-controlled labor confederations agreed to forego real pay increases and business limited price hikes (which were nonetheless higher than pay increases). The drive to privatize public firms was stepped up, and banks that had been nationalized in 1982 were re-privatized. As state-owned firms were privatized, sometimes after declaring bankruptcy (and therefore ceasing to exist legally), the new owners were free to negotiate new pay and productivity packages, with precarious employment becoming the norm. Jobs were no longer secure, part-time employment became more common, "out-sourcing" to smaller firms became a general practice, and workers and employees were asked to perform more duties in order to remain at work.[10] The pacts, entailing lower inflation, lower capital costs and a renewal of modest but consistent economic growth, revitalized the consumption of durable consumer goods and capital goods. These processes had a differential impact in distinct urban contexts. In Monterrey and Mexico City, for example, manufacturing employment began to grow and manufacturing income rose faster than prices for the first time in 10 years.

Guadalajara, which had suffered less during the first period of this transformation because the market for its consumption goods had fallen less than that of durable and capital goods, entered a more difficult period at this time, as shoes, clothes, and everyday household items began pouring in from abroad. This new importation often occurred illegally, through dumping from Asia and these small Mexican manufacturers had no way to protect themselves from unfair trade practices.

During this last stage the rural sector was hurt by policy reform. First, open markets and the end of guaranteed prices (which meant falling prices) with a revaluing *peso* (after 1988) meant Mexican agricultural crops and produce gradually lost ground at home and abroad. Second, the restructuring and privatization of the Mexican banking system put credit beyond the reach of producers who were at the same time facing increased foreign and domestic competition and lower prices. This affected commercial producers to a greater extent than subsistence producers. At the same time, however, the crops grown by subsistence producers for their cash needs fetched lower prices, and this increased their need for temporary wage employment, just as large-scale rural producers and urban labor markets became less able to provide this kind of employment. During this last stage, therefore, there were large-scale changes in the rural sector, a notable aspect of which is the impoverishment of subsistence producers and a movement of large-scale producers towards less labor intensive crops directed at internal markets.

This third stage of the Mexican restructuring process is the most controversial in terms of its impact on income and poverty because of conflicting interpretations on income and poverty. A report produced by the Mexican statistics institute (INEGI 1993)—and endorsed by the Economic Commission for Latin America and the Caribbean (ECLAC)— asserted that poverty in Mexico dropped in both relative and absolute terms from 1989 to 1992. This claim was based on a comparison of National Household Income and Expenditure Surveys. According to the report, the percentage of households in extreme poverty[11] dropped from 14.1 percent in 1989 to 11.8 percent in 1992, with absolute numbers also falling (from 14.9 million individuals to 13.6 million). "Intermediate" households (which correspond to international definitions of poor households since their earnings fall between one and two basic food baskets) made up 27 percent of the Mexican population in 1984 and 28 percent in 1992 (INEGI 1993). These results have been criticized by academic analysts who note that the total income of poor Mexican households is overestimated in the National Household Income and Expenditure Surveys because a rent equivalent is added to household income when the household owns its own dwelling. Rents rose far more rapidly than general prices in Mexico during the period,[12] which led the surveys to allocate high "incomes" to home-owning families.

Therefore, the reported increase in real incomes and relative well-being in Mexico between 1989 and 1992 may not have occurred, or at least it may be overrated. What is indisputable is that income distribution worsened in this period between the rich and all other sectors. The richest 10 percent of the population earned 55 percent more in real terms in 1992 than in 1977, and their share of national income rose from 36.7 to 47.4 percent. The real income of the upper middle class remained practically stagnant relative to 1977, and the lower middle class lost a small amount of real income compared to 1977. The working class and the poor—the bottom 40 percent of the population—experienced a small gain over 1977, but a loss in real income from 1989 to 1992. In other words, there was more inequality and more poverty and this was reflected in household incomes (Cortés 1994).

The resources derived from renegotiating the foreign debt and from the privatization of banks, public services, and industries, and the increased tax revenues derived from economic growth were partly channeled to social expenditures. Some of this took traditional forms; for example, teachers' salaries recovered somewhat. Most social expenditure, however, was channeled through a special new policy, generally known as the National Solidarity Program, or Pronasol, its acronym in Spanish.[13] Pronasol has been the subject of heated and continued debate that we cannot address in this chapter (Dresser 1991; Escobar Latapí and González de la Rocha 1991; Laurell 1994).

In any case, the remittances that Mexican migrants to the United States send back home to their families are a stronger asset against poverty than Pronasol. It is estimated that nearly $3.4 billion were sent to Mexico via migrant remittances in 1990 (Lozano Ascencio 1993). This sum was estimated at $5.5 billion in 1998 (CONAPO 1999). According to the Guadalajara daily newspaper *Siglo 21* (Oct. 29, 1994) the owners of foreign exchange houses in Jalisco (most of them in Guadalajara) recognize that most of the money that they handle is from remittances that migrants send to their families in Mexico. Remittances, however, may not have a visible impact since the money is often used for subsistence and remains hidden within the household economy. Somewhat like women's wages, remittances are an invisible income used for the purchase of basic needs.

Guadalajara: Urban Poor Households and the Social Organization of Poverty

Guadalajara is Mexico's second largest city. Of Mexico's three largest metropolitan areas, Guadalajara resembles Mexico City much more than

Monterrey, where secondary employment and the specific dynamics of large-scale manufacturing have provided the dominant force of urban development for a long time. Guadalajara, however, differs from Mexico City in several ways. Its migration hinterland is more regional in character, and government employment and expenditure are marginal. Guadalajara had, from colonial times, served as the commercial and service hub of Western Mexico. However, from 1940 onwards its manufacturing industry became national in scope, specializing in the production of food products, shoes and garments, and some chemicals (Escobar Latapí 1986). Mostly, industry located in Guadalajara belonged to the competitive sector. It was never defined as "strategic" by government policy, and it consequently received few tax, price, and market privileges. Guadalajara, a city of 3.5 million inhabitants, has been characterized as "the big city of small industry" (Arias 1985) because of the multitude of small industrial workshops which, as a sector, provided employment to large numbers of workers. Indeed, small-scale industry and low wages in the formal sector were two distinguishing traits. Before the economic crisis, the rule for working class households was to establish plurality and diversity of employment (González de la Rocha 1986; 1994a). Working-class households implemented strategies that included a variety of workers in different niches of the labor market. Households based their economies on the presence of several income earners, especially during advanced moments of the domestic cycle.

As awareness of the depth of the crisis spread through Mexico, poor urban households responded by increasing the number of workers in the family (González de la Rocha 1988; 1994a). Although real incomes fell drastically, Guadalajara households were quite successful at cushioning the impact of lower wages and a stagnant formal economy with an increased reliance on mostly informal employment. For women, this meant domestic and other personal services. For men, it most often meant self-employment of various kinds. Thus, while the real income of male heads of households in Guadalajara fell 35 percent from 1982 to 1985, real total household income dropped only 11 percent. The group showing the largest proportional increase in its labor participation were women over 15 years of age, followed closely by young men (González de la Rocha 1988).[14]

The very rich were the only ones who benefited from the economic chaos and restructuring of the last years of the decade of the 1980s. Middle income groups and the working class suffered deteriorating salaries and wages, although these strata recovered (and even gained) income after 1988 (Roberts and Escobar Latapí 1996). The middle class was hard hit in the 1980s, with falling salaries and rising real costs in land taxes, electricity and water rates, fuel, and the price of credit (Escobar Latapí and Roberts 1991). Indeed, the middle income strata suffered a larger relative drop than lower income groups (de Lara Rangel 1990; Jusidman 1987), and middle income households became more like urban working-class households (Cortés and Rubalcava 1991; González de la Rocha 1992; 1994b). This should not obscure the fact that the working class and the poor became even more vulnerable, although their incomes fell proportionately less than the middle-class incomes. Their lives became harder and mere survival became an ever-more difficult goal.

Intensification was the key to survival during the economic crisis and the years that followed. Work loads, participation in the labor market, household chores, and the use of networks increased. As Safa notes in her chapter on Dominican households, confrontations and contradictions within the household intensified also. Under-consumption, malnutrition, and ill-nesses related to poverty also increased (Langer et al. 1991). At this time, migration from Mexican cities to the United States increased dramatically as well.

In sum, household survival strategies protected total domestic incomes from falling at the same pace as individual incomes and thus cushioned the impact. The main elements of household survival strategies were:

1. Increases in the number of household members who work. Adult women played an especially important role in this (González de la Rocha 1988; 1991), followed by young males (14 years old and younger) who also turned to wage-labor and quit school. Adult females in Guadalajara increased their labor force participation by 25.9 percent, while young males increased their participation by 25.3 percent. These findings support the view that work intensification strategies fell mostly on women and the young. As a result of the increase in women's work, domestic economies saw more female incomes, and many household economies became "feminized." It could be said that this strategy was highly successful, since household incomes were protected from falling at the same pace as individual incomes.[15] This was not, however, the only change revealed during the longitudinal study carried out in Guadalajara.

2. An increase in household size (number of members per household). Households grew not only through births of new members, but through the addition of new, grown adult members. Most of the time, these new-comers were daughters-in-law and sons-in-law, as new couples began staying longer in the original home of either spouse. Although this feature was not completely new, the need to maintain income earners (from

the point of view of the receiving household) and to save some money in housing expenses and other shared expenses (from the point of view of the new couple) made this feature a more frequent phenomenon. Other relatives and non-relatives also came to the homes we studied, expanding the size of the households. Domestic chores increased as a result of the presence of more members, and so did women's responsibilities. As a means by which households gained flexibility, increased the number of workers (both in the labor market and in the domestic domain), and saved on housing, the extended household proved to be resourceful in facing economic hardship.

3. An increase in extended households during the 1980s. Larger, extended households appeared in greater numbers, since extension and the availability of workers proved to be essential assets for the household economy. When sons and daughters were married, it became more important to keep them at home with their spouses, instead of losing an economically active member.[16]

4. A rearrangement in patterns of consumption. Having more household members working and increasing household size did not fully protect households from the need to modify consumption patterns, however. Working class households protected their food consumption in the face of falling wages by reducing their consumption of other goods and services (for example, clothing and household maintenance such as plumbing repairs, bricklaying, and carpentry) and by intensifying the household's burden of work, both paid and unpaid. Although food consumption levels fell during the crisis, the severity of the decline did not approach the drop in individual real wages. Compared to the situation that prevailed in 1982, economic conditions forced households to devote a higher percentage of their total spending to food and housing. This does not mean, of course, that the population consumed more food, but simply that food prices rose so much in that period that is was necessary to allot a greater proportion of income to those products. In contrast, income spent on health and education declined during the decade and did not recover. Although one of the main goals of the changes implemented by households was the maintenance of acceptable levels of food intake, there were modifications in the patterns and levels of consumption that had been reached before the 1982 economic crisis. For instance, per capita beef consumption dropped by nearly five kilos, and milk consumption also decreased (Cordera and González Tiburcio 1991). Slight increases in the consumption of tortillas, eggs, and sugar can be interpreted as a dietary strategy to offset decreased consumption of other foods (meat and dairy

products, for example) and to provide a greater quantity of cheap energy based on sugar and carbohydrates.

5. Increased migration to the United States. International migration grew both as a result of the deterioration of material conditions in Mexico and as the outcome of the 1986 U.S. Immigration Reform and Control Act (IRCA) (Cornelius 1991; González de la Rocha, Escobar Latapí, and Martínez 1990; 1991). By 1996, the First Mexico—United States Binational Study of Migration estimated that 7.1 to 7.3 million Mexicans lived in the United States, and that the net annual loss to emigration stood at 290,000 persons (SRE/CIR 1997). Between 1982 and 1987, 28 percent of households in Guadalajara received remittances on a regular basis at one time or another from their members working in the United States. On the basis of national statistics, CONAPO (1999) concluded that in 1998, 6 percent of all Mexican households and 10 percent of all rural households depended wholly or partially on remittances, and that these households were increasing more rapidly than migration itself, reflecting a more intense dependence on migration to survive.

Migration also became more heterogeneous. It now includes urban residents (men and women) from working-class and middle-class backgrounds along with the individuals who formed part of the traditional flows (males of rural origin). The percentage of women from mid-sized cities of the state of Jalisco who participate in international migration has grown considerably. While women represented only 10 percent of international migrants in the period from 1975 to 1981, their presence increased to 17.2 percent in the period 1988 to 1992, and they now make up 20.3 percent of the total number of departures. Their lengthier stays in the United States once they leave Mexico, however, makes for close to parity in the sex composition of Mexicans in the United States (46 percent of all native Mexicans registered in the U.S. Census and in the annual CPS including country of origin are women). Most of these women are married, and although only a relatively small proportion of them participate in the U.S. labor markets (38 percent), their participation rate is double that of wives of migrants who still live in Mexico while their husbands have migrated to the United States (Arroyo and Papail 1996). Mexican women's participation rate in the U.S. labor markets is on the rise, as is school and college attendance of Mexican women over 15 years of age. Their unemployment levels, however, remain above those of Mexican men and more than double the U.S. unemployment rate (Escobar Latapí et al. 1996).

While urban contexts became part of transnational flows of workers, as has been the case of Guadalajara and other cities (Monterrey and Mexico

City included) traditional sending communities have also been the scenarios of changing patterns of international migration and changing but contradictory gender patterns and values. Jalostotitlán, Jalisco, is a town of 25,000 in a traditional *ranchero* sending area, Los Altos. The population is mainly of Spanish stock, and has for a century relied on agriculture and cattle raising for the mines of the North. Also, the region has provided an unusually large number of *cadres* both for the Church and the army. Fieldwork we conducted there in 1989 on the effect of IRCA on migration patterns showed that migration to the United States had increased after the implementation of IRCA and as a consequence of the Mexican economic crisis (González de la Rocha, Escobar Latapí, and Martínez 1990; González de la Rocha and Escobar Latapí 1991). Young women began migrating after marriage, breaking the trend of women staying behind in the village or town. These women decided not to follow in their mothers' footsteps: they rejected the life of solitude they had seen their mothers lead, and their own childhoods without fathers. Also, they were willing to become involved in wage-labor migration and work in the United States (González de la Rocha 1993b).

In this community there is no doubt that the crisis and the years of protracted adjustment that followed had a powerful impact on the population, in spite of the very useful measures taken by people at the household level. The burden, however, has not weighed equally on all. There are household members who are more vulnerable than others, especially women and children, given their subordinate position in the household. The distribution of food is one of the clearer examples of household dynamics vis-à-vis power relations. Food is distributed according to the status of the household members. The most prestigious items (like meat and poultry) are usually enjoyed by working age men, while women and children get soup, beans, and tortillas, and if they are lucky, some meat leftovers.

The intensification of work and the increasing interdependence of household members inside and outside of the migration process did not take place in a peaceful environment. Negotiations and the possibilities of conflict increased as contradictions increased. The new division of labor forced on these households by the crisis has not automatically produced changes in the norms and values that permeate Mexican society. The increasing feminization of domestic economies clashes with men's ideas (and society's norms) of women's place and women's roles (González de la Rocha, Escobar Latapí, and Martínez 1990; Kaztman 1992). This does not mean, of course, that norms and values are fixed elements of culture. It means—as Safa also shows in her chapter—that the norms and values which form part of cultural constructs of the feminine and the masculine domains (including types of socially accepted activities) are not as dynamic as other rapidly transforming domestic arrangements. Although women's work is currently the norm during long periods of the household cycle, women's relative power within the household has increased far less than their contributions to survival.

Work, Informality, and Poverty in the 1990s

Labor informality increased very rapidly during the 1980s in Mexican cities. The total number of person/hours devoted to informal work aimed at earning a living probably increased beyond even the 80 percent reported by ECLAC (1989). This is due to the long hours worked within informal employment in the late 1980s and 1990s. Married women, if they worked at all, tended to work only part-time (especially if they worked informally) in the 1960s and 1970s; by the late 1980s and 1990s self-employed women were working even longer hours than self-employed men.

The main macroeconomic reason for the increased participation in informal labor markets in Mexico is the stagnation of formal employment, together with an unsaturated market for cheap goods and services. However, to understand who works where in Mexico in the 1990s, one must understand people's different rationalities and their actions. There has been a flight of skilled workers from waged labor and, secondly, there have been changes in domestic work organization. Those working informally belong to two groups: those with no options who therefore must work informally, and those who prefer informal employment as a consequence of the worsening of wages and work conditions. Both groups have grown in the years since the crisis. The first, which consists mostly of women and youths, has grown because the decline in real household incomes as a result of falling real wages of the male head or other main household worker has forced them to seek employment. The lack of appropriate age, marital status, or school credentials pushes them toward informal employment. In fact, the participation of women is still rising: from 1987 to 1993, the participation of women rose from 33.2 to 40.0 percent in Guadalajara, for example. This increase is occurring mostly in informal occupations. This is partly due to the characteristics of the women entering the labor market: most have few years of schooling, are over 30, have children, and are married or separated (García and Oliveira 1994). In fact, 67 percent of the women working on their own account in Guadalajara in 1990 had not been active in 1982, and the average schooling of these women is less than 6 years (Escobar Latapí's data, from a 1990 CIESAS-INEGI survey).

The second group is self-employed because the relative attraction of independent work increases as formal wages decline.[17] In a small shoe factory in

Guadalajara, for example, a competent, loyal worker who is married and has children came to his employer to say that he was very sorry but he would have to quit and begin some sort of independent work because, for the first time, he could not support his family on his wages. He probably expected his employer to raise his wages. The employer replied that he would be sorry to lose him, but given the cut-throat competition in the industry he could not raise his wages. Skilled workers with family responsibilities have had to leave dependent employment in order to prevent further erosion of their incomes.

The two groups are clearly distinguishable as self-employed, informal workers in terms of their earnings and their working hours. Skilled and experienced married men working a 40 to 45 hour week earn an average of three times the minimum wage. Unskilled, married mothers, as well as young men and women, earn 1.6 times the minimum wage working about 6 hours more, on average, than the legal work week.[18] The first are most often mechanics, plumbers, carpenters, skilled shoe stitchers, or service and repair workers of various kinds. The latter most often work in market stalls, in street corner and sidewalk shops, or perform personal services.[19]

The rise in informality has also entailed a rise in the proportion and numbers of unpaid family workers. Among Guadalajara employed women, unpaid family workers comprised only 2.7 percent in 1978. In 1987 the proportion had grown to 8 percent. Since women's participation rates had increased by approximately 50 percent, this meant the total number of women doing unpaid work for their families' shops, food stalls, or workshops rose roughly 350 percent.

In this context, who was left to work formally for a wage in Mexico? Basically, employers in the manufacturing sector turned to younger, unmarried men and women with secondary education (9 years of schooling), who were not skilled but were willing to work for lower wages than the previous skilled workers. This type of labor is well suited to the *maquiladora* industry, which still demands mostly semi-skilled and schooled young women for assembly work.[20] This change also affected industry oriented toward the domestic market. In Guadalajara, for example, our 1990 survey of occupational structure and occupational mobility showed that in firms and agencies employing less than 250 workers, the mean age had dropped by about 3 years from 1982 to 1990.

The first source of added informality, therefore, has to do with people moving to self and family employment. The second source of informality is what has come to be called the rise of unprotected labor. After 1982, firms in the formal sector could directly employ unprotected labor through a variety of mechanisms, primarily by using temporary workers (Escobar

Latapí 1988). At present, firms in the formal sector and government agencies alike are providing less and less benefits and job security. Through reductions in wages and job security and increased labor turnover among firms, types of employment, industries and sectors, the Mexican urban working classes are becoming more and more homogeneous. Their households, which are forced to have more workers and tend to have them in diverse conditions of work and formality, operate as the basic force counteracting the lower wages and the segmenting influences of the labor market.

The third kind of informal work of special relevance to Guadalajara is small-scale production of mass consumer goods. Up to 1988, the main effect of the crisis and falling wages was to force workshops to lower production costs so their products could remain within the reach of workers (Escobar Latapí 1988). Since their own wages were dropping even faster than formal wages, workshops were able to produce cheaper goods by substituting raw materials of lower quality or cost and by intensification of the use of labor. They nevertheless faced more difficult financial conditions, and often fell under the control of *maquileros*, middlemen selling raw materials or buying up production. Other changes were: 1) increased informality of employment and production, as workshops tried to avoid taxes; 2) an increased reliance on the family as a workforce, which also helped lower production overheads and possible legal problems; and 3) a centrifugal tendency toward outsourcing, in which some outputting networks and workshops left major urban areas for their surrounding towns in order to lower their taxes and have access to cheaper labor pools. In sum, then, during this period informal workshops met new economic conditions by "productive involution," that is, more intensive labor, less technical division of labor, and less capital and machinery.

Since 1988, however, when GATT began to affect the domestic production of consumer goods, small workshops have faced an even more difficult situation. They have been forced to vacate some market niches and find others, as well as change production processes. In fact we may be witnessing the disappearance of a large part of informal production. Chinese imports, particularly, are sold at prices that the workshops cannot hope to match. This part of Mexican history is still being written. What can be said is that so far Mexican small-scale production has not successfully replicated the pattern of Taiwanese or Thai informal production, which is vital for the exporting industries in those countries. Some regions or industries do possess a more intricate matrix, linking small and large producers and exporters. In León, workshops employing one or two workers often have clients in ten different states.[21] In the shoe and garment industries, between one-fifth and one-third of the establishments classed as "microenterprises" perform partial production tasks for larger firms (INEGI 1994). This figure is valid for Guadalajara too.

But linkage formation is the exception rather than the rule for small Mexican industries. In a recent survey of microenterprises along the U.S.-Mexican border, Roberts (1992) found that the economic networks of those on the Mexican side were mostly local, and that they extended neither towards the interior nor to the southern United States. In Guadalajara, export producing multinationals such as Hewlett Packard, IBM, or Motorola proudly display their supplier training programs. However, in one of these cases, property is completely in the hands of the buyer. In the others, the networks are closed and concentrated rather than open so that, for example, when the U.S.-based parent company of a local electronics firm decided to sell its power supplies directly to IBM from U.S. sources, the local, partly Guadalajara-owned company could not find alternate clients. This happened in spite of the fact that, according to its general director, its product was superior both to the competition and to its own U.S.-produced counterpart. This firm, which had innovated its designs from scratch based only on its buyers' specifications, was forced to close. The positive side of this unfortunate situation is that Mexican exports are mostly produced by labor protected by at least a minimum amount of social and job security.

Today, informality is more competitive, less open and attractive, and therefore less significant as an option. Another economic slowdown combined with significant imports, lower general buying power, and a saturated market for many informal goods and services may mean that the kind of informal self-employment and dependent informal employment we are likely to see will be even more marginal and even less closely linked to the growth poles of the Mexican economy.

One or both of the following trends must happen in order to halt this tendency towards marginalized informality and deepening poverty in Mexican cities. The first is that the incomes of those working in the formal sector must recover so they can create a significant market for Mexican goods. The second is that those working informally must improve their capacity to produce and deliver significant goods and services, so their incomes also can improve.

In sum, increasing poverty and inequality accompanied by changes in the labor market in Guadalajara and other Mexican cities have important implications in terms of the social organization of urban households:

1. There is a greater need for multiple incomes, since precarious employment produces precarious household economies.

2. Women's work is a key element of survival, since their participation in local urban and international labor markets has increased and their incomes have become necessary components of their devastated household economies.

3. There is a greater dependence on grown children's incomes, and therefore the growth of extended households is likely to continue in the near future.

4. As a result of households' search for job opportunities abroad, Mexican cities have become more integrated into migration flows. More international migrants now belong to urban households in Mexico, and remittances have become important resources for urban economies.

Conclusion

The crisis, adjustment, and restructuring processes have had a strong impact on the population's welfare and on the social organization, division of labor, and coping strategies of the poor in urban Mexico. Households themselves have gone through a restructuring process, involving a high degree of flexibility and intensification of both domestic work and work for wages. Without these mechanisms and strategies implemented at the level of the household, it would have been extraordinarily difficult to survive during this period of time. To avoid a drastic reduction in food consumption, households have sent more members into the national and transnational job market. More youths, women, and children have entered the work force and have been obliged to migrate in order to earn the income needed for the survival of the household. Homemaking duties have increased as many goods and services once purchased in the marketplace must now be generated within the household (such as mending and reconditioning domestic items). As a result, women's domestic work load is greater, due both to the increase in the number of household members and to the increased dependence on at-home production.

Daily routine and individual actions within the household have become crucial to understanding popular responses to neoliberalism, since it is within the home that changes have been introduced to respond to economic difficulties outside the home. Given a quiescent labor movement unable to offer either a local or national class response, household unity and family solidarity have become the principal defense against deteriorating wages (although the crisis can certainly also exacerbate conflicts within households). The impact of a worsening economic situation is only partially alleviated while stress, conflicts, and violence within the household have increased, leaving some of its members in a more critical and vulnerable situation—as is the case of women and children (González de la Rocha, Escobar Latapí, and Martínez 1990).

Today, work and the household are both spheres of significant, if limited, agency for the poor. Both are subject to greater structural imperatives, but both depend on the visions, organizational capacity, and creativity of the people dealing with them. One of the toughest lessons the poor learn in order to survive, and one which social scientists must accept in order to understand them, is that poverty on its own does not turn neighbors into friends, relatives into contacts, or a very light purse into a meal. The poor learn to deal with new social situations. They learn to turn strangers into friends with basically no significant resources to draw on. This entails an intentional, positive, creative approach to one's own actions, which needs to be understood as part of a strategy of survival. Failure to acquire the relevant know-how is punishable by the failure to constitute a family, to school one's children, or even to survive. The daily struggle of the urban poor for survival is becoming even more arduous as urban labor markets are not conducive to the survival and reproduction of their poor populations. Resources are increasingly scarce and Mexican cities are, more now than in the past, sites of labor and social exclusion.

Employment and life in the United States are a significant escape route for Mexicans struggling against poverty. Although fraught with uncertainty and danger, migration in fact is an alternative open to many, including millions from states and regions that have previously been only marginally represented in the migratory flow.

Notes

1. This is part of a general pattern that has been analyzed by different scholars in diverse urban contexts (Benería 1992; Chant 1991; Selby, Murphy, and Lorenzen 1990; Murphy 1991; 1992).
2. For Latin America, see Ortega and Tironi 1988; Duarte 1988; Schkolnik and Teitelboim 1988; Singer 1985; McFarren 1992; Safa and Antrobus 1992; Hardy 1989; and Fortuna and Prates 1989.
3. In 1970, 66.8 percent of the total population, or 32.2 million people, lived in dwellings with two rooms or less. Nearly half (15.1 million) of these people were urban residents. Although the proportion of the Mexican population living in one-room dwellings decreased during the decades of economic growth (1950–1970), it was still very high at the end of this period, and overcrowding was one of the problems of housing in Mexico (Zepeda and Mohar 1993).
4. These subsidies comprised basic foodstuffs, urban infrastructure, cheap urban transport, fuels and utilities, free public schooling, real zero-cost credit for housing

construction (Escobar Latapí and Roberts 1991, based on Reyes Heroles 1985), and a privileged access to Social Security institutions, where the connections and know-how of the new middle class were particularly useful.

5. We use "working poor" since poverty is a condition of people who work, and is the result of very low wages and almost non-existent benefits, not the lack of work (Portes and Johns 1987).

6. Poor households in Mexico were 52.5 percent of the total number of households in 1981; by 1988 they were 62.5 percent (Hernández Laos 1992). In absolute numbers there was also an increase, with an additional 4 million households (22 million people) in the poverty category. In 1990, 41 million Mexicans were unable to satisfy their basic needs (were poor) and 17 million lived in extreme poverty (Tello, 1991, 59).

7. In 1990, poverty encompassed 39 percent of the urban population in Latin America (116 million people), compared to 35 percent in 1980 (CEPAL 1992a; CEPAL 1991).

8. In the seven countries of Latin America (including Mexico) which comprise 80 percent of the region's economically active population (EAP), during the period 1980–1989 the number of employed persons rose faster than the total population, and faster than the population of working age. Employment in the informal sector and in small industries rose twice as fast as the population of working age and triple the rate of population growth (CEPAL 1992b, Table 4; González de la Rocha 1993a).

9. By 1987, public sector investment in rural infrastructure had fallen to one-seventh of what it was in 1980.

10. PEMEX, the State-owned oil firm, gradually cut its payroll from 200,000 to 100,000, but retained its former production and export levels.

11. Households in extreme poverty are those whose total income is below the basic food basket value, which means that the sum of all household wages is not enough to satisfy the members' food needs.

12. Gilbert (1991, 237) reports that in 1988, while the minimum wage rose 11 percent and prices rose 52 percent, rents rose 84 percent. In 1989, minimum wages increased 14 percent, prices 20 percent, and rents 48 percent. A generalized scarcity of rental housing drove rents up and affected the survey (particularly in 1992) by placing poor homeowners in much higher income brackets than those corresponding to their cash income.

13. This program sought to avoid the government's social welfare apparatus, delivering targeted subsidies and public infrastructure directly to state and municipal governments which in turn channeled some of the specific programs to the target populations directly, provided they organized to supply labor and to negotiate with Pronasol officials and their local or state governments. It replaced general subsidies, such as low maize prices in urban areas, with programs that require qualifying for aid. According to government reports, Pronasol received only between 0.4 and 2 percent of total federal expenditure (Escobar Latapí and González de la Rocha 1991; Laurell 1994).

14. This finding met with disbelief and a skeptical appraisal of González de la Rocha's panel of 100 households, originally studied in 1982 and followed in 1985 and 1987. Later, however, independent studies and various re-analyses of official sources came to the same conclusion (Selby, Murphy, and Lorenzen 1990; De Barbieri 1993; Cortés and Rubalcava 1991).

15. Information from other Latin-American contexts shows the same phenomenon as that found by our studies in Guadalajara. Total income of urban households in Venezuela fell 22 percent and individual wages 34 percent between 1981 and 1986. The same happened to urban households in Uruguay and Costa Rica, whose total incomes dropped 14 percent while individual incomes fell by 22 percent from 1981 to 1989 (CEPAL 1991). Available information from urban Latin America shows that the importance of household income contributed by members who are not household heads increased during the 1980s (CEPAL 1991).

16. Many references to the advantages of extended households during economic hardship can be found in the literature, with a special emphasis in the flexibility that this type of household structure provides (Chant 1994; González de la Rocha 1988; 1991; Selby, Murphy, and Lorenzen 1990).

17. This is true provided informal income opportunities exist and are accessible, and as long as the market for them does not collapse as formal employment declines.

18. Escobar Latapí's data, from a 1990 survey of 5,000 Guadalajara workers.

19. There are significant differences according to gender and occupational category in the relative attraction of dependent wage employment versus self-employment. In general, men leaving a dependent occupation will earn more as independent workers. Women, on the contrary, will lose a significant part of their income, particularly if they leave professional or managerial occupations (Escobar Latapí 1995). Timing is also significant. Those who left dependent employment before the outbreak of the crisis earned significantly more than those who did not; those who left dependent employment after 1982, when competition in the informal market for goods and services was becoming harder, tended to earn less than immobile dependent workers.

20. Since 1988, analysts have announced a "second wave" of *maquiladora* expansion, consisting of more skilled, more complex labor and production processes, which would also be more closely linked to Mexican industry (Shaiken 1994). There is such a tendency, but it has not yet significantly affected the skill contents of that kind of work, although it has produced a significant shift in some of the sociodemographic characteristics of the labor force. The proportion of men working in the *maquiladoras*, for example, rose from 10 to 35 percent between 1978 and 1988 (Brannon and Lucker 1989).

21. Christopher Woodruff, personal communication

References

Arias, Patricia, ed. 1985. *Guadalajara: La Gran Ciudad de la Pequeña Industria*. Zamora: El Colegio de Michoacán.

Arroyo, Jesús and Jean Papail. 1996. *Migraciones internacionales y desarrollo regional en Jalisco*. Guadalajara: Universidad de Guadalajara.

Benería, Lourdes. 1992. The Mexican debt crisis: Restructuring the economy and the household. In *Unequal Burden: Economic Crises, Persistent Poverty, and Women's Work*, edited by Lourdes Benería and Shelley Feldman. Boulder: Westview Press.

Boltvinik, Julio. 1987. Ciudadanos de la pobreza y la marginación. *El Cotidiano*. 19 (Sept.–Oct.): 305–326.

Brannon, Jeffery T. and G.William Lucker. 1989. Impact of Mexico's economic crisis on the labor force of the maquiladora industry. *Journal of Borderlands Studies 4.* 1:39–70.

Brydon, Lynne and Sylvia Chant. 1989. *Women in the Third World: Gender Issues in Rural and Urban Areas.* Aldershot: Edward Elgar.

Castells, Manuel and Alejandro Portes. 1989. World underneath: The origins, dynamics, and effects of the informal economy. In *The Informal Economy: Studies in Advanced and Less Developed Countries,* edited by Alejandro Portes, Manuel Castells, and Lauren A. Benton. 11–37. Baltimore: The Johns Hopkins University Press.

CEPAL (Comisión Económica para América Latina y el Caribe). 1992a. El perfil de la pobreza en América Latina a comienzos de los años 90. LC/L.716.

———. 1992b. Hacia un perfil de la familia actual en Latinoamérica y el Caribe. Serie A, No. 247.

———. 1991. La equidad en el panorama social de América Latina durante los años ochenta. LC/G. 1686.

Chant, Sylvia. 1991. *Women and Survival in Mexican Cities: Perspectives on Gender, Labor Markets, and Low Income Households.* Manchester: Manchester University Press.

CONAPO. 1999. *La situación demográfica de México.* Mexico City: author.

Cordera, Rolando and Enrique González Tiburcio. 1991. Crisis and transition in the Mexican economy. In *Social Responses to Mexico's Economic Crisis of the 1980's,* edited by Mercedes González de la Rocha and Agustín Escobar Latapí. 19–56. La Jolla: Center for U.S.-Mexican Studies, University of California, San Diego.

Cornelius, Wayne A. 1991. Los Migrantes de la Crisis: The changing profile of Mexican migration to the United States. In *Social Responses to Mexico's Economic Crisis of the 1980's,* edited by Mercedes González de la Rocha and Agustín Escobar Latapí. 155–194. La Jolla: Center for U.S.-Mexican Studies, University of California, San Diego.

Cortés, Fernando. 1994. La evolución en la desigualdad del ingreso familiar durante la década de los ochenta. Mimeo.

Cortés, Fernando and Rosa María Rubalcava. 1991. Autoexplotación forzada o equidad por empobrecimiento. Mexico City: El Colegio de México.

De Barbieri, Teresita. 1993. Crisis y relaciones de género en América Latina. *Demos: Carta Demográfica sobre México.*

de Lara Rangel, Salvador. 1990. El impacto económico de la crisis sobre la clase media. In *Las clases medias en la coyuntura actual,* edited by Soledad Loaeza and Claudio Stern. *Cuadernos del CES.* 29–49. Mexico City: El Colegio de Mexico.

Dresser, Denise. 1991. *Neopopulist Solutions to Neoliberal Problems: Mexico's National Solidarity Program.* La Jolla: Center for U.S.-Mexican Studies, University of California, San Diego.

Duarte, Isis. 1988. Crisis, familia y participación laboral de la mujer en la República Dominicana. Paper presented at the 37th *Annual Latin American Conference [on the] Demography of Inequality in Contemporary Latin America.* University of Florida, Gainesville, Florida, Feb. 22.

ECLAC (Economic Commission for Latin America and the Caribbean). 1989. *The dynamics of social deterioration in Latin America and the Caribbean in the 1980's.* San José, Costa Rica: ECLAC.

Escobar Latapí, Agustín. 1986. *Con el sudor de tu frente: Mercado de trabajo y clase obrera en Guadalajara.* Guadalajara: El Colegio de Jalisco.

————. 1995. Movilidad, restructuración y clase social en México: el caso de Guadalajara. In *Estudios Sociológicos, El Colegio de México.* Vol. XIII: 38, May-August: 231–259.

Escobar Latapí, Agustín and Bryan Roberts. 1991. Urban stratification, the middle classes, and economic change in Mexico. In *Social Responses to Mexico's Economic Crisis of the 1980's,* edited by Mercedes González de la Rocha and Agustín Escobar Latapí. 91–114. La Jolla: Center for U.S.-Mexican Studies, University of California, San Diego.

Escobar Latapí, Agustín and Mercedes González de la Rocha. 1991. Introduction. In *Social Responses to Mexico's Economic Crisis of the 1980's,* edited by Mercedes González de la Rocha and Agustín Escobar Latapí. 1–18. La Jolla: Center for U.S.-Mexican Studies, University of California, San Diego.

Escobar Latapí, Agustín, Frank D. Bean, and Sidney Weintraub. 1996. *The Dynamics of Mexican Emigration.* Monograph prepared for the International Organization for Migration.

Feldman, Shelley. 1992. Crisis, poverty, and gender inequality: current themes and issues. In *Unequal Burden. Economic Crises, Persistent Poverty, and Women's Work,* edited by Lourdes Benería and Shelley Feldman. 1–25. Boulder: Westview Press.

Fortuna, Juan Carlos and Suzana Prates. 1989. Informal sector versus informalized labor relations in Uruguay. In *The Informal Economy: Studies in Advanced and Less Developed Countries,* edited by Alejandro Portes, Manuel Castells and Lauren A. Benton. 78–94. Baltimore: The Johns Hopkins University Press.

García Brígda and Orlandina de Oliveira. 1994. *Trabajo femenino y vida familiar en México.* Mexico City: Colegio de México.

Gilbert, Alan. 1991. Self-help housing during recession: the Mexican experience. In *Social Responses to Mexico's Economic Crisis of the 1980's,* edited by Mercedes González de la Rocha and Agustín Escobar Latapí. 221–242. La Jolla: Center for U.S.-Mexican Studies, University of California, San Diego.

González Block, Miguel Ángel. 1991. Economic Crisis and the Decentralization of Health Services in Mexico. In *Social Responses to Mexico's Economic Crisis of the 1980's,* edited by Mercedes González de la Rocha and Agustín Escobar Latapí. 67–90. La Jolla: Center for U.S.-Mexican Studies, University of California, San Diego.

González de la Rocha, Mercedes. 1994a. *The Resources of Poverty: Women and Survival in a Mexican City.* Oxford: Basil Blackwell.

————. 1994b. Reestructuración social en dos ciudades metropolitanas: un análisis de grupos domésticos en Guadalajara y Monterrey. Paper delivered at the panel "New Perspectives on Gender, Family and Work in Urban Mexico," XVIII LASA International Congress, 10–12 Mar., Atlanta, Georgia.

————. 1993a. Familia urbana y pobreza en América Latina. Document prepared for the Economic Commission for Latin America and the Caribbean (ECLAC). Presented at the "Reunión Regional Preparatoria del Año Internacional de la Familia," organized by ECLAC, United Nations, Aug. 10–13, Cartagena de Indias, Colombia.

————. 1993b. El poder de la ausencia: mujeres y migración en una comunidad de los Altos de Jalisco. In *Las realidades regionales de la crisis nacional*, edited by Jesús Tapia. 317–334. Zamora: El Colegio de Michoacán.

————. 1992. Los matices de la diferencia: patrones de organización doméstica entre los sectores medios y los sectores populares urbanos. Paper delivered at the conference "Sociodemographic Effects of the 1980s Mexican Economic Crisis," Austin: University of Texas at Austin, Apr.

————. 1991. Family well-being, food consumption, and survival strategies during Mexico's economic crisis. In *Social Responses to Mexico's Economic Crisis of the 1980's*, edited by Mercedes González de la Rocha and Agustín Escobar Latapí. 115–128. La Jolla: Center for U.S.-Mexican Studies, University of California, San Diego.

————. 1988. Economic crisis, domestic reorganisation, and women's work in Guadalajara, Mexico. *Bulletin of Latin American Research.* 7, 2:207–223.

————. 1986. *Los recursos de la pobreza: Familias de bajos ingresos de Guadalajara, Guadalajara.* Jalisco: El Colegio de Jalisco/CIESAS/SPP.

González de la Rocha, Mercedes. and Agustín Escobar Latapí. 1991. The impact of IRCA on the migration patterns of a community in Los Altos, Jalisco, Mexico. In *The Effects of Receiving Country Policies on Migration Flows*, edited by Sergio Díaz-Briquets and Sidney Weintraub. 205–232. Boulder: Westview Press.

González de la Rocha, Mercedes, Agustín Escobar Latapí, and María de la Martínez. 1990. Estrategias versus conflicto: Reflexiones para el estudio del grupo doméstico en época de crisis. In *Crisis, conflicto y sobrevivencia:. Estudios sobre la sociedad urbana en México*, edited by Guillermo de la Peña, et al., comps. 351–367. Guadalajara: Universidad de Guadalajara/CIESAS.

Hardy, Clarissa. 1989. *La ciudad escindida: Los problemas nacionales y la región metropolitana.* Santiago: Sociedad Editora e Impresora Alborada, S.A.

Hernández Laos, Enrique. 1992. *Crecimiento económico y pobreza en México: Una agenda para la investigación.* Mexico City: Centro de Investigaciones Interdisciplinarias en Humanidades, Universidad Autónoma de México.

Instituto Nacional de Estadística, Geografía e Informática (INEGI). 1993. Informe sobre la magnitud y evolución de la pobreza en México, 1984–1992. Mexico City: ONU-CEPAL, INEGI.

INEGI. 1994. *Encuesta Nacional de Micronegocios.* Aguascalientes: Instituto Nacioal de Estadística, Geografía e Informática.

Jusidman, Clara. 1987. Evolución del consumo en el medio urbano. Paper delivered at the Seminario Científico de la H. Asamblea General de Asociados de la Fundación Mexicana para la Salud, Mexico City.

Kaztman, Rubén. 1992. ¿Por qué los hombres son tan irresponsables? *Revista de la CEPAL.* 46:87–95.

Langer, Ana, Rafael Lozano, and José Luis Bobadilla. 1991. Effects of Mexico's economic crisis on the health of women and children. In *Social Responses to Mexico's Economic Crisis of the 1980's*, edited by Mercedes González de la Rocha and Agustín Escobar Latapí. 195–220. La Jolla: Center for U.S.-Mexican Studies, University of California, San Diego.

Laurell, Asa Cristina. 1994. Pronasol, o la pobreza de los programas contra la pobreza. *Nueva Sociedad 131* (May-Jun.): 156–170.

Lozano Ascencio, Fernando. 1993. *Bringing it Back Home: Remittances to Mexico from Migrant Workers in the United States.* Transl. by Aníbal Yáñez. Monograph Series, 37. La Jolla: Center for U.S.-Mexican Studies, University of California, San Diego.

McFarren, Wendy. 1992. The politics of Bolivia's economic crisis: survival strategies of displaced tin-mining households. In *Unequal Burden, Economic Crises, Persistent Poverty, and Women's Work,* edited by Lourdes Benería and Shelley Feldman. 131–158. Boulder: Westview Press.

Morris, Lydia. 1990. *The Workings of the Household.* Cambridge: Polity Press.

Murphy, Arthur. 1991. City in Crisis: Introduction and Overview. *Urban Anthropology* (Special Issue) 20, 1: 1–13.

———. 1992. Crisis and change in a regional city: The case of Oaxaca, Mexico. Paper prepared for the conference "Sociodemographic Effects of the 1980s Economic Crisis in Mexico," Institute of Latin American Studies, University of Texas at Austin, Apr. 23–25.

Ortega, Eugenio and Ernesto Tironi. 1988. *Pobreza en Chile.* Santiago de Chile: Centro de Estudios del Desarrollo.

Pérez-Alemán, Paola. 1992. Economic crisis and women in Nicaragua. In *Unequal Burden. Economic Crises, Persistent Poverty, and Women's Work,* edited by Lourdes Benería and Shelley Feldman. 239–258. Boulder: Westview Press.

Portes, Alejandro and Michael Johns. 1987. The polarization of class and space in the contemporary Latin American city. mimeo.

Reyes Heroles G.G., Jesús. 1985. Política económica y bienestar social: elementos de una estrategia para redistribuir el ingreso en México. In *Igualdad, desigualdad y equidad en España y México.* 405–442. Madrid: Instituto de Cooperación Económica/El Colegio de México.

———. 1983. *Política macroeconómica y bienestar en México.* Mexico City: Fondo de Cultura Económica.

Roberts, Bryan. 1992. Enterprise and labor markets. The border and the metropolitan areas. *Working Paper No. 32.* New York: Russell Sage Foundation.

Roberts, Bryan R. and Agustín Escobar Latapí. 1996. Mexican social and economic policy and emigration. *Population Research Center.* University of Texas at Austin.

Safa, Helen and Peggy Antrobus. 1992. Women and the economic crisis in the Caribbean. In *Unequal Burden: Economic Crises, Persistent Poverty, and Women's Work,* edited by Lourdes Benería and Shelley Feldman. 49–82. Boulder: Westview Press.

Schkolnik, Mariana and Berta Teitelboim. 1988. *Pobreza y desempleo en poblaciones: La otra cara del modelo neoliberal. Colección Temas Sociales, 2.* Santiago: Programa de Economía del Trabajo, Academia de Humanismo Cristiano.

Selby, Henry, Arthur Murphy, and Stephen Lorenzen. 1990. *The Mexican Urban Household: Organizing for Self-defense.* Austin: University of Texas Press.

Shaiken, Harley. 1994. Advanced manufacturing and Mexico: a new international division of labour. *Latin American Research Review.* 29(2):37–72.

Singer, Paul. 1985. *Repartição da renda: Pobres e ricos sob o regime militar.* 2d ed. Rio de Janeiro: Jorge Sahar Editor.

SRE/CIR. 1997. *First Bi-national Mexico-U.S. Study of Migration*. Mexico City and Washington, D.C.: authors.

Tello, Carlos. 1991. Combating poverty in Mexico. In *Social Responses to Mexico's Economic Crisis of the 1980's*, edited by Mercedes González de la Rocha and Agustín Escobar Latapí. 57–66. La Jolla: Center for U.S.-Mexican Studies, University of California, San Diego.

Tuirán Gutiérrez, Rodolfo. 1993. *Estrategias familiares de vida en época de crisis: el caso de México*. (Serie A-CELADE, n. 246) Paper presented at Workshop Trabajo sobre Familia, Desarrollo y Dinámica de Población en América Latina y el Caribe, Santiago, 27–29 November 1991.

Zepeda, Pedro and Alejandro Mohar. 1993. *Vivienda para pobladores de bajos ingresos: Políticas e instituciones*. Mexico City: Consejo Consultivo del Programa Nacional de Solidaridad/ El Nacional.

9

Space, Power, and Representation in Yucatán

Oriol Pi-Sunyer

All cultures tend to make representations of foreign cultures the better to master or in some way control them. Yet not all cultures make representations of foreign cultures and in fact control them (Said 1994, 100).

Foreword

This chapter is on how locations are transformed into touristic destinations. I will look at what is taking place in Quintana Roo, in southeastern Mexico, and more specifically at how the construction of tourist sites is instrumental in foreclosing—limiting, erasing, simplifying—an understanding of complex cultural and political universes. It is also a discussion of globalization in previously marginal and isolated places and of how the material conditions of the poor (typically peasants or post-peasants) put constraints on their ability to participate in transnational systems.

The attraction of such destinations for the Western visitor is grounded in an idealization and romanticization of the exotic, whether this be represented by landscapes, "appropriate" indigenous peoples, or the ruins of ancient civilizations. This phenomenon no doubt reflects a growing ignorance of real rural life and of non-urban environments in general. The call for the protection of such spaces is often accompanied by a desire to control or denigrate peripheral people who live in them. Chaia Heller (1999, 17), in her discussion of ecological ideologies, notes that the same radical ecologists who express a romantic desire for "Mother Earth," often reduce third world women through a discourse on overpopulation "to masses of faceless bodies devouring the scarce resources of the world." Needless to say, people so positioned are unlikely to be thought worthy of agency or voice. Much the same critique has been made by Conrad Kottak (1999, 27) when he identifies developmentalism and environmentalism as related Euro-American belief systems, and decries the fact that "local people, their landscapes, their ideas, their values, their traditional management systems are being attacked from all sides." In Quintana Roo, pressures of this type are directly related to the penetration of tourism, which is not simply a new industry, but a transnational intervention with claims to knowledge and authority about the places in which it intervenes.

Introduction: Geographic Imaginations

In a 1998 article, Sherry Ortner discusses how "public culture," which she defines as "all the products of art and entertainment . . . as well as all the texts of information and analysis," aspires, through images, claims, and representations, "to speak to and about actual people in the United States" (414). She proceeds to note how theories of representation compel us to think about representations "as produced and consumed within a field of inequality and power" (Ortner 1998, 434), and elaborates on the role—actual or potential—of ethnography in understanding "modern" phenomena.[1]

In much the same way that Ortner claims that public culture, with its array of models, metaphors, and stereotypes, functions as a master narrative to explain, describe, and represent how the American social and cultural world is put together, it can be argued that tourism has become one of the principal mechanisms through which our knowledge of the world and other societies, past and present, is shaped (Mowforth and Munt 1998, 6–7; Kirshenblatt-Gimblett 1998; Lowenthal 1985). Here, "tourism" is used to describe not only leisure travel itself, but a massive industry catering to travelers and would-be travelers.[2] The explicatory role of the travel narrative (more or less factual, more or less fictional) dates at least to the European age of discovery (Elliott 1989). In an essay on nineteenth-century North American travel narratives, Salvatore (1996, 86) has discussed how travel writing "was a fecund site for the construction and organization of difference" and how travelers, through the act of writing, were engaged in a constant redefinition of self and other. This task not only involved a great deal of simplification, but commonly produced narratives that effaced or homogenized native peoples, as was the case with a great deal of the writing on the American West (Greenfield 1992; on artists and the West see Rodríguez 1989; Hughes 1997, 137–205) and with much of the literature on colonial Africa (Pratt 1992; Davidson 1964).[3]

If the travel narratives and related narrative fiction of an earlier time (see Said's [1994, 62–80] discussion of narrative and social space) characterized the outlying world for the domestic consumer, a body of more recent cultural products perform a comparable role for distant places, particularly "exotic" ones.[4] Imaginative spaces themselves—"non-Western" for example—must be filled, even if the content undergoes some change over time (Clifford 1988; on the role of museums see Price 1989). But what is striking is the degree to which very old themes are redeployed with relatively minor alteration. Lutz and Collins (1993, 89–90) in their account of the role of the National Geographic, for over a century middle-class America's lens on the world, explain that "the eye of the National Geographic . . . looks for cultural difference. It is continually drawn to people in brightly colored, 'different' dress, engaged in initially strange-seeming rituals or inexplicable behavior." The National Geographic's world, populated for the most part by young, healthy, and handsome-looking people (typically brown-skinned younger women and children) is depicted as essentially unproblematic, easily comprehensible in terms of common humanity. Images (and text) mediate nature and culture, provide material for stories of race and gender, modernity, and primordialism. Elements of this geographical imagination have long formed part of European travel lore (Trouillot 1991). Finally, the National Geographic not only portrays the outside world, but claims to speak about it with authority, a characteristic that it shares with many other institutions and products of popular culture.[5]

Tourism, perhaps less obviously because of its characterization as a leisure activity, is engaged in essentially the same task. As Crick (1989, 329) has stated, "the imagery of international tourism is not, for the most part, about socioeconomic reality at all." And he proceeds: "The places in the glossy brochures of the travel industry do not exist; the destinations are not real places, and the people pictured are false." Touristic spaces play many different roles. Thus, Errington and Gewertz (1989, 42) have described how Melanesia serves some visitors as the proper backdrop for self-realization quests, encounters "with what was seen as 'primitive'" which contribute to the traveler's sense of "individuality, integration, and authenticity." Again, what stands out is the degree to which the visitor uses travel not as a road for intellectual growth, but as therapy or a mechanism for the reaffirmation of established categories of alterity and inequality—while concurrently feeling virtuous about the whole endeavor. In short, examined from the consumption end of the business, contemporary tourism supports inter- and intra-class differentiation by helping to construct cognitive systems—"habitus" or "lifestyles"—which give people and class segments a sense of their place in the world (Mowforth and Munt 1998, 128–136; Bourdieu 1984; Lamaison 1986, 118–119).

Two related issues have drawn the attention of researchers and commentators. The first, by now thoroughly developed in the literature, is the extent to which the industry is involved in the transformation of cultural meanings (Clifford 1997, 188–219, 220–237; Rojek 1997), or as Greenwood (1989, 179) expresses it, "all the 'natural resources,' including cultural traditions, have their price, and if you have the money in hand, it is your right to see whatever you wish;" and, one might add, change it to your liking. The other concern is grounded in the recognition that this transformation of touristic spaces is due to something more than the inevitability of change, or to a nostalgic search for a supposedly simpler existence. In many places, it also encodes a socio-spatial framework for reproducing a topography of boundedness and difference. Especially in third-world environments, colonial ontologies give rise to discursive practices that obscure the complexity of "host society" social relations and naturalize the cartography of power (Edensor 1998; Escobar 1995, 10–11; Gordon 1992; Goswami 1996, 55–56; Hall 1994).

By "cartography of power," I have in mind those processes and practices that entail the social reorganization of space; changed meanings of knowledge, social group, and power; and the consequences of commodification (Low 1996, 399). More generally, the concept points to the social construction of the spatial as a product of both collective mythologies— "wilderness," "primitive society," etc.—and concrete interventions in the landscape (Cooper 1999, 377–379). In Quintana Roo, the most obvious interventions take the form of resort development and the establishment of protected zones such as the Sian Ka'an Biosphere Reserve. While "cartography" is metaphorical shorthand, the means by which social relations and social practices are situated in social space have a material dimension: the terrain itself and the manner of its allocation, supported by an array of maps, literature, and pictorial representations. Although spatial categorization and segregation antedates by centuries the contemporary global system, the commodification of space in locations such as Quintana Roo reflects the power and influence of neoliberal economic and social values grafted onto much older constructs.

Mapping Mexico's South

As a consequence of extensive resort development, of which Cancún is the most evident example, Quintana Roo has, since the early 1970s, experienced rapid and uneven social and economic change (for programs and economic projections see Quintana Roo 1987). A measure of this change is demographic: in 1930 the total population of Quintana Roo, then a Federal Territory, was just over 10,000, a figure that would increase to more than 50,000 by 1960 (Dirección General de Estadística 1962, 7), and is now well over 700,000. From the 1960s to the present, the state has been transformed from what one observer (Joseph 1995, 269) describes as "a dependent territory, ethnically homogeneous, agricultural and isolated" to a region based on tertiary industries (chiefly tourism), ethnically heterogeneous and "marked by deep socioeconomic contrasts." One of the most obvious consequences of this transformation is a physical environment that reflects the ascendancy of an extreme modernizing agenda. As one traverses a patchwork of ethnoscapes (Appadurai 1990; 1991) and landscapes, the evidence of how Quintana Roo is being reconfigured—massive public works projects, resort development, theme parks, supermarkets, foreign franchises—is overwhelming and puts into stark relief the decline of village-based communities.[6]

But more is taking place than the displacement of the old by the new. Less evident is appropriation and contradiction, the emergence of new social groups, divisions within indigenous communities (political and religious), struggles over land and resources, the role of the state, and the influence of still-powerful collective sentiments. A setting of this type is not easily rendered in linear forms that seldom have room for complex local responses. As Zárate Hernández (1998, 139) suggests with respect to another part of Mexico, "local societies are not totally autonomous, but neither are they simply passive recipients of the grand projects of modernization."

What I am proposing is that Quintana Roo, because of its history (recent and not so recent) and its social and ethnic composition, offers myriad spaces for negotiation and contestation, as well as a particularly rich environment for the elaboration of modes of geographic imagination. These universes coexist, but influence one another only in indirect ways. I will first discuss how national elites and foreigners conceptualized this region, indeed all of the southern Mexican frontier. I will later examine how local people understood this same world, and the policies to which it has been subjected. Consequently, my "mapping" shifts in focus.[7] The initial discussion of metropolitan views is of a general order and considers the role of peripheries for national directorates and foreign observers. Later, the focus narrows to examine how past and present are interpreted by the Maya—or at least some of them. The essay concludes with a discussion of peripheries in the formulation of political and economic policies. Implicit in the whole discussion is the assumption that ethnographic knowledge can make a contribution to a serious understanding of national and transnational processes and the assumptions that underlie them.

From colonial times to a few decades ago, Quintana Roo was positioned at the outer edge of the Mexican imagination. It is a telling irony that the *presidio* of Bacalar, the southernmost military outpost of New Spain, was also the last fragment of Mexican territory abandoned by the Spanish crown (1826). The fort was so isolated that for years the garrison had little to fear from newly-independent Mexico.[8] In 1847, on the eve of the War of the Castes, the most serious and protracted Indian rebellion in the postcolonial New World, Mexican troops garrisoned Bacalar. The rebellion broke out through much of Yucatán and during the long war Indian rebels needed to control the Bacalar fort, the town that it protected, and in particular the trade routes to the British settlement on the coast of Honduras, source of British-made weapons (Sullivan 1989, 115–123). Bacalar fell to Indian insurgents in 1848, was recaptured a year later, and came under Mayan control after a long siege in 1858. Eventually, and after much bloodshed, the Mexican army retook it.

The siege of Bacalar is one episode—a telling one, to be sure—in a conflict that dragged on for decades and slowly wound down as the balance of military power shifted to the Mexican army. Following their failure to take the city of Mérida, capital of all of Yucatán, the Mayan insurgents retreated east and south and established their headquarters and religious center at Chan Santa Cruz (now Felipe Carrillo Puerto), which only fell to the Federal army in 1901. But state control remained tenuous much beyond the main lines of communication. The Maya, for their part, never conceded defeat. Farriss (1984, 19) is of the opinion that "perhaps the conquest was not complete until 1969" with the death of the last indigenous leaders of this long struggle.

What is significant for our purposes is that the war, and the protracted insurgency that followed it, helped define the region for generations of Mexicans. Draconian campaigns by Federal troops well into this century reinforced the Mayan sense that the agents of the state were brutal and untrustworthy, in no sense different, and perhaps even worse, than the Spanish who preceded them.[9] The other side of the coin is that the directing classes of Mexico—to the extent that they gave the matter much thought—regarded Quintana Roo as "an unhealthy place full of hostile Indians" (Villa Rojas 1945, 29; see also Sapper 1904) that contributed little of value to national society. Typical of this perspective is the opinion voiced by a former Mexican army doctor interviewed by the American journalist John Kenneth Turner (1969, 123) in the early 1900s: "Quintana Roo is the most unhealthy part of Mexico... for every soldier killed by a Maya at least one hundred die of starvation or sickness." For much of the nineteenth century, the official policy can be summed up as the classic colonial enterprise of "wresting from the barbarous Indians the lands that they occupy" (*Revista de Mérida*, April 1, 1875, 2, quoted by Sullivan 1989, 169).

This long period of war in a distant and supposedly unhealthy place framed the region for the Mexican directorate. It is significant that from the 1870s onwards—the long presidency of the modernizing Porfirio Díaz—official Mexico placed its hopes on the controlling and civilizing possibilities of technology, particularly on rail- and road-building projects. Technological advance against adverse nature and recalcitrant populations is a common enough colonial trope, but it takes on particular salience when we remember that contemporary plans for the "integration" of Quintana Roo would similarly be based on the technologies of the era: computer-assisted modeling, state investment in infrastructure, and large-scale resort development.

All of this has a bearing on geographical imagination, perhaps most notably on the place assigned to the contemporary Maya. Surprisingly perhaps, they have been given or offered no significant role in touristic representation and are minimally visible even as recipients of government services. To claim that this erasure is a consequence of the War of the Castes and its aftermath is a simplification, but there are continuities evident in stereotypes of the Maya as backward, ignorant, uncivilized, and a danger to the state—an image that has been powerfully reinforced by events in Chiapas. Also, as Geertz (1994; see also Tsing 1993) has commented with reference to Southeast Asia, marginal post-primitives are often an embarrassment to modernizing national elites: they may remind them of their own neo-modernity and do not fit contemporary representations of progress. The options may be reduced to transforming the natives into folkloric performers (MacCannell 1992) or pretending that they are hardly there.[10] We can add two further elements that reinforce invisibility. One is the historically deep cleavage between indigenous peoples and *ladinos*[11] throughout southern Mesoamerica, a separation that manifests itself in a marked social distance and an etiquette of inequality (van den Berghe 1994, 36–37). The other is the longstanding reluctance on the part of the Mexican state to treat members of indigenous communities as other than individual citizens. As Hvalkof discusses with regards to Peruvian Amazonian indigenous groups in his chapter, this Enlightenment-inspired policy effectively defines indigenous cultural identity as a matter of custom: archaic, superficial, even inimical to modern political culture. Policies of this type are fully compatible with an official *indigenismo*, an Indianist imaginary that seeks the roots of national identity in the glories of pre-Columbian cultures now safely in the past.

The ideological use being made of the Maya is profoundly disturbing. Invisibility transforms a substantial sector of the population into "a people without history" (Wolf 1982, 4), stripped of significant role or voice for modern times. But the conceptual vacuum also offers space for foreign (and foreign combined with domestic) geographical imaginations.

Quintana Roo, and other southern zones, have for more than a century and a half fascinated a certain type of foreign traveler (for a general discussion of eighteenth-century travelers, see Löfgren 1999, 16–40). Probably the most important visitors—though not the first—in elaborating a durable image of place were the American John Lloyd Stephens (a diplomat in search of a mission) and his traveling companion, the English illustrator

Frederick Catherwood (Stephens 1841; 1843; Catherwood 1844).[12] Stephens, while not insensitive to such matters as the forced labor extracted from Mayan peasants, records an undifferentiated mass of humble peasants "trained to the most abject submission" (1843, 120; Farriss 1984, 538). The Mexican archaeologist Ignacio Bernal (1980, 121) is no doubt correct in noting that he was a man of his time, little concerned with the sociology of peripheral places, who "set himself wholeheartedly to the study of Mexican antiquities." What emerges from Stephens' four volumes of travel and adventure is the insistence on the grandeur of southern Mesoamerica's ancient civilizations. Arriving at the forest-enveloped site of Copán—which he later "bought" for the grand sum of $50 (Stephens 1841, 128)—he comes face to face with a Mayan *stela*:

> The sight of this unexpected monument put at rest once and forever, in our minds, all uncertainty in regard to the character of American antiquities, and gave us the assurance that the objects we were in search of were interesting, not only as the remains of an unknown people, but as works of art proving, like newly discovered historical records, that the people who once occupied the continent of America were not savages (Stephens 1841, 1, 102).

For Stephens, the importance of this find (and others that would follow) is two-fold: it establishes the idea of monument-as-document, and less explicitly, traces a divide between past and present. If the people who had previously lived in southern Mesoamerica were "not savages," it is by no means clear that the same can be said of contemporary inhabitants. In fact, at one juncture in the "purchase" of Copán he makes a show of status—"I opened my trunk, and put on a diplomatic coat, with a profusion of large eagle buttons" (Stephens 1841, 1, 127)—the better to impress the owner of the land, who was thus made to realize that his visitor was "an illustrious incognito" (Stephens 1841, 1, 128). Stephens likens this encounter to that of British officers treating with African potentates.

Stephens' books remain in print (in the first nine months *Incidents of Travel* ran through nine editions!) because they so thoroughly encapsulate a particular construction of place. The dominant motif is that of the forest-buried city deep in hostile and mysterious territory. It is an early example of what Said (1994, 210–212) has called "exploration narrative," essentially a description of a quest, of how that which is wild and dangerous is made to reveal its deepest secrets to the intrepid explorer. Catherwood's superb engravings depict sites that are not just surrounded by trees, but appear to emerge from the tropical forest itself, locales which are thus part natural history, part archaeology. Catherwood's illustrations are also rich with "fauna:" obligatory natives, monkeys, snakes, and other denizens of this exotic world.

Stephens and Catherwood did not invent the travel tale, and were not the first outsiders to visit the Mayan lowlands, but they contributed greatly to a particular way of seeing and interpreting. As authors, they straddled the worlds of popular writing and the beginnings of serious archaeological research and, in the latter category, have been credited with setting "the tone for Maya archaeology during the following century" (Henderson 1981, 35–36). Certainly, almost a century later, we detect a very similar tone in Sylvanus Morley's (1920, 431) description of Copán: "Copán may be aptly called 'the Athens of the New World,' a title the writer has been wont to bestow upon her in drawing analogies from the ancient cities of the Old World." Again, no question that the ancient residents were a civilized people—comparable to Athenians.

Stephens and Catherwood, and those who followed them, were not simply visitors, but visitors with a purpose. At first, what foreign explorers most eagerly sought was the location of archaeological sites, and "later visitors sought a much wider range of information—about social life, farming, hunting, language, religion, history" (Sullivan 1989, 128; see also Castañeda 1996, 109–110, 280–285). The Maya, for their part—in the course of seeking foreign allies—revealed much of themselves and helped to "construct an image for foreigners to write down and take home with them" (Sullivan 1989, 130). However, this was hardly equal exchange. For outsiders, it often entailed a highly instrumental approach: they knew what they wanted and the trick was to persuade the inhabitants to come forth with the desired information. In the interests of "science" and "objectivity," many visitors hid their real intentions and were not above deceit and lying (Castañeda 1996, 54–55, 113–122).

This past has helped to fix an image of people and place that in many respects persists in both popular and professional forms. Ethnographically, it transformed the Maya themselves into the case example of "closed corporate communities" and "folk cultures"—structures and identities in opposition to "modernity" (Redfield 1941; 1947; 1950; Redfield and Villa Rojas 1934). Somewhat later, the spatial-social theory of a folk-urban continuum was designed to account for a dichotomy between preliterate, religious, and familial peasant life and a literate, secular, individualized, and depersonalized modern urban society. The sense of a Yucatán composed of villages, some certainly more "modernized" than others, but all substantially removed from "civilization" lingers to this day. Granted that conditions were very different 60 or more years ago, what we can term the Redfield paradigm is not explicable by the passage of time alone. It is essentially a model of gradients: the different degrees to which various communities have been exposed to "schools, roads, and economic exploitation" (Redfield and Villa Rojas 1934, 1); it assumes that a village can "choose progress" and that there is a relatively well defined "Road to the Light" (a chapter title in A Village *that Chose Progress* [Redfield 1950]). Perhaps because the future seems so clear and inevitable, transition from one social formation to another is described in terms of steps and contrasts. Certainly there is very little attempt in this extensive ethnographic literature to understand how villagers "make sense" of the "outside" world or engage in their own process of selection and incorporation of alien elements.

More recent writing has stressed the degree to which those cultural characteristics and identities commonly referred to as "Indian" or "traditional" are in good measure a product of four centuries of colonial control followed by national policies that have not been significantly different (Annis 1987; Friedlander 1975; Frye 1996). However, this theoretical reorientation has found it difficult to overcome a long-established model of boundedness, difference, and stasis. Altogether, this facilitates the positioning of indigenous societies somewhere beyond, or on the outer fringes of, the modern world.

Finally, contemporary geographical imaginations of southern Mesoamerica have been strongly influenced by environmental ideology and practice, a powerful socio-political movement devoted to "the preservation of nature," and which in various ways is engaged in furthering so-called "biocentric" ecologies. In this scheme of things as well, people are typically secondary, and certainly the needs of poor local inhabitants are all too easily overlooked. The link between contemporary environmentalism and past history is a matter that we will address later in this chapter.

Maya Ethnoscapes and Dreamscapes

In this section we will be discussing some Mayan responses to the forces at work in the material and ideational space that they inhabit, and increasingly share with others. In part, these responses reflect the ways in which changes in society, culture, and territory reconfigure group identity in late twentieth-century Mexico. Now as in the past, the Maya respond to the external in diverse ways that include marshaling and realigning perspectives on time, history, religion, and the social order. As Appadurai (1991, 197) has commented, "we live in a world of many different realisms" in which the products of the imagination—"dreams, songs, fantasies, myths, and stories"— acquire new power, while the boundaries between different forms of realism become blurred.

To speak or write of "the Maya" is itself something of a distortion. The contemporary Mayan-speaking societies of Mesoamerica occupy an extensive territory in southern Mexico, Guatemala, and Belize. They live in very different physical environments—the highlands of Guatemala and Chiapas, the lowlands of the Yucatán peninsula, including parts of Belize—and their recent experience reflects specific historical events in these countries (Vogt 1969, 21–23). While not generally thought of as a diasporic people, wars, repression, and upheavals have sent them far from their homelands, not only across the borders of southern Mesoamerica, but to such distant places as the United States. It is estimated that over 50,000 Mayas (a much larger number were internally displaced) were among the refugees who fled Guatemala in the 1980s; some 20,000 have settled in Los Angeles and other southern California communities (*The New York Times*, October 4, 1998, 23). Like other Native American groups—and for a longer period than most—the Maya are the survivors of "an apocalyptic history of European and Euro-American contact, colonialism, territorial disenfranchisement, attempted cultural genocide, persecution, and prejudice" (Erlandson 1998, 478).

This experience and memory bears very directly on how Mayan people engage in the task of reshaping their universe, and in the process are constantly reinventing their own culture. Farriss (1984, 6) has called it "a collective enterprise in which man, nature, and the gods are all linked." The capacity both to resist and to change was indispensable under colonial rule, and the pattern remains roughly the same, although with a different mix of elements and, hardly surprisingly, some ultra-modern features.

As earlier indicated, the village of Chan Kom in the southern part of the state of Yucatán (across the Quintana Roo border) is one of those anthropological locations that carries the burden of decades of anthropological research and a corresponding weight of anthropological theory. It is useful to consider how very differently ethnographers currently working in the area conceptualize the elements of diversity present in the community and the region. In contrast to a set of oppositional "traits" positioned in taxonomically different spaces, there is a sense of merging elements and what at first may seem anomalous situations. For example, in a fascinating passage in her ethnography of Chan Kom, one of Alicia Re Cruz's narrators explains that the *aluxes*, forest guardian spirits of Cancún, are not amused by what has been done to their domain:

> The Yuntziles, *aluxes* of Cancún, don't want anyone to live there because it [Cancún] is theirs. It is said that all Cancún is going to be flooded, not even the cars will be able to escape. Everyone is going to drown, until no one is left there, even the hotels, everything is going to disappear (Re Cruz 1996, 140).

The image of the Ritz-Carlton Cancún, the Hyatt Cancún Caribe, and another 140-odd hostelries following the fate of the Titanic at the instigation of dwarf-tricksters is not without irony; after all, it is the most flashy products of western material culture that are destined to be swallowed up by the lagoon. But, fundamentally, the role of this tale is explanatory: a way of "internalizing"—and thus in part controlling—a dominating urban presence that is both necessary and destructive. Re Cruz explains at some length that for the people of Chan Kom Cancún functions as a "second *milpa*" (corn field), an alternative or supplementary source of livelihood. However, temporary employment in, or migration to, this city carries with it severe cultural and spatial dislocation:

> Among the urban challenges that the migrant faces, the factor that stands at the core of the changeable representation is the basic relation between home and workplace. All the imagery encapsulated in *milpa* production, the quintessence of socioeconomic and symbolic Maya identity, is based on the unit of production and consumption, the household. Migration breaks this connection between a household that is no longer a unit of production, and the workplace, the city (Re Cruz 1996, 149).

How to manage the reality of an urban workplace that is no longer the site of social value and where the migrant is rewarded by wages and situated at the very base of a hierarchy of power and control? One way is to recognize, symbolically and materially, both the importance of boundaries and the fact that people today live and work in a world of shifting and overlapping realities. In Chan Kom and most other Mayan villages, labor migration is hardly a choice, but it is a culturally decentering experience for people who until very recently had very substantial control over the means of production. Pérez-Taylor (1994, 234), an anthropologist who has conducted fieldwork among the poor (some Maya, others not) in Cancún describes the situation:

> The informants, from their position as workers, offer [an image of] Cancún as a society covered by a simulacrum—one sees what is not [real]—but they also express how their lives . . . have been affected; [how] the lack of security. . . leads to distrust and fear (my translation).

Distrust and fear may be manifested, and to some degree managed, in a variety of ways. As an example, we offer the comments made in June 1998 by one of our Mayan interlocutors. These words were not offered in answer to a particular line of inquiry, but simply as a response to the type of query— How have you been, how is your family?—one makes after a long absence. Our friend is a middle-aged corn farmer from an interior village who assigns a great deal of cultural value to the making of *milpa*—the whole cycle of slash-and-burn agriculture that has underpinned communal life for centuries.[13] He has had considerable experience working outside the community, mostly as a construction worker on projects linked to coastal resort development. Not remarkable for indigenous Mexico, he is a member of an evangelical congregation, one of the several Christian churches that have contributed so much to the transformation of Middle American religious environments. Finally, he lives close to a major Classic Mayan site and, together with his family, is an avid television viewer; in fact, watching programs in his house—and discussing them afterwards—is an experience to which we always look forward.

This sketchy biography may help contextualize our friend's response. He began by telling us that he was well in health, and so were the rest of his family (we had brought news from one of his sons working on the coast). He then proceeded to tell us that life had been very difficult in the village and elsewhere:

This has been a terrible year for the fields: there has been a great drought, nothing will grow. The seeds die in the ground and the leaves of the new plants dry up, burned by the sun. We have had only two good years in the last five, and in some years it hasn't even been worthwhile to plant corn or other crops.

And then he proceeded to elaborate:

On top of all these problems, the general conditions are bad, very bad. There is lots of crime, high prices for everything, insecurity. Without food from the *milpa,* people are forced to seek work elsewhere, something that is increasingly necessary, and for longer periods of time. All of this uncertainty makes me think of what happened to the Old Ones and their great cities. It is said that famine and war finished most of them off, and that a small number—our ancestors—survived in the forest. It is also written in the Bible that pestilence, war, and disarray will end the world as we know it. After the Apocalypse those who survive will enjoy peace and plenty. There will be no crime, no corruption. The Millennium, some say, is close at hand.

All of this was expressed quietly, with little apparent emotion, but with great sincerity, while sipping a Coca-Cola; an utterance invested "with the highest moral character" (Gutiérrez-Estévez 1998, 322). It is a remarkable statement that links past, present, and future, joining the great Mayan collapse of more than 1,000 years ago to scriptural prophecy, the problems of the present, and how these might resolve themselves on a cosmic scale.[14]

This commentary was not without its touch of ecological concern. It was not just the cultivated plants that were suffering, but also the forest: "One sees far fewer animals today, far fewer deer." Perhaps uneasy that we might find the prospects disturbing, he smilingly assured us, "But, of course, you will all be fine, you are good people."

Although it was certainly unstudied, this account fits comfortably the canons of Mayan oral literature whose "greatest emphasis in oratory is on sermons . . . which are usually prophetic and apocalyptic" (Edmonson and Bricker 1985, 58). Now, and in the past, the Maya have set great store by their books and their prophets, and for our friend the Bible is the book of knowledge and revelation. Writing of the corpus of secret post-Conquest Mayan literature, Inga Clendinnen (1987, 135) notes that "that Maya conviction that all things have pattern, however little obvious that pattern may seem to be, provided the dynamic for the Books of Chilam Balam," and later on comments (1987, 161) that "a shared understanding of the past," as recorded in this literature, "enabled the Maya to confront a dangerous present and a problematic future with something close to equanimity." The colonial Maya, powerfully influenced by the Spaniards, and utilizing their script (but not their language), wrote syncretic narratives that remained true to their past while providing a much-needed sense of continuity.

The commentary of our friend, of some 20 minutes duration, we believe, represents not only a personal opinion, but also opens a window on matters that preoccupy Mayan villagers. This is an environment whose workings are hard to fathom, but whose consequences are felt every day. Physical and psychological security, or lack thereof, is the permanent concern of villagers and, in different forms, of most of the inhabitants of Quintana Roo. What, presumably, is supposed to reassure the citizenry, often accomplishes the opposite. This is true of optimistic government bulletins that repeatedly stress improvements and bright futures, and of the heavy military presence—roadblocks, patrols along the beaches and through residential areas—that has become an integral part of daily life. Up to a point, one learns to live intermingled with soldiers and their convoys. It is much harder to determine what they are doing, and certainly explanations are few. Perhaps it is not too extreme to speak of a geography of fear, an upside-down universe that is the antithesis of that idealization of order, structure, and predictability so fundamental to Mayan cosmologies.

Central to the dislocations is the impact of economic restructuring, foreign investment, and privatization. These are issues that I have addressed in earlier publications (Daltabuit and Pi-Sunyer 1990; Pi-Sunyer and Thomas 1997; Pi-Sunyer, Thomas, and Daltabuit 1999) and that touch all of Mexican society. In brief, incorporation into the global market system through NAFTA (North American Free Trade Agreement) has increased socioeconomic inequality to an extent revealed in the government's own figures which show that, by the mid-1990s, real wages had declined by more than half of their 1980 value, and half the labor force lived below the poverty line (Valdez 1996, 109). Of particular significance for Mayan agriculturalists is the virtual revocation of Article 27 of the Constitution, which permits and encourages the privatization of communally-owned *ejido* land, dismantling a multipurpose institution that reproduces key elements of agrarian society (Simpson 1937). It is hardly remarkable that these very genuine threats induce responses that include prophecy and the hope that Cancún—a place of fear, although also a place of work—will be swallowed up by the waters of its lagoon.

What should come through from this too-brief discussion is the richness of Mayan life and imagination. In Quintana Roo ordinary corn farmers travel through time and knit together ancient tragedies, Biblical lore (adapted to Mayan needs), and the genuinely unfathomable world of Mexican crony capitalism and foreign entitlement. None of this richness forms part of standard geographical imagination, or even of fairly sophisticated travel writing.

Peripheral Places, State Formation, and Transnationalism

At the beginning of this chapter I asked how locations are transformed into touristic destinations. Numerous factors contribute to this reconfiguration, not the least the redeployment for the contemporary traveler of an extensive repertoire of long-established images and fantasies. The argument that I will develop in this final section is that an understanding of tourism in locations such as Quintana Roo requires not only a recognition of the power of such images, but a sense of how they are linked to the processes of state formation and the economics of transnationalism. This discussion is premised on the assumption that landscapes and places can be read as texts: their organization is intended to communicate meaning. Typically, they are intertextual sites, because texts and discursive practices are inscribed in institutions and landscapes.

One of the paradoxes of our increasingly globalized, ever-more diasporic world is the degree to which the more privileged members of Western societies seem to require the reassurance of political, cultural, and ethnic demarcations and hierarchies (Wilson and Donnan 1988). Why this should be is debatable, but Salman Rushdie (1991, 102)—much like Edward Said—is of the opinion that such constructs satisfy "certain longings in the Western psyche;" "longings," he believes, grounded in the experience and imagination of colonialism.[15] For its part, tourism continues to be influenced by the longing to experience "Otherness," a desire heavily dependent on the global circulation of mass-mediated images.

The view of a compartmentalized social and cultural universe is constantly confronted by the reality that contemporary societies are inextricably joined together; or, as Appadurai (1994, 413) phrases it, "identities and identifications now only partially revolve around the realities and images of place." However, it is also evident that global processes do not in themselves lead to a diminution of boundaries. In a recent paper, the Mexican anthropologist Esteban Krotz (1997, 238–239) draws attention to the irony of an American anthropology "dedicated particularly to cultural diversity," and, at the same time, prone to annul this diversity and see the world in its image. Talal Asad et al. (1997, 720) comments on the "great historical transformation" in people's ways of living, but also insists that "this change involves not the permanent elimination of boundaries but new ways of making and unmaking them."

Engaging both the transformations and continuities requires that we pay some attention to national political cultures (Pi-Sunyer 1998). This has not always been anthropology's strong suit, for as Brosius (1999, 285) notes, "we have been so fixed on local social movements, transnational NGOs, and globalizing processes that we seem to have forgotten about the need to understand how national political cultures might mediate between these." For instance, any discussion of contemporary Quintana Roo has to recognize that for generations it was not simply a national periphery, but a highly vulnerable region without firm southern boundaries.

This history has a direct bearing on tourism development given that the onset of mass tourism was accompanied by changes that, theoretically at least, should reinforce state authority. Most obviously, infrastructure investment in power grids, roads, and airports, afford the agents of the state an expanded degree of control. We can add a variety of state and quasi-state agencies and institutions—schools, agricultural extension services, clinics, radio and television stations—that also function to mark state influence. In Quintana Roo, these physical and institutional changes have been accompanied by massive and rapid migration from other parts of the country (most of it since the early 1970s), so that today it looks and feels much more "Mexican"—and consequently less indigenous—than it did 30 or 40 years ago. Tourism, however, is not free of political risks and public relations complications. It was obviously a carefully thought through strategy that led the rebel Zapatistas in Chiapas to occupy San Cristóbal de las Casas, the old colonial capital, on January 1, 1994. Tourists woke up to the sight of a disciplined, mostly indigenous, force of armed young men and women patrolling streets and plazas. In the words of George Collier (1994, 2), "treating startled tourists and civilians with courtesy [the rebel army] pronounced itself in rebellion against the government, the army, and the police."

They did not—then or later—declare themselves in rebellion against the idea of Mexico or the integrity of the Mexican state; in fact, Zapatistas have been punctilious in their respect for national symbols, particularly the Mexican flag. While this surely is evidence of pragmatic politics, it also reflects a struggle for the meaning of the nation. The Zapatistas, making their own the mythic figure of Emiliano Zapata, stress a populist and revolutionary Mexico, while in their numerous communiqués they depict their struggle as the most recent episode in a 500-year battle for human dignity. In short, they portray themselves as representing the authentic, if often voiceless, nation.[16]

Related to developments in Chiapas, and to pan-Mayanist mobilization in neighboring Guatemala (Warren 1998), is the growing demand of Mayan people for greater equity and voice coupled to a deepening fear of the loss of place. This is strongly reflected in our interviews, which record overwhelming support for the implementation of Mayan language and history courses in the schools. Parents are almost universally in favor of schooling, but many fear that the educational system will alienate their children from family and community. At the same time, we became aware of a growing, and sometimes quite explicit, valorization of the Mayan experience on the part of certain sectors of the non-Mayan middle class, among them community organizers, local intellectuals, and some environmentalists. Consequently, the possibility of a counter-hegemonic discourse is present, but it must confront social constructs of nation and society that continue to imagine indigenous people as the antithesis of all that is modern and progressive.

The Mexican model of state, with its claims to moral authority and emotive power, has its antecedents in 18th-century creole nationalism. It underwent modernization during the period of 19th-century liberal reforms, and was substantially reformulated during the Revolution. While hardly static, the Mexican state remains a philosophical and political edifice of the Enlightenment. In a country like Mexico, this means it is primarily the work of an educated metropolitan minority. Both as organization and as ideology it has drawn legitimate criticism. The Mexican intellectual Bonfil Batalla (1996) refers to Mexican state formation as "the construction of a fictitious state from whose norms and practices the majority of the population is excluded" (see also Johnson 1971, 180; Anderson 1991, 198). But what remains the most remarkable and hopeful feature of this political discourse is that those on the margins of the system—peasants, the unemployed, indigenous groups—continue to articulate demands that are reformist rather than radical (see also Hvalkof, this volume, on Peruvian indigenous organizations).

The state's considerable efforts to reinforce its presence and represent itself in Quintana Roo must be understood in the aforementioned context of a history of geographical and political distance from the capital (Vernon 1963, 53–54; Cumberland 1968, 217–218). Probably because it was for so long the periphery of a periphery, Quintana Roo exhibits a particularly insistent elaboration of national symbology, and nowhere more so than in capital city of Chetumal. Until the 1960s, the majority of the houses were built of wood, and the town motto remains "Chetumal—*de buena madera*," a pioneer sentiment signifying that literally and figuratively the community was built of "good timber." Only a handful of these porched frame houses remain. All other structures, from dwellings to office buildings, are built of concrete or cinder-block, and what was once a picturesque Caribbean town has been transformed into a generically "modern" administrative and commercial center. This process has been accompanied by a conscious and over determined attempt to fix national memory on urban space. The main thoroughfare, Avenida de los Héroes, is dedicated to national heroes, the most important portrayed in busts and statues. Héroes is in turn crossed by streets commemorating national figures and events: presidents Obregón and Cárdenas, the heroic defenders of Chapultepec castle, and so forth. At another level, the whole of Quintana Roo is defined as national space through its designation as *la cuna del mestizaje*—the cradle of racial mixing—a unique interpretation for a region which until very recently was overwhelmingly indigenous.[17]

Before tourism and its related changes, the chief Mayan strategy for managing outside forces was dispersal and escape, if possible. In fact, much of Quintana Roo can be thought of as a classic example of what Gonzalo Aguirre Beltrán (1979) aptly termed a "region of refuge," a cultural and physical space protected from outside pressures by distance and inaccessibility. The situation on the ground is now similar to that described by Frank Cancian (1996, 217) for Zinacantán where he attributes the proximate cause of social change to the Mexican government and other organizations "that paid for the construction of new schools, roads, water and light systems, community buildings, jails, and churches." However, the most critical, though not the most visible, change that is occurring in rural (or previously rural) settlements is that the material underpinnings of community life—forest, field, and kitchen gardens—are being lost as the result of specific government plans and policies. Given the close symbolic and material connections linking religion with smallholder agriculture, the consequences for local people go far beyond the economic (Nutini 1996, 87). As customary socio-religious organizations lose their power to manage outside intervention, new religious syntheses, or competing cosmologies, emerge. Finally, as landlessness increases and more individuals work for wages, reciprocity and pooling of resources, once the bulwarks of village social life, come under growing pressure (Rosenbaum 1993, 31; Gudeman and Rivera-Gutiérrez, this volume).

This is but the briefest sketch of how national and transnational policies, including tourism promotion and environmental programs, influence the lives of peasant and post-peasant Maya. Both villagers and those who have moved into urban areas change, at least in part, in order to remain the same. This is an old strategy, with new twists. It helps to shed light on different matters, including the success of Protestant evangelical denominations and the skill with which the Maya have utilized modern information technology, most notably the success of "Cyber Zapatistas" with the Internet and advanced communications in general. Nelson (1966, 295) quotes one Guatemalan Mayan leader as saying, "the Maya give thanks for food, for air, for the tools that serve us, the office machines, the computers."

What this chapter has attempted to explore, chiefly through an examination of tourism, is how the global, in its multiple dimensions, manifests itself in this corner of the Mexican state. One strand, the one that opened the chapter, is linked to the growth of new middle classes in industrialized societies and their protagonism in "a Western imaginary which projects assumed qualities onto places and maps increasingly mobile desires and fantasies onto the globe"(Edensor 1998, 14). These desires and fantasies are disseminated through electronic and printed transmission—brochures, magazines, and television programs—and in the process become incorporated into global "mediascapes." There is a very tangible political dimension to how global forces—specifically global capitalism—construct and commodify cultures and sites. Many of the responsible agents in this process are recognizable with little difficulty: multinational corporations, including those engaged in tourism and media; governments and international bodies; financial institutions.

Less obvious, but no less important, are what Mowforth and Munt (1998, 158) call "new socio-environmental movements" for whom "environmental issues are still widely equated with ecology rather than society or culture" (Mowforth and Munt 1998, 159). Escobar (1995, 194–195) asks us to consider how well the ideology of sustainable development meshes with "environmental managerialism," and points out that

> Over the years, ecosystems analysts have discovered the "degrading" practices of the poor but seldom recognized that the problems are rooted in development processes that displaced indigenous communities, disrupted peoples' habitats and occupations, and forced many rural societies to increase pressure on the environment.

We (Daltabuit and Pi-Sunyer 1990, 10–11) made a similar point early in our research:

> Under the blanket of environmentalism, the options open to local populations could be further restricted, for in places like Quintana Roo—if history

and experience are any guide—a "managed" environment is bound to translate into an environment managed by outsiders chiefly to satisfy the needs of outsiders.

If an example is needed, one need only look across the border at Belize where "the environmental movement, so rapidly exported to Belize, has since the early 1980s not only sequestered 40 percent of the land-mass of Belize into preserves but also appointed itself the 'manager' of this land" (Sutherland 1998, 140; see also de Onis 1992, 219–243). What Sutherland refers to as "NGO hegemony" not only poses problems for local people, whose customary forms of resource use may be redefined as criminal activity, but for third-world governments who may be pressured to impose conservationist regimes.

While the situation in Quintana Roo is unlikely soon to approach that of Belize where approximately 70 to 90 percent of the country's freehold land is owned by foreigners (Lundgren 1993), international conservation agencies define environmental policy, and 65 percent of the members of the Belize Tourism Association are non-Belizeans (McMinn and Carter 1998), there are similar geopolitical forces at work. As a result of structural adjustment policies, what have been termed "ecological distribution conflicts" (Azar and Sterner 1996)—essentially disputes over land and resources—are increasingly common in Quintana Roo and are bound to grow.

For working people in the region—whether peasants, wage workers, or a combination of both—the most critical concern is simple survival: the need for land, employment, housing, and food, but also for intangibles such as recognition, respect, and access to education (see the discussion by Díaz Barriga 1996). This search is responsible for much of the mobility and fluidity, the shifts in roles, categories, and identities. Many people and their families cross back and forth between "peasant" and "worker," "rural" and "urban," and perhaps even between "Maya" and *ladino*. Much of this mobility, it was explained to us, was dictated by employment considerations.

Observers of the condition of postmodernity draw attention to hybridity—the blurring of genres and categories—and the extent to which personal and national borders are becoming ambiguous, not least along the peripheries of postcolonial nation-states (Kearney 1991; Stepputat 1999; Polier 1999; Errington and Gewertz 1995). In such locations, which also constitute the capitalist frontier, modernity and postmodernity have led to an accelerated compression of time and space (Harvey 1992, 240). In Quintana Roo, indigenous communities first experienced campaigns of state terror (Taussig 1984; Margold 1999), later a Revolutionary dispensation that granted them land and relative security, and more recently expropriation and full-scale capitalist penetration (compare Yetman and Búrquez 1998). As for space, the shift has been from an underdeveloped margin (and sanctuary) to something close to an extension of South Florida.

The postmodern has numerous connotations, but from its inception it has been conceptualized in relation to the post-industrial, one of whose key characteristics is the dominance of the service sector. This economic reorientation is in turn linked to new forms of consumption, of which tourism is an excellent example. With respect to political economy, a dominant feature of "late capitalist" neoliberal systems is the extent to which the interventionist, welfare-oriented state has lost ground and is being displaced by the globalization of economic, as well as social and cultural, relations. As Grillo (1998, 224) notes, "the globalization, or transnationalization, of production, distribution, and exchange . . . accompanied by new forms of international organization" have important implications for states and regions. In Quintana Roo, it sometimes seems that everything of value in the transnational system has been transformed into a commodity.

We also encounter pluralism of various types: tourists by the hundreds of thousands, of course, but also many immigrants from the Mexican interior, New Age pilgrims, an emerging middle class, expatriate homeowners, and Mayan cultural activists. One may reasonably ask whether pluralism itself is in some degree a product of late capitalism, a cultural and economic formation that both homogenizes and (re)codifies. The matter is important because "diversity" by itself begs the question. In Quintana Roo, the dominant postmodern and "diverse" presence is foreign: tourists and others attracted by the tropics, the ruins, and the low prices. Foreigners come in, but poor people are restricted to a much more circumscribed orbit. Perhaps, as Stuart Hall (1992, 309) has written, globalization does have the potential of "producing a variety of possibilities and new positions of identification, and making identities more positional, more political, more plural and diverse." Without in the least underestimating the initiative of many of our friends, their role in the global scheme of things remains severely circumscribed by poverty, nationality, and ethnicity. This is unlikely to change.

Notes

Much of the research on which this contribution is based was carried out between 1993 and 1998 in five different Quintana Roo communities. I am indebted to the many people of the area who have helped me understand the complexity of this corner of Mexico, but the reader will understand that it is more prudent not to reveal their identity. I want to thank my friends and colleagues in an ongoing collaborative project, R. Brooke Thomas, Magalí Daltabuit, and Henry Geddes Gonzáles, for their support and the stimulus of years of shared research and writing on

Quintana Roo. Fieldwork was made possible by support from the Wenner-Gren Foundation for Anthropological Research (Grant 5618), a University of Massachusetts Faculty Research Grant (Summer 1994), and a Latin American Studies Faculty Research Grant (Summer 1998). The "we" of portions of the text is recognition of the collective nature of much of the research.

1. A strength of ethnography is that "it derives from the richness of ethnographic data, a product of doing long-term, in-depth fieldwork," which Ortner contrasts with the extreme opposite of this type of understanding "to be seen in some forms of television journalism, with its reliance on quick visual cuts and chopped sound bites" (1998, 434).

2. This includes, among others, specialty magazines, official tourism organizations, travel agencies, airlines and cruise ship companies, television travel programs, travel writers and their publishers, and advertisers' copywriters—even when the subject is not not explicitly related to travel.

3. Goswami's (1996) study of Victorian "Mutiny Tours" argues that "Englishness" and the rationale for imperial domination were constructed not only in the metropole, but equally in imperial peripheries. On the construction of national polities and identies on the borders of states see Sahlins (1989) and Douglass (1998).

4. Of course, virtually any location can be exoticized, and if necessary—as in the case of theme parks—exotic elements can be imported or invented.

5. Needless to say, the *National Geographic* styles itself as a scientific publication. But its authority among the public probably owes more to its subscription rate, the third largest for magazines in the United States, and more recently, to its television nature programs—an animal kingdom in which humans play only guardian roles.

6. Appadurai (1990) suggests that contemporary transnational culture be conceptualized as a series of "scapes," among them ethnoscapes, technoscapes, and mediascapes. We could add leisurescapes to the list. There is no obvious hierarchy in Appaduri's roster and the approach is designed to highlight a global integration in which place is secondary. We would argue that some "scapes"—sundry colonial tropes, for example—continue to play a critical role in popular imagination and the construction of the global cultural economy.

7. While this mapping owes something to Appadurai's "scapes," the exercise is meant to relay how an imagination of colonial derivation segmented and rationalized southern Mexican space. This is then contrasted to very different indigenous formulations and contestations.

8. Bacalar was built to reinforce Spanish claims to southern Yucatán and to protect the colony from the English settlement on the coast of Honduras.

9. The Maya did not normally differentiate between Spaniards and Mexicans, both of which were designated as "White."

10. The Maya, in fact, have been folklorized at a major theme park that contains a "Maya village" and produces light-and-sound shows more reminiscent of Polynesia than of southern Mesoamerica.

11. *Ladinos* are people of mixed descent who are more likely to identify with their European ancestry than with indigenous societies, past or present.

12. On other early visitors to the Mayan area see Bernal (1980) and Parsons (1993).

13. *Milpa* (slash-and-burn) agriculture among the Maya has material, societal and religious dimension (Annis 1987; Kintz 1990; Re Cruz 1996; Daltabuit 1992). Until a few decades ago, the communities of Quintana Roo were essentially self-sufficient and needed only a few outside inputs, a situation which increased the importance of *milpa* in a system of family-centered production. *Milpa* has been described as "an agronomic system that operates by producing a very large number of very small quantities" (Annis 1987, 36), a mode of production that encourages reciprocity (corn is mixed with various intercrops; exchange buffers individual adversity). Cosmographically, *milpa* and corn played—and continue to play—a central role in religion and identity, sufficient to note that the "first people" were produced by the gods from *masa*, corn dough.

14. This narrative is certainly consciously informed by Biblical eschatology, echoing themes found in both the Old and the New Testaments. Clearly, our friend believes that we may already be living in the End Time, a period of disruption and chaos presaging the final conflict against evil and the return of the Messiah. It is also congruent with an indigenous sense of time and history, a historicizing cyclicity that links the present to a past—and a future—of which it forms part (Warren 1998, 145).

15. The extent to which tourism is enmeshed in a colonial imaginary can be quite explicit. A recent (1999) full-page advertisement in the New Yorker—"Tahiti by Gauguin"—for the cruise ship *Paul Gauguin* features a tropical landscape and a reclining cinnamon-colored young woman. The reader is informed that these "breathtaking" worlds are "closer than you imagined" and "more than you dreamed."

16. The rhetoric of the Zapatistas is significantly different from that commonly used by indigenous activists in the United States or Canada. Most obviously, policies and positions are more consciously revolutionary than those espoused by many Native American leaders. At the same time, Mexican indigenous movements, while certainly making social and cultural demands, are not characterized by cultural separatism. On the contrary, they typically attempt to forge alliances with peasants and workers, and do not reject support from allies in other sectors of national society.

17. Particularly clear, of course, with respect to the contemporary Maya. The Museum of Maya Culture in Chetumal deals only with the pre-contact Maya.

References

Aguirre Beltrán, Gonzalo. 1979 [1969]. *Regions of Refuge*. Washington, DC: Society for Applied Anthropology, Monograph 12.

Anderson, Benedict. 1991. *Imagined Communities*. London: Verso.

Annis, Sheldon. 1987. *God and Production in a Guatemalan Town*. Austin: University of Texas Press.

Appadurai, Arjun. 1990. Disjuncture and difference in the global cultural economy. *Public Culture* 2:1–24.

———. 1991. Global ethnoscapes: notes and queries for a transnational anthropology. In *Recapturing Anthropology*, edited by Richard G. Fox. 191–210. Santa Fe, NM: School of American Research Press.

———. 1994. Patriotism and its futures. *Public Culture* 7:411–429.

Asad, Talal et al. 1997. Provocations of European ethnology. *American Anthropologist.* 99:713–730.

Azar, C. and T. Sterner. 1996. Discounting and distributional considerations in the context of global warming. *Ecological Economics.* 19:169–184.

Bernal, Ignacio. 1980. *A History of Mexican Archaeology.* London: Thames and Hudson.

Bonfil Batalla, Guillermo. 1996. *México Profundo.* Austin: University of Texas Press.

Bourdieu, Pierre. 1984. *Distinction: A Critique of the Judgment of Taste.* London: Routledge & Kegan Paul.

Brosius, J. Peter. 1999. Anthropological engagements with environmentalism. *Current Anthropology.* 40(3):277–309.

Cancian, Frank. 1996. The Hamlet as mediator. *Ethnology.* 35(3):215–228.

Castañeda, Quetzil E. 1996. *In the Museum of Maya Culture.* Minneapolis and London: University of Minnesota Press.

Catherwood, Frederick. 1844. *Views of Ancient Monuments in Central America, Chiapas, and Yucatan.* London: Bartlett and Welford.

Clendinnen, Inga. 1987. *Ambivalent Conquests.* Cambridge and New York: Cambridge University Press.

Clifford, James. 1988. *The Predicament of Culture: Twentieth-century Ethnography, Literature, and Art.* Cambridge, MA: Harvard University Press.

———. 1997. *Routes.* Cambridge, MA: Harvard University Press.

Collier, George A. 1994. *Basta! Land and the Zapatista Rebellion in Chiapas.* Oakland, CA: Food First Books.

Cooper, Mathew. 1999. Spatial discourses and social boundaries. In *Theorizing the City,* edited by Setha M. Low. 377–399. New Brunswick, NJ: Rutgers University Press.

Crick, Malcolm. 1989. Representations of international tourism in the social sciences: Sun, sex, sights, savings and servility. *Annual Review of Anthropology.* 18:307–344.

Cumberland, Charles C. 1968. *Mexico: the Struggle for Modernity.* Oxford and New York: Oxford University Press.

Daltabuit, Magalí. 1992. *Mujeres Mayas.* Mexico, DF: UNAM, Instituto de Investigaciones Antropológicas.

Daltabuit, Magalí and Oriol Pi-Sunyer. 1990. Tourism development in Quintana Roo, Mexico. *Cultural Survival Quarterly* 14(1):9–13.

Davidson, Basil. 1964. *The African Past: Chronicles from Antiquity to Modern.* London: Longmans.

de Onis, Juan. 1992. *The Green Cathedral.* Oxford and New York: Oxford University Press.

Díaz Barriga, Miguel. 1996. Necesidad: Notes on the discourses of urban politics in the Ajusco foothills of Mexico City. *American Ethnologist.* 23(2):291–310.

Dirección General de Estadística. 1962. *Octavo Censo General de la Población, 1960 (Resumen General).* México, DF: Estados Unidos Mexicanos, Secretaría de Economía.

Douglass, William A. 1998. A Western perspective on an Eastern interpretation of where North meets South: Pyreneean borderland cultures. In *Border Identities,* edited by Thomas M. Wilson and Hastings Donnan. 62–95. Cambridge: Cambridge University Press.

Edensor, Tim. 1998. *Tourists at the Taj*. London and New York: Routledge.

Edmonson, Munro S. and Victoria A. Bricker. 1985. Yucatecan Maya literature. In *Literatures, vol 3, Supplement to the Handbook of Middle American Indians*, edited by Munro S. Edmonson. 44–63. Austin: University of Texas Press.

Elliott, J.H. 1989. The discovery of America and the discovery of man. In *Spain and Its World 1500–1700*. 42–64. New Haven, CT: Yale University Press.

Erlandson, Jon McVey. 1998. The making of Chumash tradition (CA Forum). *Current Anthropology*. 39 (4):477–485.

Errington, Frederick K. and Deborah Gewertz. 1989. Tourism and anthropology in a post modern world. *Oceania*. 60:37–54.

———. 1995. *Articulating Change in the "Last Unknown."* Boulder, CO: Westview Press.

Escobar, Arturo. 1995. *Encountering Development*. Princeton, NJ: Princeton University Press.

Farriss, Nancy M. 1984. *Maya Society Under Colonial Rule*. Princeton, NJ: Princeton University Press.

Friedlander, Judith. 1975. *Being Indian in Hueyapan*. New York: St. Martin's Press.

Frye, David. 1996. *Indians into Mexicans*. Austin: University of Texas Press.

Geertz, Clifford. 1994. Life on the Edge. *The New York Review of Books*, April 7. 3–4.

Greenfield, Bruce R. 1992. *Narrating Discovery*. New York: Columbia University Press.

Greenwood, Davydd J. 1989. Culture by the pound: an anthropological perspective on tourism as cultural commoditization. In *Hosts and Guests: The Anthropology of Tourism*, edited by Valene L. Smith. 171–185. Philadelphia, PA: University of Pennsylvania Press.

Grillo, Ralph D. 1998. *Pluralism and the Politics of Difference*. Oxford (UK): Clarendon Press

Gordon, Robert. 1992. *The Bushman Myth*. Boulder, CO: Westview Press.

Goswami, Manu. 1996. "Englishness" on the imperial circuit: Mutiny tours in Colonial South Asia. *Journal of Historical Sociology*. 9(1):54–84.

Gutiérrez-Estévez, Manuel. 1998. Plurality and perspectives in the literary genres of the Yucatec Maya. *American Anthropologist*. 100(2):309–325.

Hall, Colin Michael. 1994. *Tourism and Politics*. John Wiley: Chichester and New York.

Hall, Stuart. 1992. The question of cultural identity. In *Modernity and its future*, edited by Stuart Hall, D. Held, and T. McGrew. 274–316. Cambridge (UK): Polity Press.

Harvey, David. 1992. *The Condition of Postmodernity*. London: Blackwell.

Heller, Chaia. 1999. *Ecology of Everyday Life*. Montréal, New York, London: Black Rose Books.

Henderson, John S. 1981. *The World of the Ancient Maya*. Ithaca, NY: Cornell University Press.

Hughes, Robert. 1997. *American Visions*. New York: Alfred A. Knopf.

Johnson, Kenneth F. 1971. *Mexican Democracy: A Critical View*. Boston: Allyn and Bacon.

Joseph, Fritz-Pierre. 1995. Quintana Roo. In *Marginación y pobreza en México*, edited by Gloria Vázquez Rangel and Jesús Ramírez López. 269–277. México, DF: Editorial Ariel.

Kearney, Michael. 1991. Borders and boundaries of state and self at the end of empire. *Journal of Historical Sociology.* 4(1):52–74.

Kintz, Ellen R. 1990. *Life Under the Tropical Canopy.* Forth Worth: Holt, Rinehart and Winston.

Kirshenblatt-Gimblett. 1998. *Destination Culture.* Berkeley and Los Angeles: University of California Press.

Kottak, Conrad P. 1999. The new ecological anthropology. *American Anthropologist.* 10:123–35.

Krotz, Esteban. 1997. Anthropologies of the South: their rise, their silencing, their characteristics. *Critique of Anthropology.* 17:237–251.

Lamaison, Pierre. 1986. From rules to strategies: an interview with Pierre Bourdieu. *Cultural Anthropology.* 1:110–120.

Löfgren, Orvar. 1999. *On Holiday.* Berkeley, Los Angeles, London: University of California Press.

Low, Setha M. 1996. The anthropology of cities: imagining and theorizing the city. *Annual Review of Anthropology.* 25:383–409.

Lowenthal, David. 1985. *The Past is a Foreign Country.* Cambridge: Cambridge University Press.

Lundgren, Nancy. 1993. Women, work, and "development" in Belize. *Dialectical Anthropology* 18:363–378.

Lutz, Catherine A. and Jane A. Collins. 1993. *Reading National Geographic.* Chicago: University of Chicago Press.

Margold, Jane A. 1999. From "Cultures of fear and terror" to the normalization of violence. *Critique of Anthropology.* 19(1):64–88.

MacCannell, Dean. 1992. *Empty Meeting Grounds.* London and New York: Routledge.

McMinn, Stuart and Eriet Carter. 1998. Tourist typology: Observations from Belize. *Annals of Tourism Research.* 25(3):675–699.

Morley, Sylvanus G. 1920. *The Inscriptions at Copán.* Washington, DC: The Carnegie Institutution of Washington.

Mowforth, Martin and Ian Munt. 1998. *Tourism and Sustainability.* London and New York: Routledge.

Nelson, Diane M. 1966. Maya hackers and the cyberspatialized nation-state: modernity, ethnonostalgia, and a lizard queen in Guatemala. *Cultural Anthropology.* 11(3):287–308.

New York Times. Mayan Immigrants without Spanish are in Language Limbo. October 4, 1998. Section 1, Page 23, Column 1.

Nutini, Hugo G. 1996. Mesoamerican community organization: preliminary remarks. *Ethnology.* 35(2): 81–91.

Ortner, Sherry B. 1998. Generation X: anthropology in a media-saturated world. *Cultural Anthropology.* 13(3):414–440.

Parsons, Lee Allen. 1993. *Columbus to to Catherwood.* Kislak bibliographic series, publication one. Miami Lakes, FL: Jay I Kislak Foundation.

Pérez-Taylor, Rafael. 1994. *Entre la tradición y la modernidad: antropología de la memoria colectiva.* Unpublished doctoral dissertation. Barcelona: University of Barcelona, Faculty of Geography and History, Department of Social Anthropology.

Pi-Sunyer, Oriol. 1998. Ethical issues for North American anthropologists conducting research in Mexico: the national dimension. *Human Organization.* 57(3):326–327.

Pi-Sunyer, Oriol and R. Brooke Thomas. 1997. Tourism, environmentalism, and cultural survival in Quintana Roo. In *Life and Death Matters*, edited by Barbara Rose Johnston. 187–212. Walnut Creek, CA: Altamira Press.

Pi-Sunyer, Oriol, R. Brooke Thomas, and Magalí Daltabuit. 1999. *Tourism and Maya Society in Quintana Roo, Mexico.* Latin American Consortium of New England, Occasional Paper No. 17.

Polier, Nicole. 1999. Culture, community, and the crisis of modernity in Papua New Guinea. *Political and Legal Anthropology Review.* 22(1):55–65.

Price, Sally. 1989. *Primitive Art in Civilized Places.* Chicago: University of Chicago Press.

Pratt, Mary L. 1992. *Imperial Eyes.* London: Routledge.

Quintana Roo. 1987. *Quintana Roo: Cuaderno de Información para la Planeación.* México, DF: Instituto Nacional de Estadistica, Geografía e Informática.

Re Cruz, Alicia. 1994. Lo sagrado y lo profano de la identidad maya entre los emigrantes de Yucatán. *Nueva Antropología* 14(46):39–48.

———. 1996. *The Two Milpas of Chan Kom.* Albany: State University of New York Press.

Redfield, Robert. 1941. *The Folk Culture of Yucatan.* Chicago: The University of Chicago Press.

———. 1947. The folk society. *American Journal of Sociology.* 52: 237-251.

———. 1950. *The Village that Chose Progress.* Chicago: The University of Chicago Press.

Redfield, Robert and Alfonso Villa Rojas. 1934. *Chan Kom, a Maya Village.* Washington DC: The Carnegie Institution of Washington.

Rodríguez, Sylvia. 1989. Art, tourism, and race relations in Taos: toward a sociology of the art colony. *Journal of Anthropological Research.* 41(1):77–99.

Rojek, Chris. 1997. Indexing, dragging, and the social construction of tourist sites. In *Touring Cultures*, edited by Chris Rojek and John Urry. 52–74. London and New York: Routledge.

Rosenbaum, Brenda. 1993. *With Our Heads Bowed.* Albany, NY: SUNY Institute for Mesoamerican Studies, Studies in Culture and Society, Volume 5.

Rushdie, Salman. 1991. *Imaginary Homelands.* London: Granta Books.

Sahlins, Peter. 1989. *Boundaries: The Making of France and Spain in the Pyrenees.* Berkeley: University of California Press.

Said, Edward W. 1994 [1993]. *Culture and Imperialism.* New York: Vintage Books.

Salvatore, Ricardo D. 1996. North American Travel Narratives and the Ordering/Othering of South America (c. 1810–1860). *Journal of Historical Sociology.* 9(1):85–110.

Sapper, Karl. 1904. Independent Indian states of Yucatan. In *Mexican and Central American Antiquities, Calendar Systems, and History. Bureau of American Ethnology Bulletin.* 28: 623–624. Washington, DC: Smithsonian Institution.

Simpson, Eyler. 1937. *The Ejido, Mexico's Way Out.* Chapel Hill, University of North Carolina Press.

Smith, Carol A. 1995. Race-class-gender ideology in Guatemala: modern and anti-modern forms. *Comparative Studies in Society and History*. 37(4):723–749.

Stephens, John Lloyd. 1841. *Incidents of Travel in Central America, Chiapas, and Yucatán, 2 Vols*. New York: Harper and Brothers

———. 1843. *Incidents of Travel in Yucatán, 2 Vols*. New York: Harper and Brothers.

Stepputat, Finn. 1999. Politics of displacement in Guatemala. *Journal of Historical Sociology*. 12(1):54–80.

Sullivan, Paul. 1989. *Unfinished Conversations: Mayas and Foreigners Between Two Wars*. New York: Alfred A. Knopf.

Sutherland, Anne. 1998. *The Making of Belize*. Westport, CT: Bergin and Garvey.

Taussig, Michael. 1984. Culture of terror—space of death: Roger Casement's Putumayo report and the explanation of torture. *Comparative Studies in Society and History*. 26(3):467–497.

Trouillot, Michel-Rolph. 1991. Anthropology and the savage slot: the poetics and politics of otherness. In *Recapturing Anthropology*, edited by Richard G. Fox. 17–44. Santa Fe, NM: School of American Research.

Tsing, Anna. 1993. *In the Realm of the Diamond Queen: Marginality in an Out-of-the-Way Place*. Princeton: Princeton University Press.

Turner, John Kenneth. 1969 [1910]. *Barbarous Mexico*. Austin: University of Texas Press.

Valdez, Norberto. 1996. Land reform and the two faces of development in rural Mexico. *Political Anthropology Review*. 19(2):109–120.

Van den Berghe, Pierre L. 1994. *The Quest for the Other*. Seattle and London: University of Washington Press.

Vernon, Raymond. 1963. *The Dilema of Mexico's Development*. Cambridge, MA: Harvard University Press.

Villa Rojas, Alfonso. 1945. *The Maya of East Central Quintana Roo*. Washington, DC: Carnegie Institution, Publication 559.

Vogt, Evon Z. 1969. The Maya introduction. In *Handbook of Middle American Indians,Volume 7, Part 1*, edited by Evon Z. Vogt. vol. 21–29. Austin: University of Texas Press.

Warren, Kay B. 1998. *Indigenous Movements and Their Critics*. Princeton, NJ: Princeton University Press.

Wilson, Thomas M. and Hastings Donnan. 1988. Nations, state, and identity at international borders. In *Border Identities*, edited by Thomas M. Wilson and Hastings Donnan. 1–30.Cambridge: Cambridge University Press.

Wolf, Eric R. 1982. *Europe and the People Without History*. Berkeley and Los Angeles: University of California Press.

Yetman, David and Alberto Búrquez. 1998. Twenty-seven: a case study in Ejido privatization in Mexico. *Journal of Anthropological Research*. 54(1):73–95.

Zárate Hernández, José Eduardo. 1998. Ethnography, cultural change, and local power. *Journal of Historical Sociology* 11(1):138–149.

Contributors

Jacquelyn Chase is Assistant Professor of Geography and Planning at California State University at Chico. Her work in Brazil has focused on global influences on regional change, and has included research on the flexibility of local labor markets in agricultural regions, household responses to the privatization of state-run companies, and fertility decline in restructured regions. Her papers include "Controlling labor commitment in Brazil's global agriculture: the crisis of competing flexibilities" (*Society and Space*), "Managing urban settlement in Brazil's agroindustrial frontier" (*Third World Planning Review*), "Trapped workers, urban freedoms, and labor control in Brazilian agriculture" (*Journal of Rural Studies*), and "The politics and experience of rural loss in Brazil" (*Sociologia Ruralis*). Chase also worked on research on fertility decline, gender, and regional culture in Brazil and has written a recent article in *Gender, Place, and Culture*.

Carmen Diana Deere is Professor of Economics and Director of the Center for Latin American, Caribbean, and Latino Studies at the University of Massachusetts in Amherst. She holds a Ph.D. in Agricultural Economics from the University of California, Berkeley. Dr. Deere is past President of the Latin American Studies Association (1992–94). She is co-author with Magdalena León of *Empowering Women: Land and Property Rights in Latin America* (Pittsburgh, 2001), *Women in Andean Agriculture: Peasant Production and Rural Wage employment in Colombia and Peru* (ILO, 1983). She co-edited with León *Rural Women and State Policy: Feminist Perspectives on Agricultural Development in Latin America* (Westview, 1987).

Agustín Escobar Latapí is regional director and professor-researcher at CIESAS Occidente, in Guadalajara. He has worked mostly on employment, labor markets, and social policy, but has also dealt extensively with various aspects of Mexico-U.S. migration. His most recent book on this subject is *La Dinámica de la Emigración Mexicana*, published by Porrúa-CIESAS.

Mercedes González de la Rocha is Researcher at the Centro de Investigaciones y Estudios Superiores en Antropología Social de Occidente, in Guadalajara, Mexico. She holds a Ph.D. from the Faculty of Social and Economic Studies at the University of Manchester. González de la Rocha is the author of the book *The Resources of Poverty: Women and Survival in a Mexican City* (Blackwell, 1994), and of numerous papers and articles on household economies, migration, and gender in Mexico.

Stephen Gudeman is Professor of Anthropology at the University of Minnesota. His principal interests revolve about culture and social organization, and especially economic anthropology. In anthropological economics, he focuses on the dialectics of market and community, and local models that are different from, provide a critique of, and sometimes give rise to formal economic models. He has carried out fieldwork in Panama, Colombia, and Guatemala. Gudeman's books include *Conversations in Colombia* (with Alberto Rivera, 1990), *Economic Anthropology* (ed., 1998), and *The Anthropology of Economy* (2001), which explore the interrelations of community, market, and culture.

Søren Hvalkof is Senior Anthropologist at the Nordic Agency for Development and Ecology, NORDECO, a Copenhagen-based company specializing in natural resource management in developing countries. His theoretical interest is mainly within the framework of political ecology with a regional focus in the Amazon basin. He has done extensive fieldwork as well as being actively involved in indigenous land titling and other indigenous projects. Hvalkof is co-editor with Peter Aaby of *Is God an American? An Anthropological Perspective on the Missionary Work of the Summer Institute of Linguistics* (1981). He also wrote "Nature, political ecology, and social practice: toward an academic and political agenda" (with Arturo Escobar), in *Building a New Biocultural Synthesis: Political-Economic Perspectives in Biological Anthropology* edited by Alan Goodman and Thomas Leatherman (1998), and *Liberation through Land Titling in the Peruvian Amazon*, co-edited with Alejandro Parellada (1998).

Cristóbal Kay studied at the University of Chile in Santiago and at the University of Sussex. He started his academic career as a researcher in the University of Chile and from 1974 to 1989 was a lecturer at the University of Glasgow. Since then he has been an Associate Professor at the Institute of Social Studies in The Hague, Holland. His research interests are development theory and rural development, with particular emphasis on Latin America. For many years he has been the editor of the *European Journal of Development Research* and currently is an editor of the *European Review of Latin American and Caribbean Studies*. He has done fieldwork on agrarian and peasant matters in Chile, Peru, and Cuba. He is the author of *Latin American Theories of Development and Underdevelopment* (London and New York: Routledge, 1989 and 1993). He has edited *Globalisation, Competitiveness, and Human Security* (London: Frank Cass, 1997), *Latin America Transformed: Globalization and Modernity* (London: Arnold and New York, Oxford University Press, 1999) and *Disappearing Peasantries?* (London: Intermediate Technology, 2000).

Magdalena León is Professor in the Faculty of Humanities and Social Sciences and former Director for the Center for Documentation of Women and Gender of the National University of Colombia, Bogotá. Professor León was formerly Director of Research at the Colombian Association for Population Studies (ACEP) where she directed national-level studies of urban and rural women. She served as advisor to the Colombian governmental delegation to the IV United Nations Conference on Women in Beijing (1995), and has been a consultant to many U.N. agencies, NGOs and academic women's studies program. With Carmen Diana Deere she coauthored *Empowering Women: Land and Property Rights in Latin America* (Pittsburgh, 2001), and *Women in Andean Agriculture: Production and Rural Wage employment in Colombia and Peru* (ILO, 1983). She co-edited with Carmen Deere *Rural Women and State Policy: Feminist Perspectives on Agricultural Development in Latin America* (Westview, 1987).

Oriol Pi-Sunyer teaches at the University of Massachusetts, Amherst. His interests in the anthropology of tourism date to the early 1970s when he returned to his native Catalonia to study Costa Brava fishing communities. He contributed a chapter on tourism and its consequences to Valene L. Smith's *Hosts and Guests: The Anthropology of Tourism* (1977), followed by other articles in journals and edited volumes. He received his undergraduate degree in Mexico and later conducted fieldwork on grass-roots economic change. This research resulted in several publications, including the monograph *Zamora: A Regional Economy in Mexico* (1967). His work on tourism in Mexico began in the late 1980s. Together with R. Brooke Thomas and Magalí Daltabuit he has written several pieces that explore the cultural, economic, and political dimensions of tourism in southern Mexico, most recently "Tourism, Environmentalism, and Cultural Survival in Quintana Roo," a contribution to Barbara Rose Johnston's *Life and Death Matters* (1997). One of his major theoretical concerns is the relationship between structures of domination and forms of representation.

Alberto Rivera-Gutiérrez is the Latin America Program Director for HECUA (Higher Education Consortium for Urban Affairs) and heads a sustainable development project in the Guatemalan Highlands. He is interested in social change, development, and the environment and how these issues are modeled and used to make social life meaningful. His book, *Conversations in Colombia* (with Stephen Gudeman, 1990), examines peasant livelihoods from the perspective of economic anthropology. Rivera Gutiérrez has done research among the Wayuu in northern Colombia and has consulted for indigenous organizations, governments, and international agencies.

Helen I. Safa is Professor Emerita of Anthropology and Latin American Studies at the University of Florida. She was Director of the Center for Latin American Studies at UF from 1980–85 and President of the Latin American Studies Association from 1983–85. Her research has focused on gender, development, and poverty, particularly in the Caribbean, where she has done research for more than 40 years. Her most recent publications include *The Myth of the Male Breadwinner: Women and Industrialization in the Caribbean* (Westview 1995) as well as an edited collection on race and national identity in the Americas (*Latin American Perspectives*, May 1998).

Index

Also from Kumarian Press...

Global Issues

Capitalism and Justice: Envisioning Social and Economic Fairness
John Isbister

The Cuban Way: Capitalism, Communism and Confrontation
Ana Julia Jatar-Hausmann, Named 'Outstanding Academic Title' by CHOICE Magazine

Inequity in the Global Village: Recycled Rhetoric and Disposable People
Jan Knippers Black

Where Corruption Lives
Edited by Gerald E. Caiden, O.P. Dwivedi, Joseph Jabbra

Conflict Resolution, Environment, Gender Studies, Globalization, International Development, Microfinance, Political Economy

Advocacy for Social Justice: A Global Action and Reflection Guide
David Cohen, Rosa de la Vega, Gabrielle Watson for Oxfam America and the Advocacy Institute

Bound: Living in the Globalized World
Scott Sernau

Exploring the Gaps: Vital Links Between Trade, Environment and Culture
James R. Lee

Going Global: Transforming Relief and Development NGOs
Marc Lindenberg and Coralie Bryant

The Hidden Assembly Line:
Gender Dynamics of Subcontracted Work in a Global Economy
Edited by Radhika Balakrishnan

Mainstreaming Microfinance:
How Lending to the Poor Began, Grew and Came of Age in Bolivia
Elisabeth Rhyne

Managing Policy Reform: Concepts and Tools for Decision-makers in Developing and Transitioning Countries
Derick W. Brinkerhoff and Benjamin L. Crosby

Reconcilable Differences: Turning Points in Ethnopolitical Conflict
Edited by Sean Byrne and Cynthia L. Irvin

War's Offensive on Women:
The Humanitarian Challenge in Bosnia, Kosovo and Afghanistan
Julie A. Mertus for the Humanitarianism and War Project

Kumarian Press, located in Bloomfield, Connecticut, is a forward-looking, scholarly press that promotes active international engagement and an awareness of global connectedness.